About 1400 hours that afternoon, John Hennigan called me back to Kontum. We now had assigned B-52 strike plots and times, along with an insertion point and time for the Mike Force battalion. Everything was going to happen between 0700 and 0900 hours the next morning, 03 April. I was selected to bring the news to Dak Seang and to make sure that the camp held through the night. There was still real worry that the NVA might try to take the camp, and we couldn't allow that to happen.

Before I left to prepare for a combat assault into Dak Seang, Lieutenant Colonel Hennigan talked to me. He told me that I was his direct representative on the ground and that if I felt it necessary, I could relieve the detachment commander and assume command myself. We agreed that I wouldn't tell the A-245 commander of my authority, but if I had to assume command, Lieutenant Colonel Hennigan would back me up by radio. I thought that that would be the most serious step I could expect to take, but it could only be a last resort. Relieving the commander of a team that had been continually fighting for thirty-six hours would heavily impact morale. . . .

Books published by The Ballantine Publishing Group are available at quantity discounts on bulk purchases for premium, educational, fund-raising, and special sales use. For details, please call 1-800-733-3000.

BATTLE FOR THE CENTRAL HIGHLANDS

A Special Forces Story

George E. Dooley

BALLANTINE BOOKS • NEW YORK

horized. If this
...blisher as "un-
...isher may have

A Ballantine Book
Published by The Ballantine Publishing Group
Copyright © 2000 by George E. Dooley

www.randomhouse.com/BB/

Library of Congress Catalog Card Number: 00-104861

ISBN 0-8041-1939-2

Manufactured in the United States of America

First Edition: September 2000

10 9 8 7 6 5 4 3 2 1

To Nina Smith, my wife; and Ed Sprague—
my two best friends.
And to all the 5th Special Forces Group (Airborne)
KIA and MIA. We still remember.

He which hath no stomach to this fight,
Let him depart; his passport shall be made,
And crowns for convoy put into his purse:
We would not die in that man's company
That fears his fellowship to die with us. . . .
He that shall live this day, and see old age,
Will yearly on the vigil feast his neighbours,
And say, To-morrow is Saint Crispian:
Then he will strip his sleeve and show his scars. . . .
This story shall the good man teach his son;
And Crispin Crispian shall ne'er go by,
From this day to the ending of the world,
But we in it shall be remembered,—
We few, we happy few, we band of brothers;
For he to-day that sheds his blood with me
Shall be my brother; be he ne'er so vile,
This day shall gentle his condition:
And gentlemen in England now a-bed
Shall think themselves accurs'd they were not here,
And hold their manhoods cheap, while any speaks
That fought with us upon Saint Crispin's day.

—William Shakespeare, *King Henry the Fifth*

Acknowledgments

Books aren't written alone. A lot of people end up helping even though they may not be aware of it. A few of the many who helped me are:

Max Lund, my friend from Michigan, who provided most of the detail given in chapter 15. Max also assisted in describing what Ed Sprague was doing in the early seventies. Max would have made a good Special Forces soldier if he'd had the inclination.

Jim Steele for convincing me not to quit writing and for putting me in touch with Owen Lock at Random House. In many respects, Jim's short career mirrored a Special Forces tour but without the benefits and support. Jim is another person who would have made a good SF soldier.

John Southworth gave me more information than I could hope to use about Ed Sprague, particularly about Ed Sprague and his team on a winter training exercise in Norway. Maybe the material can be used in another manuscript.

The members of Chapter 73, Special Forces Association. Every few months, I need to get back with real men, men with honor and values who have proved their worth. They give me that.

Amy Olson provided some of her computer skills and artistry. She patiently taught me the subtleties of Quark and Adobe Photoshop. Dave Buckner acted like a proper English teacher and corrected my grammar.

Finally, the folks at Enfield who keep me engaged.

Preface

I've always been intrigued about the difference between *history* and *story* in English. Learned scholars write history, while people who experienced it and were there write stories. I was there during some of the Vietnam Central Highlands fighting and don't recognize the official "history" that has since been written. In German *Geschichte* means both history and story/tale.

This is my *Geschichte*.

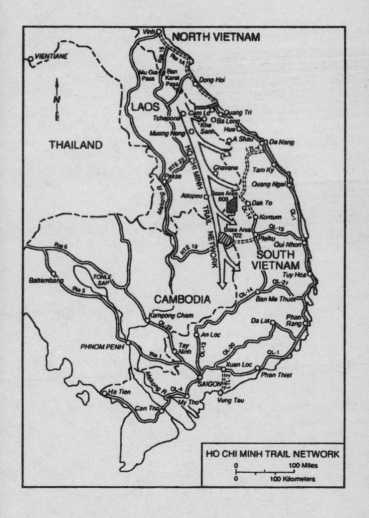

HO CHI MINH TRAIL NETWORK

0   100 Miles

0   100 Kilometers

Prologue

It was good to see the guys once again.

Some were heavier, some balder, and some grayer. All were older. Yet this crowd was different from a gathering at a typical sales convention or industrial show. Sure there were wives and girlfriends among them, but the men still seemed distinct. They weren't boisterous or loud but projected an air of confidence. How do you put your finger on that undefinable quality that made those men unique?

Ed Sprague was there, surrounded by friends and family, a minigroup within the larger crowd. Ed looked distinguished and healthy, talking to others in his deep, south-Boston accent. He looked as he always did, like a kindly old uncle whom everyone liked. Nobody meeting him for the first time would recognize a man who retired as an army master sergeant and went on to a second career with the State Department, finally retiring at ambassadorial rank as an FSO-1. Nobody would recognize him as a ferocious warrior responsible for the deaths of hundreds of Viet Cong in the Central Highlands of Vietnam during the 1960s and 1970s. Perhaps the presence of Ed and the others in the reception room combined to create a noticeable aura that indicated this group was different from others.

Jim Stewart was there with his wife, Cara. Jim spent twenty years in Special Forces and related duty. Quiet and unassuming, few would guess that he was one of the original soldiers who joined Special Forces. Even fewer know about his covert assignments. Jim doesn't look like a Rambo, but a Rambo doesn't survive in the real world of special operations.

The annual Special Forces Association convention was taking place, as it does in a different city every year. Many former Special Forces soldiers go to every convention; others just periodically visit. The primary bonds of those men reached back to mutual worldwide service during the Cold War of the fifties, sixties, and seventies. Some of the men had trained the Cuban guerrillas that had harassed Fidel Castro for thirty years; others had a part in the elimination of Che Guevara as an insurrectionary threat in Latin America; and still others had worked in classified missions in Europe and other parts of the world. Some had assisted the Afghanistan rebels to defeat the Soviet Union. The most common bond, however, was service in Southeast Asia during the Vietnam War, where almost every Special Forces soldier had at least one tour, and most had multiple tours in Vietnam or Thailand. Many of those men had clandestine time in Cambodia, Laos, and North Vietnam.

But still, what makes that group and gathering exceptional? To explain, we have to look back at the events that caused the formation of Special Forces.

When the Office of Strategic Services (OSS) was formed by Col. William "Wild Bill" Donovan in World War II to conduct unconventional warfare in Europe and Asia, the founders had to search throughout the entire armed forces to find capable people. Then the recruits had to be trained in languages, clandestine communications, guerrilla warfare, sabotage, espionage, demolitions, and the other requirements of unconventional warfare. After first finding candidates with foreign language skills, the OSS trained them with the skills that they would need to operate behind enemy lines, including parachuting as a means of infiltration. The OSS did remarkably well in World War II and was promptly disbanded when the war ended. But the unconventional warfare mission requirements didn't go away. In fact, after World War II, the mission requirements increased in direct proportion to Soviet subversion throughout the world.

After World War II, unconventional warfare became a cheap way to foster insurrection, and the U.S. Army had no capability on hand to either foster or contain it. The Greek civil war and Korean War provided the impetus for the army to get involved in special warfare, and in 1952, Special Forces was born.

Every Special Forces soldier had to be a triple volunteer. He had to volunteer for the army (draftees were not welcome or recruited), volunteer for Airborne training, and volunteer for Special Forces. Then there were stringent physical and swimming tests, psychological evaluation, and mental achievement qualifications that were as high as those for Officer Candidate School (OCS). From the start, it was predicted that the army would not look kindly on Special Forces' draining talented soldiers from the rest of the army. And such was the case.

Over the years, Special Forces was underfunded by the army, denied support personnel, and generally treated as an unwanted stepchild. Special Forces soldiers purposely maintained an image different from their paratrooper and Ranger cousins. They didn't spit shine their boots; they grew long hair and mustaches; they did all those things that would bother a conventional-warfare officer. They even did nonarmy things like being loaned to the CIA for classified missions and to NASA to secure Gemini capsules. For the officer or noncommissioned officer who volunteered for Special Forces, it was generally acknowledged that the transfer was not a career-enhancing move. Yet people still volunteered to serve, and the army continued to tolerate Special Forces; the unconventional missions continued to accrue, and someone had to perform them.

After a while, it became normal to assign difficult to almost impossible missions to Special Forces and to expect that they would be accomplished. The missions were all accomplished, and the Special Forces legend continued to grow.

Perhaps then this partially explains why that group is uncommon. They served as members of an elite force somewhat

rejected by its parent service, but mission oriented and dedicated to accomplishing any assignment. We'll see more as we
go along.

CHAPTER 1

What Am I Going to Be When I Grow Up?

I saw the North Vietnamese lieutenant standing in the wood line to my right. The man in front of me saw him that same moment and instinctively fired, hitting the lieutenant in the abdomen. The lieutenant had a grimace on his face and was bending slightly forward when I finished the job by putting an M-16 round through his left cheek and blowing his brains out the back of his head. Still operating on instinct and training, I switched to full automatic and sprayed left and right into the wood line, killing another North Vietnamese soldier. In five seconds in the summer of 1966, I had my first confirmed kills in Vietnam. Fortunately, the two North Vietnamese Army (NVA) soldiers were the only two enemy there, and the contact ended.

Along with a Civilian Irregular Defense Group (CIDG) company of mostly Jarai montagnards, we were finding our way out of the operational area to Cung Son, a Special Forces camp in the Central Highlands of Vietnam, when the contact occurred. I was one of two Americans with the montagnard company, both of us Special Forces men, sometimes known as Green Berets. Ed Sprague was the other American, and we've been lifelong friends since 1965.

Walking as third man in the point squad of the company, I was following a compass azimuth to the northeast, checking my map against the terrain to the front, when the NVA lieutenant appeared. Although busy with the map and compass, I let them both fall as I fired. The compass was tied to my patrol harness and the map wasn't going anywhere. But there's more to the story.

5

Ten days before, Ed Sprague and I accompanied the CIDG company from Trai Mai Linh, our base camp in the Central Highlands, to Cung Son, another Special Forces camp about fifty miles south. The U.S. 1st Cavalry Division had found an NVA regiment to the south of Cung Son and wanted help from the Vietnamese army to hold blocking positions around the NVA. The Vietnamese army had declined to assist, and the tasking was given to Special Forces. Three montagnard CIDG companies were flown out of three different camps to help with the cordon operation. Supposedly, as we and other units of the 1st Cavalry held the NVA in the encirclement, the NVA would be hunted and killed within the cordon.

It proved to be a boring ten days, with the montagnards anxious to operate against the NVA but limited to local security around the blocking position that we occupied. Occasionally, we'd spot an NVA or two and fire on them, but that was all. The 1st Cavalry brought B-52 strikes onto the supposedly trapped NVA, but as was often the case throughout the war, the NVA seemed to have vanished. Nobody thought about turning the tables: the montagnards ought to have been the hunters looking for the NVA, and the 1st Cavalry Division should have occupied the blocking positions. But that was the Vietnam War in 1966.

When we were inserted, we spent the rest of the day and night with a rifle platoon from the 1st Cavalry. It was interesting to contrast our two totally different ways of operating. They carried extra water in five-gallon cans; we found water throughout the land and purified it with iodine tablets before drinking it. The U.S. troops carried heavier loads than we did, but seldom traveled as far as we normally went. They were much more dependent on helicopter resupply, getting at least one resupply each day; we usually went three days before needing a resupply. Not that the U.S. troops were better or worse than we were; they were just different in how they approached the job.

While we sat in our blocking position, the Cav maneuvered within the cordon. They found base camps, caches, and very few enemy. Periodically, air strikes would bomb targets, but there just weren't very many enemy around, although the signs and indicators were abundant.

Perhaps the officers of the 1st Cavalry Division were frustrated at their lack of success. Maybe there were other reasons. But as anxious as the Cav was to fly us from Mai Linh to Cung Son and then by helicopter out to the cordon position, they just couldn't seem to find the helicopters to fly us back to Cung Son when the operation ended. So we walked out, without benefit of maps for most of the area. It didn't matter; we had radios, a fully armed and aggressive montagnard CIDG company, and the NVA just weren't as good as we were.

So what was a young American man from the south side of Chicago doing in a place like this? I was where I ought to have been. By virtue of custom, history, and birth, I was needed in Vietnam in 1966, and that's where I was.

I was born in the back-of-the-yards neighborhood of Chicago, in the area south of the Union Stock Yards on Chicago's south side. In the summer, a welcome cooling wind from the north would bring the smell of the yards, but that was a given. In books that I've read since, the neighborhood has been described as tough and poor, but I don't remember it that way. The neighborhood that I remember was full of ethnic Irish, German, Polish, and a few other groups. Sure, you had to have a few fights as a young boy and teenager, but I didn't know that that was terribly abnormal.

My parents took their children to the local Methodist church, and I was a Boy Scout. I enjoyed scouting, particularly camping. Used to city blocks, I loved the openness of nature and doing all the things required to gather merit badges. As one of my birthday presents, my parents gave me an annual membership to the YMCA where I learned to swim and to shoot a rifle. My younger sister and brother didn't seem to share my passions. But we were all encouraged in whatever we wanted to achieve.

Growing up in the forties and fifties, I was always amused (or amazed) by the values of the times. My grandfather, an Irish Catholic, who had served in World War I, had married the daughter of German Lutheran immigrants. My father, the first offspring, was considered the result of a mixed marriage. I don't suppose that things got better when my father married a German-English-Scotch amalgam, and I was the first offspring.

But growing up, the closest influence on me was my Irish grandfather. Sure, he sometimes spoke in a fake brogue: "B'jaysus now, why would you do such a thing (or act that way)?" But he guided me through my early years, probably more than my own parents. Grampa was my ideal. He treated me more as an equal than as a child. Grampa encouraged my love of reading, often letting me read his paperbacks. My parents didn't want me reading comic books as they considered the content to be corrupting; instead, I read *God's Little Acre*, *From Here to Eternity*, and other books probably less suitable than comic books for a preteen.

Grampa, however, was a complex person. He had only a sixth-grade education but read three newspapers a day. He worked for the city of Chicago, first as a driver, then as a laborer, but he detested politicians. In his youth, he was what we would call today a gang member (Reagan Colts, a politician-sponsored alleged athletic club). Later, after he was discharged from the army, he drove a truck in the stockyards and was also a union organizer, a somewhat hazardous occupation in the 1920s.

My grammar school, Holmes Elementary, was burned down by the son of a Chicago firefighter and was quickly rebuilt. I attended Tilden Technical High School, at that time, the best school on the south side. Although I was an indifferent student, I knew that I was receiving a very good education. In January 1954, I entered Tilden and found myself in one of the first honors programs in the school system. I never thought of myself as smart, but as someone who could grasp an idea quickly and retain it. Without doing a lot of homework and studying, I managed to graduate in the top third of my class.

I was fortunate to be educated by some no-nonsense teachers, many of whom were World War II veterans. But of course, World War II was the defining event of the 1940s and 1950s. When I was a child, almost every adult male that I knew had served in the military in World War II. It was expected that the entire family would attend the American Legion convention in downtown Chicago each summer. My father was a veteran of the 1st Infantry Division in World War II, and he and my grandfather were both members of the same American Legion post. At family gatherings and picnics, the talk among the men would typically refer to the war. War, or at least service in one of the armed forces, was a manhood rite of passage. And the Selective Service System helped to see that as many males as possible were afforded the opportunity to perform the rite.

The draft was an ever-present fact in the life of every male from age eighteen to twenty-four. If you went to college after high school, you could expect to be drafted when you graduated. If you married and didn't immediately have children, you could expect to be drafted. If you were lucky enough to find a good job, you could expect to be drafted and lose the job. Outside of marriage and children, there was little chance of escaping the draft. We all knew that draft exemptions were available, or that it was possible to become a conscientious objector, but those options were not even considered among the young men with whom I grew up.

While going to high school I became a rebellious teenager like so many of my peers. Although I had lettered on the swimming team, I quit to find a part-time job after school. Through the school work-study program, I worked two to three hours per day at Commonwealth Edison, the electrical utility company. Perhaps the pocket money fueled my rebellion, or maybe it was just a natural part of growing up and becoming an adult. My father attempted to control me, and of course, I resisted.

When I graduated from high school, I entered the Chicago branch of the University of Illinois, then a two-year campus located at Navy Pier, in an engineering curriculum. Although I had the aptitude for the field, I really wasn't interested in being an engineer. My father thought that his son's becoming an engineer would be a great step. I suspect that he wanted me to live my life under his direction. My growing rebelliousness led to arguments. It wasn't a good home life in 1958.

Midway through my second semester, in the fall of 1958, I was already on academic probation for poor grades and about to fail more courses. I decided to drop out of school and join the army.

I visited the local recruiter and asked if I could enlist. The recruiter asked how old I was and what I wanted to enlist for. I told him that I was seventeen and I wanted to be a paratrooper. The recruiter explained that I could certainly enlist for Airborne school, but that I would have to get permission from my parents to enlist as I wasn't eighteen.

By that time, the animosity between my father and me was to the point that he would deny me anything that I wanted, just to show that he could control me. So he refused to sign the enlistment papers.

The next day, I went to a different recruiting station, filled out a new set of papers and told the new recruiter that I would get my father to sign. I forged my father's signature and had an aunt, who was a notary public, notarize the forms for me. I figured that once I had left home, my parents would assume that I had run away and just accept my absence. I wasn't very slick.

The next day, I was in the downtown Chicago Armed Forces Entrance and Examining Station, waiting to take some tests, when my original recruiter came in and spotted me. He asked me what I was doing there when my father wouldn't give his consent. When in doubt, tell the truth, and I did. The recruiter took me out of there and brought me home.

That night, the recruiter and my father talked. I wasn't privy to the conversation, but I suspect the recruiter said something like "Mister Dooley, I think that you know by now that your son intends to leave home and enlist, with or without your permission. If you don't give permission now, he can enlist without your permission in two months when he turns eighteen. Why don't you give your consent and rebuild some of the trust and respect between you and your son?"

Whatever was said, it worked. On November 12, 1958, I

enlisted in the army. I knew that I'd miss my girlfriend, buddies, and family, but I needed adventure. Besides, if I didn't
enlist, the draft would have taken me in a few years anyway.

Basic Training was at Fort Leonard Wood, Missouri. Sometimes referred to as Fort Lost-in-the-Woods or Little Korea,
the post was isolated in the Missouri Ozarks. It was cold in
winter and hot in summer. In the winter, the snow was covered with a gray layer from the soot of a thousand coal-
burning stoves. The barracks were "temporary" World War II
buildings, still in service, and each had its own coal furnace
and outside coal pile. In warm weather, we didn't have to
worry about soot, but there was no air-conditioning.

The first step in the army process was the reception station,
where uniforms were issued and the Army Classification Battery (ACB) of tests was taken. Then, of course, there were the
first inoculations, which made almost everyone sick. Adding
to the bewilderment of my group of new recruits was the
seemingly illogical process that we went through.

When we first arrived, we were given fatigue uniforms,
underclothes, and towels. But we weren't given boots. That
was common, so you could track the progress of a platoon of
recruits by the state of their clothing. The newest guys had
only uniforms, but no boots. In the next day or so, brown
boots were issued, which had to be dyed black. So we had
boots which couldn't be worn while we waited for the dye to
dry so we could polish them to protect the dye. Then, we were
given the rest of our uniforms. All of that was interspersed
with testing, details, make-work projects, medical examinations, and seemingly endless immunizations. About five days
into the army, I experienced the ultimate humiliation: my parents visited me.

On their way to a vacation in the West, my parents were
driving down U.S. 66 through Missouri and decided to visit
their son. I was on KP (kitchen police) when they found me,
and I was wet and dirty from working in the mess hall. Of
course they were concerned about me, but I was embarrassed
to be visited and thought that I was being checked out by my

parents. That is not esteem enhancing to a teenager. Perhaps they sensed my discomfort because they quickly resumed their trip.

During the in-processing, I was interviewed by a bored specialist four (E-4) as part of the personnel assignment process. I was asked what I wanted to do in the army, what kind of a job did I want? I said that I had enlisted for Airborne. The bored interviewer asked me again: "But what do you want to do in the Airborne?" He explained that Airborne soldiers drive trucks, cook, keep personnel records, and all the other things that the rest of the army does.

I was amazed. I thought that I would jump out of airplanes all the time and do the things that the 82d and 101st Airborne Divisions did at Normandy. I had no idea that I would have a job in addition to being a paratrooper. So after about five seconds' consideration, I said that I wanted to be a truck driver.

Since the reception station was my first glimpse of the army, I wondered about all the noncommissioned officers (NCOs). I knew that NCOs didn't make as much money as civilians, but the NCOs that I saw seemed to have all the things that civilians had. They had families, houses, cars, and I just couldn't figure out how. Later I learned about the additional allowances, subsidized shopping, and free medical care. I also had a thought that I didn't share with my fellow recruits. Would I stay in and become one of these NCOs, and what would life be like in twenty more years, in 1978?

Basic training was exciting but uneventful. I had been raised on stories about basic training and looked forward to experiencing everything. We were armed with the M-1 Garand rifle and carried that rifle everywhere. But those old M-1s had been used for years and were no longer very accurate. It was still the Eisenhower administration, and not a lot of money was spent on defense. A recruit, paygrade E-1, earned seventy-eight dollars per month.

Early in the course, we were given a one-hour orientation by the Airborne recruiting team. I was much impressed with their presentation and figured that most of my company would volunteer. However, only about twenty-five people volunteered. There was an immediate physical training (PT) test and two-mile run. Only twelve of us passed. Although everyone should have been in good enough physical condition to meet the criteria, I suspect a lack of motivation by those who failed the test. For those with a mercenary bent, the extra fifty-five dollars per month in jump pay should have been a sufficient motivator, but even that wasn't. I began to realize that an Airborne or elite path wasn't for everyone.

A number of us were called to the dayroom one evening and told that we were eligible to apply for Officer Candidate School (OCS). Other than what I had seen so far, I didn't know very much about army officers. I thought that they were pompous swagger-stick-carrying martinets, and I didn't want to be one of them. Some of the group applied, but I didn't.

In the eighth week of basic, we received orders for Advanced Individual Training (AIT). Many of the draftees were sent to combat engineer training. I was sent to light-vehicle drivers school, which was eight more weeks at Fort Leonard Wood. So far, I was getting everything that I asked for in the army.

Light vehicles in the army consisted of everything from 2½-ton trucks on down. So we started with quarter-ton jeeps, moved to three-quarter-ton vehicles, and then on to deuce-and-a-halfs. Unlike those in basic training, the cadre were more laid-back, and there was less harassment. There were the usual Saturday morning inspections, and we could get passes to go to Waynesville or Rolla on Saturday afternoons. Waynesville had a population of about five hundred people and consisted mostly of bars and military stores designed to part new recruits from their money. Rolla was bigger, more sedate, but still a country town in comparison with Chicago. After exploring both towns once, I never bothered to go back.

I finished AIT in April 1959, drew advanced travel pay, and followed my orders to report to the 101st Airborne Division at Fort Campbell, Kentucky.

* * *

Fort Campbell was the real start of my military career. When I first passed through the main gate (Gate 4), the extremely neat and polished MPs were impressive. I knew that I was joining a unit that had made history, and I was going to become part of that organization. There were signs and names all over the installation reminding where the 101st had been and what its men had done. Jumping into Normandy during the early hours of D day, 06 June 1944, the 101st played a key part in the Allied landing. Later, the division's defense at Bastogne in the Ardennes (December 1944) broke the back of the German offensive known as the Battle of the Bulge. My first stop was the replacement detachment, where the 101st received replacements, processed them, and sent them forward to divisional units. But there was another aspect; the 101st Replacement Detachment also housed quitters and terminators pending their reassignment to non-Airborne units elsewhere in the army. Any individual could quit jump school at any time, and the quitter was gone from jump school and his unit within hours. Terminators were men who had become Airborne qualified but decided to terminate their jump status. Like quitters, they were sent from their units within hours.

Sadly, the quitters and terminators housed at the replacement detachment reminded one of a leper colony. Many of those people were losers who could not take the rigors of an Airborne unit and, like bad apples, had to be removed from the barrel immediately so they wouldn't spoil the remaining good soldiers. It also helped to keep the typical Airborne unit 100 percent deployable. But many of the terminators were old NCOs who had served in Airborne units for years. Some just became tired or wanted an easier job, and terminating their Airborne status was one way of getting reassigned. Once they terminated, however, they could never return to jump status. Although I hadn't yet gone to jump school, I knew that I would never quit or terminate.

At that time the 101st and the 82d maintained their own jump schools. There was also the Army Airborne School at Fort Benning, but that school mostly graduated officers. Some officers did attend the divisional jump schools, so it obviously wasn't mandatory that officers had to go to Benning.

The commander at Fort Campbell in 1959 was Maj. Gen. William Westmoreland. He was an impressive man who double-timed whenever he was outside in public. He set the tone for the division and was respected and loved by almost every-one. It was his concept of the Airborne that it was not just paratroopers; Westmoreland had been experimenting with helicopters to move troops about. So my first ride ever in a helicopter was in an H-34 to Support Group, my new unit in the 101st. I expected to be assigned to the 426th Supply and Transport Company, but that was not to be.

Support Group of the 101st consisted of the 801st Mainte-nance Battalion, the 521st QM Parachute Supply and Main-tenance Company, the 326th Medical Company, the 426th Supply and Transport Company, and a small Headquarters and Headquarters Detachment. Compared to the divisional support command of a mechanized or armored division, the 101st Support Group wasn't very large, but Airborne units have to be light and portable.

When I reported into the personnel office, the personnel sergeant major pulled me aside. He said: "Dooley, do you really want to be a truck driver?"

I didn't know if this was a test or trick question, so I replied: "I don't know, Sergeant. It's what the army sent me to school for."

"Can you type?"

"I took typing in high school and got up to about forty-five words-per-minute."

"I'm thinking about making you a clerk and having you work right here in this office."

With that short conversation, my career in the army took another direction. The personnel sergeant went on to explain that I was too smart to be a truck driver and that clerking was better for me. I didn't have the vaguest idea what he was talking about, but I did have experience changing truck tires and helping to load and unload cargoes, so I figured that being a clerk might not be too bad. I was assigned to the Headquarters Detachment. About two weeks later, I started jump school.

Jump school was three weeks of pull-ups, push-ups, and running, interspersed with training on how to jump and land with a parachute. It was designed to be physically challenging, but it also instilled a particular mental attitude. I learned very early that attitude was everything. As more than one jump-school cadreman told us: "It's all mind over matter. I don't mind, and you don't matter."

At the time, I didn't know about Pavlov and learned response, and B. F. Skinner's work in the same field. I learned, though, that you could train someone to the point that you could get a reflexive response from that individual, causing that person to do something that he might otherwise want to think about. How else do you get people to exit an aircraft flying at over 100 miles-per-hour, 1,250 feet above the ground? But it was still all fun.

Every morning at jump school, we'd have to stand inspection in formation. The cadreman would step in front of us, look for about five seconds, and announce to the platoon sergeant taking notes: "Ropes on patch, belt buckle not polished. Give me ten." The "ropes" might be a loose thread or two on my 101st shoulder patch, and the belt buckle comment could have been for anything. Doing ten push-ups was the punishment.

After each day at jump school, we'd all drag back to our barracks, shower, and prepare our uniforms for the next day. To avoid too many gigs, we would break starch each day (i.e., wear a newly laundered and starched set of fatigues), polish belt buckles and boots, and still expect that something wrong would be found. It was all a game, and if you approached it that way, you'd remain sane.

One person in our platoon was a thirty-five-year-old Catholic chaplain. He was harassed more than anyone else precisely because he was an officer and a chaplain. The jump school cadre expected more of officers than us enlisted peons. The cadre would constantly ask the chaplain if he wanted to quit, and they encouraged him to do so. He didn't quit, but was recycled to another class for medical reasons.

The culmination of our ground training was a five-mile run in the early morning hours in late May 1959 while it was still cool enough to avoid heat injuries. After everything else that we had been through in jump school, the run wasn't very hard and most made it.

The following week, we made the required five jumps from C-119 flying boxcars. The first jump was the hard one. As I advanced toward the door of the aircraft where the jumpmaster was putting each jumper out individually, I was sure that I'd balk. But when the jumpmaster said, "Stand in the door!" and "Go!" everyone, me included, automatically did so. That Pavlovian stuff worked.

We graduated in Mann Theater (named after a World War II 101st Medal of Honor winner), and we were all newly certified paratroopers. Some didn't make it, though. The attrition rate was around 20 percent, with most being recycled to later classes. To quit jump school was a shameful act, and very few would even consider it. Some did, but as I learned throughout my career in the army, people who don't belong in an organization ought to leave.

I enjoyed working in Support Group personnel. I kept getting better jobs, and I learned more as I went. But the real education was listening to the NCOs who had served in World War II and during the Korean War. Without ever spending a day in the infantry, I began to learn about what the infantry was like and how things were done. My professional education was coming along.

Headquarters Detachment didn't have a morning physical training (PT) program like most other units. Before the days of computers, we had to manually prepare monthly payrolls, keep track of promotions, reclassifications, temporary duty, jump manifests, and a wide assortment of other administrative tasks. So PT became an individual thing. We'd often run in small groups in the evenings, usually to the west, out to the weapons ranges. The remainder of the evening would usually be devoted to spit shining boots and preparing for the next day.

The 101st was a member of the Strategic Airborne Corps or STRAC. At the time, to be a STRAC soldier meant that you had extremely short hair, always wore starched and tailored fatigues, and spit-shined boots, and we all bought into it. We didn't realize that we were being perfect garrison soldiers because we all were just doing what was expected. Some said that STRAC stood for "Stupid Troopers Running Around in Circles."

In the spring of 1960, I came out on a levy to Germany. My unit didn't want to lose me, and I lucked out. I had just returned from the personnel administration course at the Adjutant General School at Fort Ben Harrison, Indiana, just outside of Indianapolis. The personnel sergeant used the opportunity to promote me to specialist four (E-4) and reclassify my MOS (military occupational specialty). While I was at Fort Harrison, I was selected as the unit soldier of the month, so maybe that helped, too. But things got better.

Also in the spring of 1960, most of the clerical personnel were taken out of Headquarters Detachment and assigned throughout the units of Support Group. Before that happened, the personnel office was losing each man one day every two weeks to KP at the 426th Supply and Transport Company where we ate. The idea was to farm everyone out to other units and bring us back to work in personnel each day, and we would be made SD (special duty) at our unit of assignment, which meant no more KP or other details. I ended up in the 326th Medical Company, the primary medical unit for the 101st. It had three clearing platoons, which operated clearing stations, each of which was the first stop enroute to an evacuation hospital. The remaining platoon in the 326th was the evacuation platoon, where I ended up.

Evac platoon was the largest platoon in the company and was responsible for moving wounded from the field back to the clearing stations. It also had a real job in peacetime in that it covered drop zones with medical support for every parachute jump. On almost every jump, someone would be injured. Typically, someone would land wrong, breaking a leg. Often, a jumper's parachute would have a partial inversion, called a Mae West because the parachute looked like a bra as it descended rapidly; or worse, someone might streamer in. The reserve parachute was supposed to remedy those situations but might compound them. Sometimes, the reserve chute only partially deployed and wrapped around the main chute, causing it to collapse completely. Other times, the trooper might land in strong winds and be dragged, unable to recover control. Regardless, injuries occurred.

I wasn't a medic, but I got to live with them and hear about what they experienced. My education continued. By osmosis, I began to learn what my fellow soldiers already knew about injury, disease, and treatment. I also learned about other ways to advance in the army. But maybe, the most important lessons I learned in 326th Med came from 1st Sgt. Wilbur Childress.

First Sergeant Childress was a master sergeant (E-7) at a time when the two new "super grades" had been introduced into the army. Too young to be promoted to master sergeant (E-8), Childress was a young anachronism. NCOs promoted to E-7 in 1959 and 1960 were being promoted to sergeant first class (E-7) with five stripes, while at the same time there were plenty of sergeants first class (E-6), also with five stripes. If the situation sounds confusing, it was.

Wilbur Childress was one of the real characters of the 101st. He was an extremely effective first sergeant, and nobody wanted to see him bumped out of his position. The group sergeant major protected him and wouldn't allow him to be replaced. Wilbur was good. I recall standing an evening formation one day when Childress, out in front of the formation, said: "We got to GI (clean) the dayroom tonight. I want one NCO from each of the clearing platoons, and fifteen enlisted swine from Evac." Yet despite his arrogant attitude, most of his troops loved him.

* * *

The only Ranger School allocations that came to Support Group went to 326th Med. There were no more Ranger units left in the army, but the extremely demanding Ranger training was looked upon as a leadership school for young NCOs and officers. But the formal emphasis of the school was on patrolling, mountain, and other operations, particularly in swampy areas. No combat patrol went out without a medic.

I wanted to go to Ranger School, because graduation from that course was accompanied by an automatic promotion to sergeant (E-5). When I asked First Sergeant Childress if he would send me to Ranger School, he said he would if I first went to Recondo School.

Recondo School in the 101st was the idea of General Westmoreland. Recondo was a contraction of recon and doughboy, and the school was meant to expose every small-unit leader in the 101st to operational patrolling. The school was unique in the army at the time and probably helped to advance Westmoreland's reputation. Heading the school was Medal of Honor winner Lew Millett. It wasn't an easy course, and wasn't designed to be. In two weeks, it taught everything that Ranger School did. But it was an effective discriminator. If you could pass Recondo School, the odds were that you'd pass Ranger School.

So, I went to Recondo School; twice in fact. I failed the first time because I didn't have an infantry background and wanted to guide my patrol along Jordan Springs Road after a helicopter assault. In the process, I learned that the guy with the clerk background was always assigned to carry the heavy things, such as the Browning automatic rifle (BAR), the A-6 machine gun, or the radio. Through adversity comes knowledge. The second time around I passed and was awarded Recondo number 996.

But when it came time for me to go to Ranger School, the personnel officer, who was a warrant officer parachute rigger, said no: "I don't need any Ranger clerks, and I won't release you to go." So be it. Buddha must have willed it.

About that time, Sgt. Maj. (E-9) Wayne Marion Price came to my rescue. Sgt. Maj. Wayne Price was one of the three original master sergeants (E-8), and one year later, one of the three original sergeants major (E-9) in the 101st. Another one of the three originals was George Dunaway, then sergeant major of the 2d Airborne Battle Group, 187th Infantry. Later on, Sergeant Major Dunaway would become sergeant major of the army. I met George Dunaway in Nha Trang when I was commissioned, years later.

Other than Ed Sprague, Sgt. Maj. Wayne Price is the individual who did most to keep me in the army and prepare me to become an NCO and, later, an officer. Looking back on things, I owe him a lot. Sergeant Major Price had me transferred down the hall to become his S-1 clerk. I didn't care, I was at a dead end in personnel. Most of the personnel leadership positions were occupied by folks who were tired and couldn't cut it anymore where they used to be. I was still young and hard charging.

Maybe First Sergeant Childress put in a good word for me. I don't know. Sergeant Major Price had me typing the daily bulletin and all the correspondence of the group adjutant (S-1). But I was also the official telephone answerer. I became a telephone middleman between the division commander and the group commanders. If I couldn't go to Ranger School and make buck sergeant, Sergeant Major Price looked out for me otherwise.

There were attempts to put me forward as the group soldier of the month. But I didn't have the time to study into all the trivia of the 101st. I was a STRAC soldier, but I wasn't very good at rote memorization. I read the history of the 101st, *Rendezvous With Destiny,* but I really was never in contention. I realize now that the attempt was a ploy by Sergeant Major Price to advance me, but I didn't deliver.

Then one day in the spring of 1961, 717 military occupational specialty (administrative specialist) opened up for promotion to E-5. Sergeant Major Price recommended me for promotion to specialist five (E-5) in MOS 717 but my old nemesis, the warrant officer from personnel, came forward with his own candidate and opposed me. The sergeant major and the warrant officer argued in front of the group commander for two hours, each pushing his candidate. With Sergeant Major Price's support, I won.

I didn't recognize it at the time, but it was then that I decided to become a career soldier. Even so, I almost became a permanent civilian, but the fates intervened. My enlistment was to be over in the fall of 1961, but the Russians decided to build a wall in Berlin to stem the tides of Germans fleeing to the West. In response to the wall, President Kennedy extended the enlistment of everyone in the armed forces. So my plans to return to college in January 1962 were thwarted, and I didn't get discharged until February 1962 after the spring semester had already started.

CHAPTER 2

Reenlistment

I went home to Chicago when my tour was up, but I found that I didn't really fit in. My friends' thrills were fast cars, while I remembered parachute jumping, wading through swamps, and rappelling down cliffs and from helicopters. Most of the people I knew were talking about how unhappy they were in their jobs, or about insurance, or the cost of housing. My path had taken me in a different direction, but some things remained the same. I returned to my father's house, but found that he still didn't want to accept me as an adult. I moved into an apartment, got a job, but wasn't happy. The solution for me was to reenlist, so I did. A little more than two months after my discharge, I was back in the army with an assignment to Korea.

The trip to Korea was by way of air to Yokohama, Japan, where we stayed at Kishine Barracks for about a week. Kishine was a small transients' compound with very few rules. For a young soldier, it was a surprise not to have formations and to have a houseboy make your bed and clean your area. It was easy to see how the American army became soft during occupation duty in Japan.

One day, it was announced that the aircraft that were supposed to fly us to Korea had been diverted to Laos for an emergency there. At the time in 1962, none of us had ever heard of Laos or knew where it was.

Instead of flying to Korea, we boarded a troopship and sailed to Inchon, Korea, by way of Taipei, Taiwan. My first time overseas, and I was getting quite a tour of the Orient. I was not terribly impressed with anything that I had seen so far and didn't even bother to take an authorized six-hour pass into Taipei. It took us about six days to reach Inchon.

There were no piers to tie up at in Inchon, so we boarded landing craft and sailed to the mainland. About a half mile out, the smell hit us. Korea smelled exactly like an outhouse! Whether it was too many people and not enough waste facilities or the use of manure as fertilizer in the rice paddies, the smell was pervasive. Everyone soon became used to it, and the smell became less noticeable. But it wasn't a good first impression.

The other pervasive smell in Korea was the garlicky odor of kimchi. Kimchi is a pickled cabbage, garnished primarily with garlic, salt, and pepper. The finished product is stored year-round in jugs where it develops a strong flavor and aroma. Kimchi is a staple eaten with rice by every Korean. When a crowd of Koreans gather, the kimchi smell is quite noticeable. Most Americans dislike the taste of kimchi, although a few consider it a delicacy.

In Korea, the American army was augmented by Korean soldiers who were attached to U.S. units. These soldiers called KATUSAs (Koreans attached to the U.S. Army) eat in the same mess halls with the Americans. It was always interesting to watch a newly assigned KATUSA pour copious amounts of sugar over roast beef and potatoes and gravy. KATUSAs must have liked the U.S. food as there was never a shortage of volunteers for the duty.

After breakfast each morning, the KATUSAs would wait for all the Americans to leave. Then they'd collect all the leftover uneaten fruit. Many oranges and bananas found their way to the black market in Taegu. But black marketeering wasn't the only sign that we weren't in Kansas any longer; corruption was a way of life in Asia, particularly in Korea. Paying bribes in Korea was the accepted practice. Raised in Chicago, I could understand bribery, which was also common when I was growing up. But in Korea, it was endemic. Later, I would learn that not even the Vietnamese were as corrupt as the Koreans.

Nothing could be left unsecured in Korea or it would be stolen; there were many cat burglars known as "slicky boys." It was rumored that a slicky boy could steal the sweat off your brow without your noticing it. Supposedly, the slicky boys came about as a result of the occupation of Korea by Japan, when stealing from the Japanese became part of the culture. I suspect, however, that slicky boys had been around for a lot longer than the forty-year occupation by the Japanese. Regardless, the slicky boys had no problem transferring their attention to their fellow Koreans and the Americans.

While we in-processed, we stayed at Ascom City, and within two days, I was on my way by train to 7th Logistical Command in Taegu. As I viewed the terraced rice paddies and the bare mountainsides, I wondered what it had been like to fight in such terrain during the Korean War. Most of the timber had been taken by the Japanese during their occupation of Korea before World War II. What little was left was under pressure from the growing population. It certainly appeared that Korea was an extremely poor country. Grave mounds dotted the hillsides. We were told that the higher up the hillside a body was buried, the more status the person had enjoyed in life.

Taegu is two hundred miles southeast of Seoul, the capital, and about one hundred miles north of Pusan, the southern coastal city. It was the newly opened headquarters for the field army logistical facilities in Korea. Actually, because of its remoteness, it was good duty.

I ended up being assigned as an administrative NCO in the adjutant general section, and within six months, I was promoted to staff sergeant (E-6). With less than four years in the army, I had attained a rank that would probably have taken me at least ten years' service to attain if I had remained in the 101st. Maybe because I was still young and enthusiastic, I was gaining rank and experience ahead of my peers. Eventually, I was named 7th Logistical Command NCO of the year. But I still felt that I wasn't in the mainstream army. I wanted to do more.

A few teams from the 1st Special Forces Group on Okinawa came to Taegu for training with the Republic of Korea (ROK) Army. When I saw my first Special Forces soldiers, I knew where I wanted to go. Thinking that I could get into Special Forces through the back door, as an administrative NCO, I applied for an intratheater transfer to 1st Group. My application was turned down, but I was getting closer when I was assigned to the 82d Airborne Division in 1963.

The 82d Airborne Division was considered the premier Airborne division in the army, but I always judged it against my experiences in the 101st. In 1964, the 82d was good and far better trained than most non-Airborne units in the army, but it suffered from close proximity with XVIII (18th) Airborne Corps and Washington.

XVIII Airborne Corps was and is the controlling headquarters for the 82d and 101st. Fortunately for the 101st, though, it was hundreds of miles away to the west at Fort Campbell. What that meant for the two Airborne divisions is that when visitors arrived to watch paratroopers in action, the 82d always got the tasking to put on a "Blue Chip" demonstration. That always involved at least an infantry battalion that had to spend valuable training and maintenance time looking pretty for the visitors.

Often presentation took precedence over substance. I remember watching a three-quarter-ton truck being towed to the heavy-drop rigging area and asking about it. I was told that the unit that owned the truck was going on alert as the division ready force and the truck had to be rigged. I asked, "But if the truck can't move under its own power, why prepare it to be dropped?"

The answer was that the unit had the requirement and that it probably wouldn't be called out. But if it was, the inoperable vehicle could have been blamed as a casualty of the drop. Besides, vehicles are luxuries that aren't really needed in an airhead. I began to think that, all things considered, I really didn't want to go to war with the 82d.

In the 82d, they took breaking starch and looking pretty seriously. Like everyone else, I played the game and went along.

In 1964, the 82d was scheduled to convert its organization from the then fashionable "pentomic" five-battlegroup configuration to a three-brigade infantry organization. The three brigades looked suspiciously like the old regiments of which the division had been composed before the pentomic battlegroup concept came in vogue, but the army could never admit it made a mistake with the battlegroup organization. So the solution was to reorganize and call the old regiments "brigades." Under the reorganization, I ended up as the personnel staff NCO of the 407th Supply and Transport Battalion.

All the personnel functions of the division had been centralized at division level. There was no longer a group personnel office. Instead, the liaison between the troops and units with the personnel people was the personnel staff NCO. I enjoyed the job and met a lot of good people, but I still wanted to go to Special Forces. I would get there eventually, but not for another year.

Many of the people that I met in the 82d Support Group I knew earlier from the 101st. We swapped stories and kept track of acquaintances. The Airborne community was still sufficiently small that we could keep track of each other. Some past friends had ended up in the 11th Air Assault Division.

The 11th Air Assault Division was formed earlier at Fort Benning, and many of its cadre came from the 101st and 82d, selected by name for transfer to Benning. But many personnel levies were not by name but by military occupational specialty (MOS) and grade requirements. So if there was a requirement to furnish a supply sergeant in the rank and grade of staff sergeant (E-6) to the 11th, you could expect that the least desirable individual would be sent. The 11th Air Assault wasn't made up entirely of castoffs from other units, but when we had the chance to rid ourselves of problem troopers, we used it.

Over many months, the 11th played with the "airmobile"

concept—heavily involving helicopters in all phases of its operations—and kept improving it. Finally, the graduating test for the 11th was an exercise against the 82d in Uhwarrie National Forest, west of Fort Bragg. There were some at the time who said that the test was rigged in the 11th's favor, but the airmobile concept was proven, and the 11th Air Assault was redesignated the 1st Cavalry Division. It would soon be sent off to Vietnam in 1965. Cold War events had been heating up, and it was obvious that the United States was getting involved deeply in Vietnam.

The Berlin Wall in 1961, the Cuban Missile crisis in October 1962, increasing activity in Laos and Vietnam, all pointed to bigger events in the near future. Everyone knew where the Cav was heading; we knew that we'd be going, too. It was time for me to figure out what I really wanted to do in the army, and where I wanted to do it.

By 1964, I had been in the army for almost six years. I had a relatively safe military occupational specialty and was drawing proficiency pay in that MOS. Although I had no formal training in the infantry, through reading and listening I knew almost everything there was to know about weapons and tactics. I had taken army correspondence courses for years, including the Special Forces course. The only thing holding me back was myself. I knew that most Special Forces soldiers had started out by serving in the 82d or 101st. In fact, the natural progression was to serve time in the Airborne divisions and then make the transition to Special Forces if you were so inclined. A non-Airborne infantryman coming from the 1st Infantry Division would be less suitable or adaptable to SF than I would be.

Everyone agreed that rank was faster in SF, but the duty was also a lot harder. I talked to many friends who had served in SF and ended back in the 82d. SF could be enjoyable and professionally challenging, but it was a killer on marriages and family life. Field training and travel were constants, but SF either produced or attracted the best NCOs in the army.

I struggled with my dilemma for months and finally realized that I had to go for it. I spoke with my battalion sergeant major and submitted my application. Clarence Mobley was the sergeant major at the time, and he had served in Germany, in Special Forces 10th Group, and became SF qualified. He understood what I wanted to do and insisted that I prepare myself. On the one hand, he wanted to keep me in his unit, but realized on the other that I needed to go on to other things. Part of his preparation was to personally administer the physical training (PT) test I had to pass as part of the application.

CHAPTER 3

Premission Training

"Who the fuck are you, and what do you want here?" Ed Sprague growled.

"I'm Staff Sergeant Dooley, and I've been assigned to your team for premission training," I replied. And, given those words of welcome to Training Team A-9, I thought that the next fourteen months might not be much fun. Even though he was an equal-opportunity grouch on first acquaintance, I learned later that Ed Sprague was a steadfast friend to everyone he liked. He proved to be a staunch protector of all of his team subordinates. Nobody, officer or enlisted, messed with Ed Sprague.

M. Sgt. (E-8) Ed Sprague was the operations sergeant of Training Team A-9 and was the ranking noncommissioned officer on the team. He was eating a brown-bag lunch in the A-9 team room with S. Sgt. Dave Boyd, an old friend of his from the 10th Special Forces Group in Germany. Dave Boyd would be killed in the Mekong Delta in Vietnam. Many others would also die there.

Ed Sprague wanted to build his new team around the nucleus of Team A-10, 10th Special Forces Group. He specifically wanted Dave Boyd as weapons, Jim Stewart as senior demo, and John Southworth as senior commo. Ed had been the team sergeant of A-10 previously, and he knew that if he had those three men, he could build the perfect A-team. Unfortunately, Boyd couldn't be released from his assignment, Jim Stewart was too ranking to serve on an A-team as a demo sergeant, and John Southworth wasn't available. All three made it to Vietnam. Eventually, Jim Stewart served a tour in

MAC-SOG (Military Assistance Command, Vietnam, Studies and Observation Group) without ever officially serving in 5th Special Forces Group. Later, Jim Stewart served on a classified assignment in Laos.

It was November 1965, and I had just reported to Company B, 7th Special Forces Group for premission training as part of a replacement packet team for later assignment to Vietnam. Like everyone else on the team, I had volunteered for Vietnam. I looked forward to my first combat tour and was glad that it was on a Special Forces A-team.

The advantage of going to Vietnam as a packet team was that everyone had trained together as a team for at least two months before going over. The alternative was going over as an individual replacement and having to work your way into an already existing team in Vietnam, proving yourself to people who had been working together for months prior to your arrival.

After lunch, Sprague told me, "You know the A-team table of organization and equipment (TO&E) has been changed for Vietnam?"

"How so?" I asked.

Sprague explained: "Well, the usual TO and E of an A-team has two of everything in six specialties: officer, operations and intelligence, weapons, communications, medical, and demolitions. For counterinsurgency purposes, one demolitions sergeant space has been dropped, and an assistant intelligence sergeant and a psychological operations/civic action officer and NCO spaces have been added."

"So what does that mean to me?"

Patiently, Sprague pointed out that my military occupational specialty (MOS) was infantry operations and intelligence NCO. I would normally be slotted as the A-team intelligence sergeant, but that I had been outranked in that position by SFC (E-7) Zane Osnoe. So, I would be assigned to the psychological operations NCO space.

Although I wasn't exactly thrilled by that, I considered my options. I could stay with the team, hoping for something better in the future, or go to Vietnam as an individual Special

Forces replacement. Since everything in Special Forces focuses on the A-team, I chose the first option and stayed with the team. I made the right decision. As with everything on an A-team, the slot that you fill matters little because everyone is cross-trained, and everybody functions as an infantryman. The medics can man mortars, the demo sergeants can communicate using Morse code, the weapons sergeants can develop and operate intelligence nets, and everyone goes on operations.

A Special Forces A-team (properly called an A-detachment) is a unique military organization. It is commanded by a captain (pay grade O-3), with an executive officer lieutenant (O-2), and it is fully staffed by noncommissioned officers. The lowest authorized ranks are sergeants (E-5), with most positions calling for staff sergeants (E-6) or sergeants first class (E-7). The team sergeant, or operations sergeant, calls for a master sergeant (E-8). Effectively, an A-team is the cadre equivalent for a typical American infantry company. A conventional rifle company of 160-plus people is commanded by a captain, who has five lieutenants working for him. The senior noncommissioned officer is a first sergeant (the pay grade equivalent of a master sergeant), and the four platoon sergeants are in pay grade E-7 (equivalent to a sergeant first class), which compares to the five sergeants first class on an A-team. So in the days of Selective Service, when all the lower ranks could be filled by the draft, each A-team meant taking away from the conventional army the talent, experience, and training nucleus of a rifle company. It's little wonder then that the army didn't look kindly upon Special Forces.

Even worse from the army perspective, Special Forces soldiers had to be capable of receiving training beyond the abilities of most officers and noncommissioned officers, thus skimming the top off the available personnel. Many SF soldiers later went on to earn baccalaureate degrees, and some obtained advanced degrees including Ph.D.s. After retirement from the army, a good many entered prestigious second careers.

An A-team usually has the mission of organizing, equipping, and training an indigenous battalion. Like the OSS of World War II, training indigenous people to fight for their homes and land is the primary mission of SF. The A-team then conducts guerrilla and other forms of unconventional warfare behind enemy lines, without benefit of the air, artillery, and logistical support normally available to a conventional battalion.

Non-SF soldiers wonder why anyone would want to serve on a small team, cut off from other units, operating in a hostile environment. The answer is that it's fun and professionally challenging. The SF soldier gets to do things that his conventional unit counterparts could never dream of. An SF soldier enjoys doing things outside the norm and doesn't consider the danger a significant factor. Of course, there is always an element of danger, but with the proper training and planning, the danger is easy to overcome. With the correct mindset, an SF soldier believes that the enemy is usually more afraid of him than the reverse. That's as it ought to be.

Serving on an operational A-team is not only professionally challenging, it's a break from the lockstep ways of doing things that the rest of the army practices. There's the freedom to perform your assignment, with obtained results being the only criteria. No chain of command looks over your shoulder, watching every move. So motivation is internal rather than external. Only in Special Forces can an NCO command a rifle company in combat.

The result of that environment is that an SF soldier is usually more self-confident than his conventional-warfare peers, better trained, more well-rounded in his cross-training, and typically arrogant. This last trait doesn't endear the SF soldier to the rest of the army. After all, General Patton was only allowed to be arrogant because he was rich and a general.

Within the enlisted ranks of an A-team, everyone is on a first-name basis. Rank is viewed as a garrison concept, as are short hair and spit-shined boots. After all, the goal is to fit in with an indigenous population, and most indigenous troops don't look like a soldier in the 82d Airborne Division.

Given my description of an A-team and a typical SF soldier, one would think that most people would want to join SF. That isn't the case. Most soldiers are content serving their time in units where they're told what to do always. And, surprisingly, most soldiers cannot adapt to living months at a time with a small group of people, having to moderate their personalities to fit in with the other members of an A-team.

It probably seems a contradiction to have confident, arrogant soldiers on one hand, but on the other hand to demand that they mesh with others. Perhaps that is where the training and evaluation sorts people out. Someone might not fit in on one A-team, but would fit perfectly on another. Evaluation (and resulting personnel transfer) is an ongoing system. Many newly assigned officers were astonished to find themselves transferred to another team because their enlisted teammates and nominal subordinates didn't think they'd fit in.

Before coming to Special Forces, I had spent a year in the 82d Airborne Division, a tour in Korea, and three years in the 101st Airborne Division. But my background was administrative, and I wanted to quit pushing paper so I could run around in the woods like a real soldier. Besides, with what was going on in the early sixties, like building the Berlin Wall, Castro's Cuba, Laos, and a growing conflict in Vietnam, I didn't need a crystal ball to know that more war was coming. We all saw that, and many career soldiers wanted to leave the infantry for easier jobs while I was going the reverse route.

I came from the 82d Airborne to Special Forces. Joining SF had always been my goal. After all, at the time, if someone really wanted to soldier, SF was the ultimate assignment in the army. Unlike today, there were no Ranger units, and the only elite warrior units in the army were SF and Airborne, and I had had my fill of the Airborne as represented by the 82d.

After a selection interview with the SF recruiting sergeant

major at Fort Bragg, I was assigned to Special Forces Training Group in early January 1965.

SF Training Group was located in the army's ubiquitous World War II temporary wooden buildings in the Spring Lake area of Fort Bragg. It was a relatively small organization commanded by a lieutenant colonel. Except for SF medical training, Training Group ran all the classroom and field instruction for the SF enlisted specialties. SF medics were trained at Fort Sam Houston and various post hospitals throughout the United States, returning to Fort Bragg only for Dog Lab, the eight-week culmination of training for SF medics. To be an SF medic then was equivalent to being a physician's assistant now, without the requirement to practice under a physician. SF medics spent the longest time in Training Group, usually about a year and a half, but Dog Lab was the biggest attrition factor. The medics in SF were usually the most intelligent people on the team. Since they had the most potential, it was always difficult to train and keep those critical people.

Building on all the medics' previous clinical work, Dog Lab gave intense instruction in everything else an SF medic needed to know. In the last weeks of the course, each student was given a dog previously rescued from a local pound. With an underpowered round so that the wound would be large but treatable, the dog was shot with a .30-caliber rifle in the rear hindquarter.* The aspiring medic then had to debride the wound, treat it, prevent infection, and nurse the animal back to health without benefit of antibiotics. When the dog could again walk, the supervising physician certified that the dog would heal, the student medic anesthetized the dog, amputated the leg, and when the physician again approved the procedure, the dog was euthanized. If the dog died anytime before being properly dispatched, the aspiring medic failed the course and might be retrained in another specialty.

---

*Animal rights activists later forced Dog Lab to quit using dogs and switch to goats. Goats aren't as lovable as dogs and don't have a human lobbying organization.

Communications, weapons, demolitions, and operations and intelligence were the other MOS courses taught in Training Group. Future communications sergeants drilled on Morse code for eight weeks, along with antenna theory, and crypto-material to encode communications. As with the other courses of instruction, there were make-break points that had to be passed. The trainees had to reach required norms for sending and receiving speeds, and had to establish stable communications, regardless of the weather conditions, interference, and skip distances involved with their antennas. Aspiring communicators were kept in separate barracks. In the evening, the code oscillators they practiced with could be heard from twenty-five feet away.

Weapons instruction concentrated on light and heavy weapons, both indirect and direct fire. Instruction was on U.S. and foreign weapons, and a particular emphasis was placed on the Soviet-bloc arms. The book *Small Arms of the World* became a weapons sergeant's bible. Field expedients were taught, one of which was that a cut-down nail could replace the firing pin in an M-79 grenade launcher. Silenced weapons and the use of subsonic ammunition and field-expedient silencers were taught as well. These were not weapons taught conventional infantrymen.

Demolition sergeants weren't limited to blowing things up, but understood both construction and destruction. Conventional demolitions were taught, along with improvised demolitions. Nuclear demolitions were also introduced. Students had to calculate minimum charges, specify the demolition material, and be able to support their choices for blowing dams, bridges of various kinds, and buildings. We learned that earmuff charges could breach concrete piers or dams, while C-4 ribbon charges could cut steel towers or other structures. For earmuff charges, equal lengths of det (detonation) cord would be the primers to each C-4 charge, and the two primers were taped together on top and further primed with a blasting cap. If everything was done right and the lengths of det cord were equal and the charges opposite each other (like two halves of an earmuff), the two explosions would reverberate off one another, turning the concrete to dust. We also learned that common items such as sugar, soap, matchheads, sawdust, wax, fertilizer, and battery acid can be used in combination with other items to create explosives or ignite extremely hot fires.

The combat engineer demolition sergeants on an A-team are often the hardest working people. They can usually be forgiven if they calculate a higher demolition charge than is necessary. Why use two pounds of C-4 when ten pounds will do just as well? Better too much than too little. But when an exact explosive effect is required, they can produce it: It takes a different explosive and amount to blow down a door than to dig a hole or cut a tree.

Operations and intelligence NCOs were taught the standard course of instruction to qualify them but received an added emphasis on POW interrogation, propaganda, photography, evasion and escape nets, and other intelligence tradecraft. After that course, they took another eight weeks at the intelligence school in Baltimore for more advanced topics. Area study and assessment and order of battle development would become reflexive job habits.

My specialty was operations and intelligence (O&I). I was constantly amazed at what you could do with ordinary things. An example: We learned how to develop a 35mm film canister without a darkroom. With the usual chemicals and a little practice, the film can be developed inside the canister in a water tumbler. But just dropping a 35mm canister into a glass of developer won't work. The method and the practice are the key.

Intelligence training at Fort Holabird, Maryland, was eight weeks of intensive instruction on interrogation, aerial photo reading and interpretation, and order of battle exercises. While a lot of the instruction was classified, most of what was taught could be learned through reading spy novels. Classes usually ended early on Friday afternoons, and most people drove the three hundred miles back to Fort Bragg for the weekends. The sixties were still the time of the one-car family, and wives and families needed to buy groceries and shop.

Fort Holabird was a rather unique post. It trained the usual assortment of intelligence analysts, interrogators, and imagery interpreters, but it also trained the "agent handlers," who all dreamed of being James Bond and going throughout the world doing exotic things. We could tell when a class received their civilian clothing allowance because they all would buy trench coats and wear them with their army low-quarters shoes. We thought of them as wimps.

But Holabird had good courses. Methods of Surreptitious Entry for example: Most people would think of clandestine entry as involving lockpicks, but there are easier ways that don't need description. Needless to say, if one man can lock or secure it, another man can open it. The Intelligence School has since been moved to Fort Huachuca, Arizona. I wonder how the agent handlers practice handoffs and urban surveillance in the desert?

Besides the MOS courses, there were two other common courses that all Training Group attendees had to undergo: Methods of Instruction (MOI) and Branch Training.

MOI was only two weeks long, but it was the first part of the winnowing process. Under the theory that every SF soldier was an instructor, we learned how to teach any subject,* using field training aids and, sometimes, interpreters. In order to challenge the novice instructor, class topics for course completion were chosen to be very dull. I had to teach the use of items in the engineer tool kit, a most boring subject.

Technical or difficult subject matter had to be presented in interesting ways so that even uneducated people could understand. Later, many of us worked with the montagnards of Vietnam, and much of what was taught in MOI helped us to train those primitive tribesmen: "bullets" would be translated as the fruit of the rifle, a rifle magazine became the pod of the fruit of the rifle. The montagnards could understand natural

---

*The burden of education was on the teacher. It was axiomatic that if the student failed to learn, the instructor failed to teach. If this same standard were applied to local schools throughout the United States, teacher unions would cry foul.

things, so complicated matters had to be placed in a simple context.

Branch Training was five weeks of classroom and garrison instruction, followed by a two-week field exercise in Pisgah National Forest in the mountains of western North Carolina.

Branch was the round-out instruction that every Special Forces soldier had to have. Survival, tactics, patrolling, ambushes, resupply, caches, and historical examples of successful and unsuccessful insurgencies were taught, along with intensive map reading and navigation. How many people know that one degree of longitude at the equator is sixty nautical miles and equals sixty-nine statute miles? Emphasis was placed on determining location by longitude and latitude since most maps do not use the military Universal Transverse Mercator (UTM) system, and there was, as yet, no global positioning system (GPS) except in the minds of science fiction authors.

The Pisgah field exercise was usually the culmination of all the SF training and thus the equivalent of the graduate orals exam. Teams assumed insurgency or counterinsurgency roles, then were parachuted into the mountains and operated against each other. Missions were assigned within the exercise, and success was evaluated according to what each team did to the other. That phase of training proved to be extremely arduous—and hungry, too, as many ration resupplies failed to appear. Opposing teams often stole each others' food. But then, the course wasn't supposed to be easy.

In the exercise, I was a team sergeant on an insurgency team. We didn't have any guerrillas with us, but we raised hell anyway. In one part of the exercise, I had to do the handoff of an evading downed airman. The exercise controllers set the situation up so that it had to be accomplished on a certain area of shoreline on Lake James. I figured that made it too easy for the counterinsurgency troops to find us and stop the handoff, so I rented a fishing boat that afternoon. Then, that evening, we rowed close to the pickup point and pretended to be fishing. When the transfer party arrived, I clearly heard over the water: "Shit, they're in a boat." The evading airman was transferred and the counterinsurgency team (wherever they were) never knew what we had done.

Throughout the training, officers and enlisted were never mixed. Officers didn't train in Training Group and went to the field in Uwharrie National Forest in North Carolina. It always seemed odd to me about the training of SF officers. In 1965, they didn't train with their potential troops, and their course of instruction was different, a "gentleman's course." Yet, when I received a direct commission in January 1967, in Vietnam, I lost my SF qualification until I could prove that I had taken the SF correspondence course, which I had finished before I joined SF. Obviously, SF officers were held to a lesser and different standard than SF NCOs. But then, maybe that wasn't bad. The qualification of an individual in SF could often be read at a glance at the flash on the beret. The beret flash is a colored background on the beret, over the wearer's left eye. The color denotes the SF group (green for 10th Group, red for 7th Group, etc.) and sometimes the SF qualification of an individual. A typical flash is about two inches long and two inches wide, with a curved bottom, and generally looks like a miniature shield.

Over the years and in different SF units, policies relating to the beret flash have varied, as have the rules on the wearing of the beret. In some units, everybody, including cooks and drivers, would wear the green beret and a full flash, regardless of SF qualification. In some other units, non-SF qualified people might wear a half flash (a half-inch tall flash in the form of a rectangle) on their beret. In other units, the green beret and full flash might be reserved for wear only by qualified people. In the early nineties, it was common to see nonqualified women support personnel wear green berets and full flashes at Fort Bragg. But that policy changed, and as of 1999, only SF-qualified men wear the green beret and full flash. But the more basic issue has always been what constitutes SF qualification?

Unlike the navy SEALs who have only one place where potential SEALs—officer and enlisted—can become trained and qualified, the army has had multiple ways to qualify SF soldiers. That leads to the conflict between Training Group flashes and "paper" flashes, which can be obtained as easily as taking the SF correspondence course and passing the written tests. Other paper flashes were awarded upon completion of on-the-job training (OJT), typically within a reserve component (Army Reserve or National Guard) unit. But in the early days of the 10th Special Forces Group in Europe, most of the qualification training was unit taught, leading to the award of paper flashes in what some have said was the best SF unit in the army. Obviously, there is a wide diversity among paper-flash qualified people.

The dialogue over real flashes and paper flashes goes on today. I don't care which is considered better because I have both. Before I ever went to Training Group, I had completed the SF extension course, which kept me SF qualified when I became an officer. But Training Group instruction for the enlisted specialties has become the standard.

In early 1965, Training Group had an attrition rate of 10 to 25 percent. Other than first completing MOI, there was no particular sequence of courses. So many went to the classroom portion of Branch before taking their MOS specialty instruction; others did it the other way around. Little thought was given to the attrition rate or sequencing of instruction as there was no impetus to graduate a large number of students. Vietnam and the Dominican Republic changed all that.

In 1965, the 5th SF Group was assigned to Vietnam from Fort Bragg. Yet the growing SF needs in country could not be met solely by the 5th, and TDY (six-months' temporary duty) teams were still being sent to Vietnam from Fort Bragg and the 1st SF Group on Okinawa. SF had been in Vietnam since 1961, and many of the SF people at Fort Bragg had already been to Vietnam on at least one TDY trip. Special Forces had to expand to meet the demands of Vietnam.

Then, the 82d Airborne was sent to the Dominican Republic in the summer of 1965, and some Training Group students began to wonder why they should study in Training Group, when they could terminate SF training and most likely be assigned to the 82d and go to war in Dom Rep. Back in those days, lots of folks wanted to go to war.

The John F. Kennedy Center for Special Warfare was the controlling headquarters for the Special Forces Groups at Fort Bragg, and they began to see that they might have a potential manpower problem. So an order went out to speed up SF training and to discourage voluntary termination at Training Group.

The order came too late to help me move out of Training Group faster; I had already completed MOI, O&I, and most of Branch. By July I was going to intelligence school at Fort Holabird, Maryland. At the end of August, I graduated Training Group and was assigned to the 7th Special Forces Group. On paper at least, I was a fully qualified Green Beret. But there's a final comment on Training Group.

Training Group only provided the basic instruction for new SF people. There were other courses of instruction throughout the army and at Fort Bragg that SF men went to. Language courses were taught at Bragg, at the Presidio of Monterey, and in Washington. HALO (high altitude low opening) parachute instruction, the military equivalent of skydiving (but quite different),* was offered outside of Training Group. SCUBA school was in Florida.

In 1965, to be SF qualified meant that you were "3" qualified, which was part of our MOS. Some said that the 3 stood for the three types of infiltration: air, land, and sea. Others said that the 3 stood for skydiving, skin diving, and muff diving.

The JFK Center and the 6th and 7th Special Forces Groups were located in the Smoke Bomb Hill area of Fort Bragg. The 3d SF Group was located with Training Group in the Spring Lake area. Other non-SF units belonged to the JFK Center,

---

*As one unnamed person said: "I don't care how many sky dives you've got. Until you've jumped from 1,250 feet into absolute darkness, carrying ninety-five pounds of equipment, using a forty-two-pound parachute, to me, you're still a leg!"

such as psychological operations battalions and civic action units, but SF people tended to look upon those other units with disdain. In return, the psychological operations people viewed us as mental midgets and fools. A popular psy ops poem in those days went:

> Strong back, and a rucksack
> Weak brained, but cross trained
> Run and play in a Green Beret
> Special Forces, strong right arm of Psychological
>   Operations

Oh well, our mothers and wives liked us.

Back then, one peculiarity about Smoke Bomb Hill was the speed limit along Gruber Road. On the rest of Fort Bragg, the usual speed limits were twenty-five or thirty miles per hour. On Gruber Road, the main artery through Smoke Bomb Hill, the speed limit was fifteen miles per hour and it was rigidly enforced by the military police. A few years before, General Yarborough's daughter had been killed by a 2½-ton truck just a few days before her wedding. Although the accident happened near the main NCO club, General Yarborough was only able to get the Gruber Road speed limit lowered. As sad as the accident was, the lowering of the speed limit shows the almost limitless power of general officers.

In 1965, things were still fairly slow at Fort Bragg, but a number of "Go" teams out of the 3d SF Group were getting Gemini space-shot missions from NASA. (A Go team was any small, specialized group with specialized skills suitable to accomplish a specific task.) Whenever a missile from the Gemini program was fired, the teams would wait in relatively plush hotels throughout Africa in case the capsule landed in Africa and had to be quickly secured.

The 6th SF Group was organizing as a counterinsurgency group, with beefed-up signal and aviation assets. The 7th SF Group was sending out training teams worldwide, running the premission program for Vietnam, and operating the

Gabriel demonstration area. Most of us had a love-hate relationship with the Gabriel demonstration area. While everyone recognized that Special Forces had to have a public relations forum to show what we could do and thus keep our slice of the army budget, almost every SF soldier hated to maintain the area and participate in the demonstrations.

Conceived as a country-fair series of briefing exhibits, followed by a mini-air show, and named after Sp5. James Gabriel, Jr., the first SF KIA of the Vietnam war on 04 April 1962, the area was the ultimate dog and pony show. Sawdust paths were meticulously maintained, while snakes and animals in the survival exhibits had to be fed twice daily, year-round. There were, however, humorous anecdotes to come out of the area.

A congressional delegation was touring the area once and was viewing the survival show. As an NCO showed how snakes could be used as food, he explained that all you had to do was cut off the head, slit the belly, and cook the critter. When one congressman asked what you would do if you didn't have a knife, the NCO bit the head off the snake and spit it out. Perhaps he was the first "snake eater," a term that later became a derisive term for SF soldiers.

In early 1965, when Gen. Harold K. Johnson was the army chief of staff, he visited the JFK Center. General Johnson was not Airborne qualified and had no great love for any allegedly elite organization. During his tour of the Gabriel demonstration area, almost everything seemed to go wrong: When a caribou aircraft made a low-level cargo extraction (LOWLEX), the extraction parachute separated from its cargo. Then a cargo-drop pallet broke apart on landing, scattering barrels all over the drop zone. Finally, an L-19 Bird Dog aircraft tried to drop a poncho parachute (a field expedient parachute made from an ordinary rain poncho), but the parachute streamered. It was not a proud day for Special Forces.

Regardless of what General Johnson might have thought of Special Forces, SF was the right organization in the right place at the right time. President Kennedy had authorized Special Forces to wear the green beret in 1961, Robin Moore wrote *The Green Berets* in 1965, and S.Sgt. Barry Sadler would soon introduce his song "Ballad of the Green Beret,"* which would eventually become the Special Forces anthem. Special Forces was hot and would not be stifled in the early days of the Vietnam War: the war they would come to be most closely associated with in the public mind. By the end of the war, almost every Special Forces soldier in the army would have had at least one tour in Vietnam and most would have multiple tours.

In an unconventional warfare situation, an A-team about to be inserted would be quarantined and begin an area study of the objective insertion area. During Vietnam, premission training took its place. Premission training was eight weeks of intensive instruction on the geography, culture, history, economics, politics, and society of Vietnam. Additionally, there was refresher training on pertinent SF topics. Half the day was spent in the classroom and the other half was devoted to Vietnamese language instruction. The content, presentation, and quality of instruction were exceptional. If the rest of the soldiers throughout the army could have received that course before going to Vietnam, the later, nagging question of "Why are we here?" would never have arisen. The United States was in Vietnam as part of the Communist containment effort that was the central focus of the Cold War, and to assist an ally to repel the invasion of North Vietnam.

Ho Chi Minh, the president of North Vietnam, after his victory over the French in 1954, decided to take South Vietnam by military force. In 1954, the country was partitioned into a Communist North and a Democratic South, and reunification elections were to be held in 1956. However, after viewing the purges, executions, imprisonments, and

---

*Part of the gallows humor of the time was expressed in an unofficial verse to Barry Sadler's song: "Back at home, a young wife waits, doing the Dog at Annex 8. Ten thousand bucks, she got today, 'cause Charlie greased her Green Beret." The Dog was a popular dance, and Annex 8 was an NCO club in the Spring Lake area. Charlie was a slang term for the Viet Cong derived from "Victor Charlie," a phonetic rendering of the phrase's initials.

expropriation of property by Ho in the north, the South Vietnamese wisely decided to have nothing to do with North Vietnam and canceled the elections. That set in motion the plan to sponsor insurgency in South Vietnam and for the eventual invasion by the North. But, although accurate, that explanation is simplistic and must be considered with the other variables of Vietnam, most notably its long and very complex history.

Vietnam history began with the original inhabitants, the Cham, who are today Muslim aborigines. The next migration of people were the montagnards who settled in the highlands and were of two distinct ethnic groups: Mon-Khmer and Malayo-Polynesian, formed into thirty-two separate tribes. The last major migration consisted of Vietnamese whose culture is closely associated with the Han-Chinese, but who have been at war with the Chinese off and on for two thousand years. Most recently, ethnic Cambodians moved into parts of Vietnam, while the French colonized all of Indochina in the 19th century.

It was also explained to us that every ethnic group hated the others. The Vietnamese hated the montagnards, whom they categorized as *moi* or savages,* while the montagnards fought among themselves. Given the opportunity, the montagnards would have taken the Central Highlands and seceded, and the Cambodians would have annexed to Cambodia large areas in the south of the country. The North Vietnamese wanted it all. But so did the Chinese.

Of course the ethnic Vietnamese religious minorities also wanted their slice of the pie. The Hoa Hao and Cao Dai were offshoot Buddhist groups that were vehemently anticommunist, but were also distrusted by the Saigon government. The Buddhist majority were not necessarily anticommunist, but did oppose the minority Catholics who governed the Republic of Vietnam.

The only unifying theme in the disparate groups com-

---

*Some Vietnamese school books characterized montagnards as having a lot of body hair and long tails.

prising Vietnam society was Special Forces. SF was specifically tasked to work with the minority groups in building paramilitary organizations to operate against the VC and NVA. They were markedly effective in doing this, returning the most enemy casualties at the least cost to the United States. SF may have been cost effective, but as usual, that didn't endear SF to the rest of the army.

After the partition of Vietnam in 1954, the U.S. Army created and staffed a huge Military Advisory and Assistance Group (MAAG) in Vietnam. True to the rule that the army always prepares to fight the last war, the MAAG in Vietnam built a conventional infantry and armor-heavy Vietnamese army. Apparently nobody told the U.S. Army advisers in Saigon that the country was mostly jungle, mountains, or swampy rice paddy.

It shouldn't then have been a surprise that by 1964, the Army of the Republic of Vietnam (ARVN) was losing a battalion a week to the insurgent Viet Cong.

Special Forces fought a different war than did ARVN. Where ARVN units maneuvered battalion-size formations (three hundred to five hundred men) through the countryside, always under the fan of supporting artillery batteries, SF concentrated on relatively small units engaging the VC in small meeting-engagements. That tactic didn't produce major battles, but it tended to keep the insurgents off balance and caused a slow attrition of their forces.

U.S. units, when committed to Vietnam, all used the conventional approach to warfare, although relying more heavily on airmobile operations.

In 1965, a public affairs team from the 173d Airborne Brigade* was touring bases in the United States. When they made their presentation at the JFK Center, there was mock trepidation that the 173d would win the war before the rest of us had a chance to participate. But in the true fashion of the

---

*Airmobile and Airborne are not synonymous. Airmobile designates troops inserted by aircraft (usually helicopter); Airborne troops are parachute inserted. However, in reality, most airborne operations were heliborne insertions.

time, the 173d with its traveling dog and pony show was only doing what other units were doing—using public affairs briefings to gain attention and budgetary dollars. The army was looking forward to its first big war since Korea, and nobody wanted to be left out of the action.

There were advantages to being in premission training. The major one was that post support details were not required if you were preparing for Vietnam. Nobody ever questioned the need to cut the grass within the Special Forces areas or to police up trash. After all, those things were universal throughout the army; although some doubted they were done at the Pentagon. The army in its infinite wisdom placed the JFK Center under the control of the XVIII Airborne Corps, the controlling headquarters for Fort Bragg. Fort Bragg then counted up the numbers of people assigned to the SF units and assigned post support details accordingly, without concern that SF had almost all NCOs and very few troops. The result was that senior NCOs were cutting grass throughout the post, loading furniture, and moving desks.

Unfortunately, nobody ever realized that as much as most NCOs wanted to be in SF, they did not, after twenty years, want to cut the grass. Many got out of the army. Alternatively, many SF people sought to serve in SF outside of Fort Bragg, primarily overseas.

With constant missions, training, and the resulting strains on family relations and finances, an SF soldier did not need more irritants. Yet we persevered; the alternative was to transfer to the 82d Airborne Division, and to most SF soldiers, that was like being demoted from college to primary school.

In December 1965, we finished premission training. Some of us already had the beginning of doubts as to how the war was being fought. After all, we had all been exposed to Mao Tse-tung and his adage that the guerrilla is a fish that swims in the sea of the population and that guerrillas need safe areas to build, train, and operate from. If that was the case, why were the Marines fighting a war in I Corps—the northern-most of the four "corps tactical zones" into which South Vietnam was divided—that differed markedly from what was happening in the other three corps areas of Vietnam?

Lieutenant General Walt was the commander of the Marine forces in I Corps. Although there were some minimal army forces there, including Special Forces, I Corps was "owned" by the Marines.

In theory, all the U.S. Forces in Vietnam were a unified command under the control of the commander, U.S. Military Assistance Command, Vietnam (COMUSMACV). However, theory didn't always equate with reality. The Marines still belonged to the navy, and the COMUSMACV, General Westmoreland, actually had to report through the navy's commander in chief, Pacific, to Washington.

One of the principles of war is unity of command, which means that no man can serve two masters and should only be responsible to one boss. In Vietnam, this principle was largely disregarded, and General Walt was allowed to fight his own separate war.* The handwriting was on the wall as early as 1965. But General Walt can't be faulted for trying to get away with whatever he could; the blame rested higher in the chain of command.

General Walt announced that his Marines would establish "coastal enclaves" in which the majority of the Vietnamese population would be protected, and that the guerrillas would "wither" in the hills. It was obvious that General Walt had never read Mao, and he generously provided that safe haven to the insurgents. Some might argue that the coastal enclave concept was only a manifestation of a Marine beachhead mentality. Regardless, the Department of Defense allowed the Marines to get away with it, and the blame can be equally

---

*Years later, I was a young major attending Command and General Staff College when retired General Westmoreland addressed our class in 1977. When asked why the Marines went their separate way in the early phase of the Vietnam War, General Westmoreland said in effect that he couldn't control them.

distributed. In a critical area of Vietnam, the majority of the terrain was freely given over to the enemy in the early stages of the war. By mid-1968, with the fall of Kham Duc, there were no Special Forces border camps left in I Corps; thus intelligence information on the infiltration of the North Vietnamese Army (NVA) into I Corps was largely limited to what the Marines could provide themselves. Later in the war, Saigon imposed an army corps into the I Corps zone, and it controlled army units within the area, but it was a case of too little, too late.

With premission training behind us, we began the tasks needed to leave Fort Bragg. We completed all our shots, made out wills, and arranged for allotments to our families. Those of us who lived on post cleared our quarters and took our families home for the holidays. When we returned to Fort Bragg in January, we drew individual and team equipment, packed it all up, and waited for our C-130 transportation to arrive.

The great adventure was to begin.

CHAPTER 4

Camp Mai Linh

On a cold Sunday afternoon in early February 1966, we loaded everything onto a 2½-ton truck, boarded a bus, and went to Pope Air Force Base. There, we loaded our equipment on a C-130 aircraft and began a three-day trip to Vietnam. All of the TO&E equipment authorized to an A-team was with us. But authorized equipment is more than any one person can use at any point in time. We probably had six hundred pounds per man of equipment. At least the army cared enough about us to authorize anything that we might need. Unlike the rest of the army, each soldier had two weapons, a .45-caliber pistol and an M-16 rifle. We also had tentage that we would never use and a typewriter that we stole from Company B, 7th Group. We weren't going in like an OSS team infiltrating France in 1943.

Nobody came to see us off, but that was okay. We all had our minds on the future. We knew that some of us wouldn't be coming back, but nobody knew which of us wouldn't make it. To hell with that—drive on! Nobody lives forever, and we're the best soldiers in the world! We really did believe.

There were two A-team packets on the aircraft. Not very many people, but with equipment, it was cramped and uncomfortable. I read *Catch-22* on the way over. Most of the other team members read, talked, or slept.

Roger Knight was our team commander. He was a captain, thirty-six years old, and, unusual for Special Forces, an armor officer. Roger was a bachelor and had just come back from a skiing vacation in New England. His executive officer was John Mullins. A career-long Special Forces soldier, John had been an enlisted medic who went to Officer Candidate School. As an infantry second lieutenant, John was going back to Vietnam for his first full tour after serving an earlier TDY tour. John knew more than most about what we were getting into.

Joe Simino was the civil affairs/psychological operations officer. A graduate of artillery OCS, Joe was formerly an infantry squad leader in the Berlin brigade in Germany. Joe and I became friends during language instruction. When my grandfather died and I had to leave early for emergency leave, Joe cleared my quarters for me.

M.Sgt. Ed Sprague ran the team. He allowed various captains to command it at one time or another, but the team was his. No officer dared screw with Ed Spague. More about Ed Sprague later.

Zane Osnoe was the intelligence sergeant. Like Mullins, Zane had had a previous TDY tour in Vietnam. A former combat engineer and an Airborne veteran of the Korean War, Zane was the one to take me on my first patrol and make sure that I was properly broken in. Zane was underutilized at the A-team level. A brilliant guy, he soon ended up on the B-team.

Jim Welsh was the light weapons sergeant. Quiet and cool, Jim didn't talk very much, but he knew his way in the woods. Jim probably forgot more about infantry operations than most people knew. I remember him one time, chasing a VC unit with his CIDG company, coolly and methodically reporting the VC casualties as he moved along.

Heavy weapons sergeant fell to Jean Uszakow. Born in Hungary, Jean had assisted the Maquis in Paris during World War II and later joined the U.S. Army. A fluent French speaker, he ended up as our primary interpreter. Jean did not survive the tour.

Henry Caesar and Wayne Summers were our medics. Caesar was senior and, of course, his nickname was Julie. Summers was a recent graduate of Dog Lab, and it was his first overseas assignment.

Our communications sergeants were John McFadden and Mike Dooley. McFadden had been in Special Forces almost from the beginning. Mike Dooley (no relation to the author) was a laid-back Californian who had graduated from Training Group in the summer of 1965. Unfortunately, Mike would be killed at Duc Lap in 1968. Mike was also an exceptionally talented cartoonist, and many of his efforts were published in *The Green Beret* magazine.*

Arnold Sims was the demolitions sergeant. He also doubled as the team supply sergeant and mess sergeant. He had no easy jobs.

The assistant intelligence sergeant was Bill Spencer. Nicknamed Barney, Spencer was so enthusiastic about the war that he was an early volunteer for Project Delta (B-52). He really enjoyed being on a six-man recon team, breaking brush in "denied territory" (an early euphemism for Cambodia, Laos, and North Vietnam). Bill was killed in 1969.

After a refueling stop in California, we island-hopped across the Pacific, stopping at Hawaii and Midway Island, and intentionally breaking down on Okinawa, for an aircrew break. We enjoyed Okinawa for twelve hours while the plane was being fixed and then flew on to Nha Trang, Vietnam.

During the long flight, the crew allowed us to observe the pilots in the cockpit. It seemed to us that the aircraft flew along on automatic pilot while the crew kept reading from checklists. The navigator had an overhead position on the right bulkhead in the cargo compartment. Maybe he got position information from the stars to double-check his radio bearings. We didn't get lost, so he did his job well. Overall, it seemed that flying a C-130 was a boring job. But the aircrew most likely wouldn't have wanted our job either.

Our crew were Air National Guardsmen who made the landing at Nha Trang sound like a combat assault. Fifteen miles out they turned out the lights and announced a combat-approach landing. I suppose they were following air force

---

*Mike Dooley had also befriended Martha Raye, who treated him like a son. When Mike was killed, Martha ensured that he didn't have an ordinary Sixth Army funeral in California, but one with a Special Forces honor guard.

procedures, but they scared us more than the threat of enemy action did. We landed at 3:00 A.M., and it was still humid and hot, and it didn't get any better as the day wore on. Later, the afternoon heat and humidity hit like a hammer.

After our initial in-processing, Col. William A. McKean, the commander of 5th Special Forces Group (Airborne), welcomed us in the makeshift Quonset hut movie theater at Special Forces operational base (SFOB). SFOB is just a fancy way of saying group headquarters, but more than that, it served as the logistic lifeline to the isolated A-camps throughout Vietnam. Supplies didn't come down through headquarters C- and B-teams, but went directly from SFOB to each A-camp.

"Gentlemen, I almost lost the camp at Plei Me last October because it took the 1st Cavalry Division a week to react. Now, MACV has authorized me to build mobile reaction forces, which I shall use as reserves. The first such Mike Force is here in Nha Trang, and soon I'll have Mike Forces in each corps area," Colonel McKean said. "Gentlemen, I promise you that I will not lose another A-camp."

Within a month, Colonel McKean lost an A-camp at A Shau in I Corps, along with a Mike Force company. This is not an indictment of Colonel McKean, but an illustration that small, isolated SF camps were tempting targets that could be overrun by massive NVA forces, particularly in overcast weather that favored the enemy's stealthy approach and hindered our air support. If the NVA were willing to pay the price in casualties, they could usually take a camp.

But A Shau was a special camp for the NVA. The camp was due west of Da Nang, hard on the Laotian border in a valley that was a primary infiltration route into I Corps. Survivors of the camp would later tell stories of watching the NVA moving in the hills at night, carrying flashlights and torches. The NVA didn't care if they were seen; they considered themselves the real owners of the A Shau.

"We have one of three possible assignments," Captain Knight said just after he came back from group headquarters and a conference with the group staff. "We can build a camp from scratch in Kontum Province. Or, we can finish a camp started by a team from 1st Special Forces Group in Okinawa, which is also in II Corps. The third possibility is to get sent to IV Corps for assignment by the C-team* there."

Ed Sprague spoke for the rest of the team: "We don't want to go to any IV Corps swamp and, even worse, risk the C-team splitting us up immediately. So that only leaves the first two possibilities."

"I agree," said Captain Knight. "The camp we would build is called Polei Kleng** and it's north of Pleiku and west of Kontum City. The other camp is called Mai Linh."

"So where's Mai Linh?" said Ed Sprague.

"It's in Phu Bon Province," replied Knight. "Generally, it's southeast of Pleiku and due south of An Khe, about fifty miles. It's close to the province capital at Cheo Reo, at the juncture of the Song Ba and Song Ayun, which is the good news. The bad news is that it's a center of FULRO activity."

Everyone knew what FULRO meant: *Front Unifié Pour La Libération Des Races Opprimées* (Unified Front for the Liberation of Oppressed Peoples) or, succinctly, the montagnard revolutionary organization, which had been fighting both the Viet Cong/North Vietnamese Army and the Republic of Vietnam.

Over the previous two years, there had been numerous examples of FULRO rebellions on the nightly television news. Typically, the FULRO leaders would rebel at a Special Forces camp by detaining the SF team and then killing all the Vietnamese, particularly the Vietnamese Special Forces counterpart team. The U.S. A-team would then be released and have to act as the middlemen between the armed FULRO insurgents and an angry Vietnamese government. It wasn't a good way to fight a war against a third party.

Sprague summed it up: "Well, no matter where we go in

---

*A C-team is a headquarters element that controls three or more B-teams. A B-team is another headquarters element which may or may not be operational and controls three or more A-teams.

**Almost four years later I had the opportunity to command the team at Polei Kleng.

the Central Highlands, we'll probably be involved with
FULRO. But we can operate against the enemy sooner if
we're not tied up in building a camp. Fighting is better than
building. I think we should take Mai Linh and handle the
FULRO problem as it arises."

Everyone agreed, and Captain Knight went off to select
Mai Linh as our choice. We were then designated as Detachment A-226.

We zeroed our M-16s and test fired our .45s and were is-
sued a personal basic load of ammunition before leaving Nha
Trang. A Caribou CV-2 army aircraft flew us to our B-team in
An Khe.

We landed at the base camp of the 1st Cavalry Division,
which they had begun building in 1965. On our way to the
B-team, the supply sergeant who picked us up in a 2½-ton
truck explained about the arrival of the 1st Cav in 1965: "An
Khe was a sleepy little village of about two hundred people,
midway between Qui Nhon and Pleiku when the Cav arrived.
On the first day, the Cav hired 150 people as camp labor, and
on the second day they hired 400. By the end of the week they
were hiring a thousand people a day from that little village. I
wonder where all those laborers came from?" Apparently
every local VC guerrilla came out of the woods to work for
the Cav.

In early 1966, B-22 was one of the few operational B-teams
in country. Located between the An Khe Pass to the east and
the Mang Yang Pass to the west on Highway 19, the area was
a central focus for the Viet Cong and NVA. During the last of
the Indochina war, the French had lost an elite regiment (Mobile Group 100) ambushed in the Mang Yang Pass, where the
rusting hulks of their vehicles could still be seen. More recently, the NVA tried to split the Central Highlands through
An Khe, which made the real estate valuable but, considering
the unfriendly neighbors, in a poor neighborhood.

B-22 welcomed us, and we attended more briefings on operational requirements and the things that we needed to do to
keep the B-team happy. It was there that we learned firsthand
about montagnard-Vietnamese relations.

B-22 sat on the south side of Highway 22 (a misnomer for what was then a two-lane dirt road), overlooking the Song Ba (Ba River). The previous day, one of the Civilian Irregular Defense Group (CIDG) montagnard soldiers was outside the camp, trying to cross the bridge across the Ia Ba (*ia* means water in Jarai; *song* is river in Vietnamese). Two Vietnamese national policemen, commonly called white mice, were guarding the bridge, and one of the policemen demanded that the montagnard surrender his bayonet before he cross the river. The montagnard gave up his bayonet, returned to his CIDG company atop the hill, and told his company commander what had happened. The company commander ordered his unit to fire on the policemen, which they did, killing both. Since there were no large numbers of Vietnamese in the An Khe area, nothing happened to the CIDG company.

In February 1966, B-22 was making arrangements to displace to Qui Nhon on the coast. The B-team had established an FOB (forward operational base) in Qui Nhon, and when they made the move, B-22 would become a more normal administrative headquarters. But as long as B-22 was still operational and had a tactical mission in An Khe, they were more tolerant of what happened at their subordinate A-camps. It was axiomatic of the Vietnam War that the more a headquarters moved into garrison mode, the more that unit distanced itself from the reality of its subordinate units in the field.

The 1st Cavalry Division gave us a Caribou ride to Cheo Reo, where we met the Okinawa team that we were replacing. Officially, Cheo Reo was named Hau Bon, and it was the capital of Phu Bon Province. Hau Bon and Phu Bon were both Vietnamese names, so the montagnard population of mostly Jarai tribesmen ignored the terms and kept the name Cheo Reo, which was Jarai. The official name didn't make a lot of sense at the time other than as an attempt to impose Vietnamese control over the montagnards and the land.

We settled in with the Okinawa team (Detachment A-112,

1st SFGA) for a three-day overlap at Camp Mai Linh, which was to be our home for the next year.

Mai Linh was a five-sided camp on the west bank of the Ba River, about ten road miles north of Cheo Reo. It was on the road to An Khe, which generally followed the Ba, but the road had long been closed by the Viet Cong by burning bridges, building abatis, and planting mines and punji stakes. North and east of Mai Linh was Indian country, inhabited by isolated Bahnar villages and NVA who used the Bahnar for forced labor.

Another oddity of the Vietnam War, Mai Linh was a replacement camp for Buon Beng, which had been opened in May 1963 then closed in June 1965. Jim Morris, author of *War Story* and *The Devil's Secret Name*, had been the executive officer at Buon Beng. At the time, however, nobody could figure out why a perfectly good camp was closed and another opened up just five miles away.

There were five CIDG companies and two combat recon platoons at Mai Linh. That organization was called a Strike Force (as opposed to Mike Force), and the individual CIDG were called strikers. Also, there were two Regional Force (RF) companies along with various Popular Force (PF) platoons under the control of the district headquarters at Phu Thien, which was also supported by Mai Linh with an additional split A-team. With over twenty SF people authorized, the team at Mai Linh was one of the largest in Vietnam. The additional "split" (or one-half A-team) at Phu Thien had come about due to FULRO.

The two RF companies at Phu Thien were mostly montagnard, but with Vietnamese in command positions. On 19 December 1965, they revolted against the Vietnamese district headquarters leadership as part of a general FULRO rebellion. In all, twenty-seven Vietnamese were killed, including the district chief. Not knowing what to do after they had revolted, the insurgents marched east to Mai Linh and surrendered. They were turned over to the provincial officials in Cheo Reo and many were held for trial in Pleiku.

That relatively minor FULRO uprising illustrated the

quandary that the Vietnamese government had. The Central Highlands could not be held by the Vietnamese alone, but the alternative was to arm the montagnards, who hated the Vietnamese, both north and south. At the urging of the United States (and particularly Special Forces), the Vietnamese government began to take some steps to solve the montagnard problem. A first and promising measure was the appointment of a montagnard camp commander at Mai Linh. Second Lieutenant Siu Broai, whose Vietnamese name was Oai, was a career Vietnamese army NCO and one of the few ethnic Jarai serving. The Vietnamese commissioned him, sent him to Vietnamese Special Forces school, and made him the commander of the Vietnamese Special Forces (*Luc Luong Dac Biet* or LLDB) team at Mai Linh. Siu Broai would end the war in 1975 as a major and a district chief, be incarcerated for "reeducation" for seven years, and eventually emigrate to the United States. But he kept the FULRO lid on at Mai Linh.

Most of the 750-plus strike force at Mai Linh were Jarai, with the next biggest group being Bahnar. The remainder were Rhade, Sedang, and a few other tribes had representation. There were no Vietnamese, so all the leadership was montagnard. In theory, that was a good situation, but theory never equates to reality because the various tribes had been warring against each other for centuries, capturing one another as slaves and generally not being hospitable.

The Jarai and Rhade were cousins, with a common language, and were Malayo-Polynesian, but the Bahnar were Mon-Khmer. Other than common sympathy for FULRO, the only thing that the Jarai and Rhade could agree on was that they both hated the Bahnar. The Bahnar refused to adopt the relatively more civilized ways of the Jarai, and many still filed their teeth to sharp points. Their women didn't wear shirts and always went bare breasted. But those traits were not why the tribes hated each other. The hatred was basic, historical, cultural, and visceral.

Special Forces was able to use the minority differences to advantage. All that was needed was to convince the tribes to work together against the predominantly Vietnamese Viet

Cong and North Vietnamese. At Mai Linh, we were lucky and were able to wage an effective war against the insurgents. We were also fortunate in replacing the Okinawa team; we inherited a well-trained CIDG, a functioning counterinsurgency program, and a camp well under way to completion. After the Okinawa team left, we were on our own and made our own mark on the area.

It was no surprise that building and operating an A-camp was never-ending work. There was so much to do that going out on combat operations became a type of rest; combat operations were always easier than staying and working in camp. There was no such thing as a typical day in camp, but some things tended to become ordinary. There was always defensive wire and bunker improvement and maintenance, resupplies to pick up, communications to improve, intelligence information to be gathered, medical patrols to operate, and camp security to provide for. Without all the benefit of the things that we take for granted at home, we learned to make do. Using field expedients became normal.

We dug a well so that we wouldn't have to scoop water into a water trailer out of the Ia Ba, but we didn't have a pump, and no hardware store from which to buy one. Instead, we traded with the air force for a C-130 fuel pump that we rigged to pump our water. Of course, the pump couldn't be powered by our 120-volt AC generators, so we had to invent a way to power the pump.

Our shower room was at the base of the observation tower, and we used an old water trailer as a cistern with a mess-hall immersion heater. Gradually, we figured out solutions for all our camp needs. Some of our solutions caused other problems. We stored one-hundred-kilogram bags of rice on pallets inside a GP-medium tent. Unfortunately, that attracted rats, which gnawed on the bottom bags to get at the rice. That problem solved itself when the concentration of rats attracted cobras, which ate them. Then some of the cobras migrated to our nearby generator bunker for warmth.

Our executive officer, John Mullins, was surprised one day

to find a swaying cobra in front of him as he entered the generator bunker. Mullins immediately shot the cobra with his M-16, and we all learned to enter bunkers with care thereafter. Over the course of a year, we found that cobras were not very aggressive and usually wouldn't strike without a reason. But that knowledge couldn't soothe Lieutenant Mullins at the time.

Fifth Group policy was that one-half of the strike force always had to be out on operation. But local security operations were above and beyond this requirement. We eventually found that we could issue shotguns to hunting details, and that solved the local security requirement. Montagnards love to hunt for food so combining the hunting with local security proved beneficial.

For close-in security we relied on obstacles of concertina wire, double-apron barbed wire, claymore mines, and implanted fougasse. As with everything else though, we found that defensive measures were evolutionary and had to be always upgraded. Fougasse were homemade napalm mines, but they eventually proved impracticable because the volatile napalm evaporated. Claymores were imbedded in concrete and their detonation wires buried; these were then fed into central switchboard devices that could be fired by single claymore, ripples, or volleys. Land mines were usually not used because perimeter grass had to be cut constantly, and most people don't like to cut grass in minefields.

Logistical resupply was mostly by airlanded loads into the airfield at Cheo Reo. Local purchase of supplies was authorized, but Cheo Reo usually didn't have what we needed. None of that mattered much, except for food for the team. Nobody wanted to live on rice, sardines, and salmon, which was the basic CIDG ration. And since we were paid a separate-rations allowance, we could buy our food locally, except that hamburgers, steaks, and potatoes were usually not available. The standard system was to purchase U.S. food at the commissary in Saigon, but the perishables would have perished by the time that we could get them back to the highlands. So we became adept at scrounging from U.S. units, primarily those in Qui Nhon.

For montagnard crossbows, tiger suits, and other goodies, we could get cases of frozen meat, ice cream, and whatever canned food we wanted. We eventually became so adept that we ordered cases of meat from the Class I depot at Qui Nhon, using various unit designations from the 1st Cavalry Division; unfortunately, our welcome at the depot ended when the B-team demolitions sergeant was caught breaking in one night. I guess that the demo sergeant thought that he had to keep up his surreptitious entry skills.

One time, John Mullins was on a food scrounging mission in Qui Nhon when he decided to have a beer in a local bar. He walked in and found a rear-echelon major sitting at a table with two American nurses. The major looked at Mullins, and in an attempt to impress the nurses said: "Lieutenant, you should shit in that hat. Then if you had another hat just like it, you could have a sandwich."

When Mullins got through punching out the major, the B-team sergeant major pulled some favors with an aviation unit and got him out of Qui Nhon in a hurry.

Other scrounging sources were the merchant marine ships in the Qui Nhon harbor. We'd visit the ships, scrounge some food from their holds, and invite the officers and crews to the bar at B-22. For the price of a few beers, we scrounged tons of food. But getting the food wasn't the hard part—moving it was.

Through favors worked out with the graves registration unit in Qui Nhon, we stored our perishables in their morgue coolers while we tried to get an aircraft to Cheo Reo. When we only had five hundred pounds or so of food, it was easy to find a helicopter ride. But when we also had a couple of pallets of beer and soda, we needed a Caribou. So we made friends in the Caribou units, which worked well until the army CV-2 Caribous were transferred to the air force and became C-7As in the summer of 1966. The air force was harder to manipulate than the army, but they, too, came around. Once back in Mai Linh, it was the usual tedious work.

* * *

The team commo men and medics were always busier than the rest of us. By the nature of their duties, at least one commo sergeant and one medic had to be in camp at all times. And quite often, even then, they might be restricted to the commo bunker or dispensary.

No communicator is ever happy with his existing setup, and John McFadden was no exception. He had multiple backup antennas rigged, an alternate commo bunker, and spare standby radios. Not content with just being able to communicate throughout Vietnam, John frequently communicated with the United States, even though that wasn't officially authorized. But then, we weren't really worried about the Federal Communications Commission finding out. What could anyone do, send us to Vietnam? Although we still had the old reliable AN/GRC-109 radios for backup use, we also had commercial, Collins single-sideband (SSB) radios that could be used for CW code transmission or voice transmission. We had commercial HT-1 FM voice radios that were marginally better than the AN/PRC-6 squad radios that they replaced. But the biggest improvement were the AN/PRC-25 radios that replaced the AN/PRC-10 sets.

The AN/PRC-25 was later modified to become the AN/PRC-77 radio. It was heavier than the AN/PRC-10 radio that it replaced but it had crystal controlled frequency tuning and you could actually communicate for twenty-five miles. You might have to climb a mountain or a tree, but that radio enabled us to operate far from Mai Linh without too much worry about getting in trouble. Many think of radios as just heavy burdens to be carried, but when you're fifteen miles away from anybody, outside of any artillery or mortar fan, and in contact with bad guys, radios assume a new dimension in your life. The same applies for medics.

Combat casualties weren't as bothersome as the normal disease that we had around Mai Linh. There was typhoid fever, typhus, hepatitis, malaria, leprosy, dengue, cholera, and plague, along with the more usual ailments and conditions. The medics had to treat a daily sick call for all CIDG and dependents, operate hygiene programs for everybody, and send out medical patrols to villages within the area of operations.

Medical patrols were our most potent asset in gathering intelligence information. While the medic treated villagers, one of the other team members would drink rice wine with the village chief and his advisers, talk about what was going on in the area, and find out what the VC/NVA were doing. We could also assess the needs of the village and make arrangements to provide other help. The Jarai and Bahnar villages didn't often ask for medical help, but when they did, it was critical.

One day Henry Caesar was called to a Jarai village to help in a birth. Usually, when a woman gave birth, it was a festive social gathering for the village women. They would shoo away the pigs and chickens, sit under the birthing mother's house in a circle and give encouragement as the mother semi-squatted while hanging onto an upright support pole. Henry had to assist in a breech birth and saved the mother but lost the baby. It's doubtful that an obstetrician could have done any better under the circumstances.

After two weeks in country, most of the team had come down with a jock-itch type of prickly heat, which we categorized as jungle rot. The medics prescribed talcum and medicated powder, but we found that the condition cleared up if we didn't wear underwear. I didn't wear shorts again until I got on the plane to come back to the States.

Since each SF camp represented a substantial investment in money and talent, we had to write a monthly show-and-tell document called a monthly operational summary, or MOPSUM. Roger Knight set the standard for creative, entertaining, and informative MOPSUMs. Roger didn't just write "summaries," Roger wrote lengthy descriptions of what A-226 had done within the last month, making sure that his writing was not typical tedious army jargon. Then he added pictures, insuring his reports were looked at.

Bunker maintenance was mundane, but a description of

how many bunkers were rebuilt or improved along with a picture showing team members shoveling dirt was eye-catching. The same applied to the gatherings of refugees; a photograph showing them getting off a 2½-ton truck caused people to look. Perhaps Roger's efforts caused him to be noticed too early, because he was transferred to Saigon after only four months or so at Mai Linh.

But Roger laid the groundwork for every commander that followed. We had four more commanders after Roger Knight, and two of them moved up to better jobs. Capt. Oscar Biehl replaced Knight and was later killed in 1967. Biehl was replaced by Capt. Bob Kvederas, who was later replaced by Capt. Jim Zachary. Captain Nichols was the last commander of the remaining original detachment. A-226 became a model of what an A-team was supposed to be, and the visitors proved that.

During the first six months at Mai Linh, we were visited only by various MACV company (lieutenants and captains) and field grade (majors, lieutenants-colonel, and colonels) officers, although the Vietnamese II Corps commander and his U.S. brigadier general adviser showed up once. In our second six months, we had visits by General Westmoreland, the lieutenant general commanding U.S. Army Vietnam, the commander of the 1st Cavalry Division, and all sorts of lesser general officers. Probably it was General Westmoreland's getting his first and only montagnard bracelet.

It was a custom among the montagnards to give proven friends a brass bracelet, the presentation being accompanied by the sacrifice of a chicken, pig, cow, or water buffalo (the animal sacrificed was based on the status of the recipient) and the plentiful consumption of rice wine, all administered by the village shaman.* It was a wonderful bonding experience

---

*Some unknowing Americans erroneously referred to the village shamans as witch doctors. They weren't. The shaman, although he was a healer and religious leader, had no problems dealing with our medics and various missionaries in the area. The shaman was revered in every village and was no more a witch doctor than a local priest or minister is in America.

between the montagnards and the United States and proved our friendly relations; significantly, none of the Vietnamese LLDB members ever received a bracelet. John Wayne, the movie star, received a brass bracelet when he did research in Vietnam for his film *The Green Berets*, and he wore his bracelet in every film that he made until he died.

Eventually, wearing a montagnard brass bracelet became a status symbol for U.S. soldiers in Vietnam. From privates to generals, everyone wanted to legitimately receive a bracelet. Not knowing any montagnards, many GIs went and got brass welding rods and made their own.

One day we received word that General Westmoreland was to visit. Captain Jim Zachary, our team commander at the time, arranged with the closest village chief and shaman to present General Westmoreland with a bracelet. Westmoreland arrived, was given a briefing and tour of the camp and then brought to the ceremonial site. Although a teetotaler, Westmoreland was persuaded to take a sip of the wine and got his bracelet. A *Time* photographer almost knocked me down taking a picture of the event.

There was a humorous aside to the ceremony though, unknown to General Westmoreland and Captain Carpenter, his aide-de-camp. Captain Carpenter (the former "lonesome end" on the West Point football team) had been a company commander in the 101st Airborne Division and while in combat had called in a napalm strike on his defensive position. He had been put in for the Medal of Honor, and while his award was pending he was made Westmoreland's aide. For the general public, calling in napalm is considered very heroic, but for infantrymen, it is looked down upon, as nape flows down into your defensive hole and burns the defender. Mike Dooley seized the opportunity.

"George, see that guy. That's Captain Carpenter," Mike said. "So what," I answered.

"Well, don't stand too close to him. He might call in nape."

Mike Dooley had a sense of humor, and Captain Carpenter's award recommendation was downgraded to a Distinguished Service Cross. There must have been some real infantrymen in the Pentagon. But General Westmoreland's receipt of a brass bracelet proved contagious among the general officer set.

After the word got out, general officers from everywhere showed up at Mai Linh to inspect the camp and, incidentally, receive a Jarai bracelet. Most, like Westmoreland, showed up in a Huey helicopter. The 1st Cavalry Division commander was a bit more ostentatious: He arrived in a Huey, with a Huey chase ship, and four gunships. No matter though, almost all the generals asked if they could do anything for us when they departed. Jim Zachary asked and we received support that we never would have gotten otherwise. Good relations with general officers help. But the most important visitor arrived rather late in our tour.

Martha Raye visited Mai Linh in late 1966. She arrived without entourage with only the 5th Group chaplain as an escort. Happily, she arrived on a montagnard festival day and there were many jugs of rice wine throughout the camp for her to sample. She was a most gracious lady, and everybody loved her. We gave her one of the Mai Linh pins that we had made up in Cheo Reo, and we all spent a pleasant afternoon with Martha.

Years later, there would be minor controversy as to whether Martha Raye was a "real" lieutenant colonel and nurse, as she had performed nursing duties at some A-camps under attack and because she wore lieutenant colonel insignia on her beret. At Mai Linh, nobody cared. Martha Raye was the only American entertainer to visit us and other small camps. She proved that somebody from the American mainstream still cared about us. Everyone respected Bob Hope, but he didn't visit A-camps. Martha did.

The USO has always done a great job entertaining troops and keeping up morale, and can't be faulted for not visiting everyone. After all, they have the most impact when they visit a large body of troops. Martha Raye was special to SF because she took the time to visit everyone. Visiting a few men at an A-camp isn't cost effective, but Martha came anyway.

Bernard Fall, in his book *Street Without Joy*, devoted more than fifty pages to the combat in the Central Highlands, particularly along the Ia (Song) Ba, axis of An Khe, Cheo Reo, Cung Son. He detailed the difficulty that the French had in holding the Central Highlands and how the French lost one of their most elite units when GM 100 was eradicated in the Mang Yang Pass. At Mai Linh, we gained the knowledge of the area that the French had, but did not repeat their mistakes. At one time or another, we operated from An Khe down to Cung Son, almost always with montagnards who had served with the French.

It's not good form to denigrate your enemy, but by and large, the VC were not very capable in the woods, and their northern neighbors, the NVA, were just short of incompetent. However, on their behalf, it must be said that they were willing to take casualties in the hundreds of thousands that the United States was not prepared to approach. There are thousands of true untold war stories concerning NVA ineptness. One of my favorites has an NVA antiaircraft crew firing six feet in front of a stationary, landed helicopter because they were taught that they always had to "lead" the fire on an aircraft. They had never been told that parked, landed, or hovering aircraft are exceptions. We never understood what the antiwar/pro-VC/NVA crowd was talking about when they tried to glorify the NVA as the heroic freedom fighters of Southeast Asia. But then, we were fighting and killing the NVA in large quantities, ten thousand miles closer than the antiwar folks were, so viewpoints tended to differ.

Usually, two Americans went out with each CIDG company, accompanied by one LLDB. Our normal patrol was three days long, because that was the amount of rations that we could carry along with ammunition, batteries, smoke, flares, 60mm mortar rounds, and the other necessary paraphernalia. Three days was also about the limit of stamina of a typical montagnard.

Because they had only relatively recently become sedentary rice growers, the montagnards were still excellent warrior/hunter-gatherers. Their culture still reflected that, and they had an affinity to the land that the Vietnamese could not approach. Almost every time that we went out, the Special Forces and LLDB accompanying the unit would say: "Let's follow an azimuth of XXX degrees for YY kilometers." The montagnard company commander would interpret that (looking at the map) and announce something to the effect: "Who knows how to go to the east of Chu Tse and stop at the Ia Ayun?" The person who responded would walk point. Different cultures and logic systems integrated.

Mostly we walked the lowlands near the streams and rivers. At night, we would find defensible high ground. We did the same things as the VC/NVA; they didn't wander too far from water, and neither did we. Going to high ground usually insured radio contact; but if it didn't, we went higher. Nobody knew back then that, within three decades, SF would tap into satellite systems for commo.

We probably only had enemy contact about 20 percent of the time, and then it would be a quick sniping and runaway. But then, that's what pacification is all about. We'd walk the woods for weeks on end, keeping the bad guys off balance. Along with that, we learned field expedients to supplement our usual battle drill.

Most of the time, the patrol on operation was out of communications with base camp. We always knew that we could violently break contact and run until we could get commo and support. But when base camp wanted to get commo with the unit in the field, all they had to do was to point a 4.2-inch mortar in the general direction of the field unit and shoot a flare at maximum distance and elevation, night or day.

An illumination round gives off a pop that can be heard for miles. Somebody would hear the pop, and the patrol would find high ground and radio back to camp. Another way was to have a Bird Dog aircraft fly in the vicinity of the patrol; we always called nearby aircraft on the II Corps air-to-ground frequency (46.00 MHz) because nobody wanted his patrol to be mistaken for a VC/NVA column. If an aircraft spotted us but wasn't up on the II Corps frequency, we always threw green smoke to identify us as friendly. Personally, I always waved when buzzed.

At night, unlike conventional U.S. and Vietnamese units, we never dug in unless in contact. Instead, we silently strung hammocks and listened to the fuck-you lizards. The fuck-you lizards were rather substantial in size, about three feet long, hung around in trees and called: "Tik, tik, tik, phuk yu!" A bit disconcerting for a boy raised in Chicago. Sometimes fuck-you lizards got captured and became food.

Montagnards knew how to live off the land. As we wandered along, they picked wild green onions, chopped bamboo shoots, and captured red ant nests using plastic battery bags. The onions and bamboo shoots were boiled along with rice, and the ants were added as protein and gave a minty taste to the meal. Quite often we'd supplement our diet with a Communist water buffalo, cow, or deer. A hand grenade in the Ia Ba would yield enough fish for a day.

It's easy to picture the montagnards as wandering savages. That impression would be wrong. They could read and hear the land unlike any American or Vietnamese. They knew when the bad guys were near and would become super silent and invisible.

Once, we were walking along a cleared area of the An Khe road, which was terribly overgrown and not a really apparent trail, when the CIDG company commander said: "Here is where the tiger went down the bank to swim to the water buffalo in the river." I looked and saw nothing out of place.

"Here is where the tiger dragged the water buffalo out of the water," said the montagnard about fifty meters beyond. I still saw nothing.

After another fifty meters, the montagnard said, pointing off to the left: "There's where the tiger ate the water buffalo." I still didn't see any sign, but followed his direction. I walked into the bushes and found the skeleton carcass of a water buffalo. You can't fault the natives in their own neighborhood. A couple of weeks later, we killed a tiger. Maybe it was the same one.

The air force had some programs where we worked together. Special Forces originally had the primary responsibility for evasion and escape (E & E) but that mission ended up being handled by MAC SOG. Other operations were more directly related to A-camps.

Early in the war, the air force paired aircraft flights with individual A-camps as defensive buddies. The result was that the two air force jets that were assigned to your camp would periodically buzz the camp when they were returning to Cam Ranh Bay from a mission. Usually, they would dive on the camp and belly out in a sonic boom putting everyone down in the dirt from the sound. But hell, they didn't know. The bad part was that we couldn't communicate. An SF camp could communicate around the world, and some did, but we didn't have the radios to talk with air force zoomies.

The air force set it up, communications-wise, so that only air force ground or air controllers could talk with their air force ground-support aircraft, sometimes known as "fast movers" if they were jets. The only aircraft that we could talk with directly were resupply ships and the close-in air-to-ground weapons platforms known as "Puff" (the Magic Dragon), Spooky, Golf-Ball, and Spectre, which were assorted gun and flare ships in AC-47, C-123, and C-130 configurations. Regardless of the communications difficulties, I will never say a bad thing about the air force; they have saved me too many times for me to count.

Sky spots were bombing missions that continued throughout the war. These were bombing missions that located a target from a known point (sometimes an SF camp) on an azimuth for an assigned distance. Usually they were in reaction to an enemy location report such as a radio transmission or other intelligence source. Often, we would get a message of a sky-spot mission to be run at 0200 (2:00 A.M.) local time at an eight-digit coordinate, which would be accurate within ten meters. Always, we'd check the map coordinates to see if we had an operation near there. What we'd usually find was that the bombing mission would be on a piece of jungle nowhere near water. That was normally a turnoff as the bad guys never operated very far from a water source, particularly during the dry season.

* * *

Detachment A-226 didn't standardize a patrol harness or rig, but we all wore the same. Two ammo pouches in front, two canteens in back, a first-aid packet on the left front, and a compass case on the right. We all carried our SOI (signal operating instructions) in our left front shirt pocket. Some wore grenades along with their ammo pouches; some didn't. Maps were usually carried in the right cargo pocket. Most hated the issue hammock and used a local version that weighed a few ounces. We also tended to leave the issue rucksack at camp; it would carry more, but then you were hauling more (and probably unnecessary) weight. Tiger fatigues were the standard uniform, and nobody ever wore a helmet. A sweat rag or towel rounded out the uniform.

After seeing pictures of supposed combat infantrymen in *Stars and Stripes* and on television before we left, everyone agreed that real infantrymen didn't clutter up the front of their harness with knives, first-aid packets, and other things that could get in the way of shoulder firing your rifle and, more particularly, from getting down into the dirt when bad things were happening. Maybe it didn't look "combatty," but practicality always came first.*

As expected, the guys on the exotic projects, Delta, Omega, Sigma, and later MAC SOG, did standardize. But mission requirements dictate what's necessary. We at Mai Linh were operating in circumstances where we almost always could achieve fire superiority or, failing that, run. Each American carried a 250-tablet bottle of dextroamphetamine, which could be used to keep the troops going if necessary.

After about six months in camp, by common consent, we went from two men on each operation to one. Between camp details and operations, we were meeting each other coming and going. Something had to give. The infantry, Airborne, Ranger, Special Forces solution is always to take the hardest

---

*Thirty years later, it's easy, watching television news, to spot who is an infantryman and who isn't. The noninfantryman is wearing knives, flashlights, survival kits, and other bulky things on the harness front.

path. But if that's the ideal solution, then to attack Moscow from Germany, the best way is to seize the Alps, go east, speed across the lowlands to the Urals, secure the high ground, move north, and swoop down from the eastern high ground. Sometimes the school solution ain't right. Nobody objected to the new way of doing things. Besides camp maintenance and operations, we were also pulling camp guard at night on two-hour shifts. We were earning our money and "killing Commies for Christ." The montagnards loved us.

Some might argue that an American alone on operation couldn't call for help if he was hit. But what if both Americans were hit? What's the difference? Besides, we grew to trust our montagnards totally. We knew they'd stand by us no matter what. Besides, the enemy just wasn't that competent. Perhaps as part of a national rationalization for pulling out of Vietnam, we have built the VC/NVA up to mythic proportions. In the viewpoint of most noncombatants and people who never went to Vietnam, the enemy was an invincible guerrilla fighter, able to traverse the hardest terrain while living on little food, always able to lure stupid Americans into ambushes and other deadly situations where the Americans would be killed in massive numbers. However, just the opposite was true.

By and large, the NVA were uncomfortable in the jungle, usually had little food and equipment, couldn't see well at night, and normally each soldier carried less than one hundred rounds for his weapon. Most of our enemy contact would be classified as meeting engagements. Minor sniping and ambushes (with us doing the ambushing) were the norm. Of course there were booby traps and mines, but the VC/NVA often tripped their own devices. One time, the NVA distributed propaganda leaflets around the jungle north of Mai Linh. The leaflets were in Korean, however, and the closest Koreans were in Qui Nhon, more than one hundred miles away.

One of their more effective tactics, although they didn't know it at the time, was the use of tetrahedrons to cause vehicle damage. A tetrahedron was two pieces of sharpened heavy gauge wire, spliced in the middle so that four prongs resulted, with each prong 120 degrees from the next. Thrown on the road, the device would always land on three prongs, leaving one prong to flatten a tire and disable a vehicle. It wasn't explosive or sexy, but it worked. But vehicle damage wasn't as critical as human casualties.

The VC/NVA did inflict casualties on us, but we inflicted far more on them than they did on us. Time, however, was on their side. After a year at Mai Linh, almost everyone had at least one Purple Heart for relatively minor wounds. We were an arrogant bunch with a bad attitude toward the enemy. I still have my official and unofficial dog tags, and they tell a lot about our attitude. Before we left for Vietnam, I saw a friend in the identification section of the 82d Airborne Division, and had him make up a third dog tag that read: IF YOU'RE RECOVERING MY BODY—FUCK YOU. After my first tour, I had a fourth dog tag made. This one read: AND LEAVE MY GODDAMN K-BAR AND ROLEX ALONE. We knew that we would suffer casualties, but nobody really expected to die.

Patrols within our own area of operations eventually became boring, and we looked forward to operating outside our AO. Every two or three months we'd get a requirement to send a CIDG company on a joint operation with the Cav or the 101st Airborne or to reinforce another A-camp. These were always good operations but sometimes had mixed results.

Ed Sprague and I went on an operation near Cung Son with the 1st Cavalry Division, and we got our first up close and personal NVA kills. On the other hand, our montagnards tended to terrorize the Vietnamese locals in the village of Cung Son, and the Special Forces camp locked us out of the camp after the operation, which was unusual for SF. But then, the Cung Son team was commanded by a quartermaster captain who had somehow finagled an A-team assignment.

On another operation with the 101st Airborne, Mike Dooley secured an artillery firebase with a CIDG company. After a few days of local security patrols, an artillery sergeant asked to accompany Mike and his patrol, and ended up KIA. They came upon a cultivated field with a fence, and Mike and the strikers climbed across the fence; but the artilleryman, not aware of the ways of the enemy, walked through a booby-trapped gate. Mike felt bad about the casualty, but knew that he could not have imparted all the ground lore that he had to a novice. Generally, we took responsibility for what happened on an operation, even though we were supposedly "advisers."

In theory, the U.S. A-team was an advisory detachment to the Vietnamese LLDB team. Like everything else the results of our cooperation were mixed. Once during the rainy season, an LLDB sergeant refused to cross a river, using the excuse that the montagnards didn't know how to swim; in reality, the LLDB sergeant couldn't swim but didn't want to lose face. Eventually, the advisory issue worked itself out with the LLDB taking out the safer operations alone, while we took out the more risky operations without benefit of LLDB presence. Regardless of whether we worked through or around the Vietnamese, the montagnards knew that it was the Americans who were helping them.

For a number of reasons, not the least of which was to flaunt our presence in the area, Roger Knight decided to make an armor sweep toward An Khe and back. Roger was a tanker, but he didn't have any tanks, so he used trucks. He took almost every vehicle that we had in camp, loaded them up with machine guns, recoilless rifles, a CIDG company, and recon platoon. He drove to within twelve miles of An Khe before returning. Along the way, he rebuilt a number of bridges, cleared abatis, freed refugees, and shot up a bunch of VC/NVA. The bad guys had to be surprised by his audacity.

Our civic action program with the montagnards was very effective. We provided them with breeding-stock rabbits but had to insure that they would raise the rabbits and not eat the breeding stock. We also obtained surplus clothing, farm equipment and seed, and ran a transportation service to the market in Cheo Reo. But our most effective means were from outside army and U.S. Agency for International Development (AID) channels.

Seeing that every montagnard man, woman, and child smoked a homemade pipe, Ed Sprague wrote his relatives back in Boston. Through the Boston media, thousands of used pipes were collected, sent to Ed, and distributed throughout the villages. For Christmas of 1966, Ed arranged the same sort of program, getting used toys and clothing for montagnard children.

How many brass bracelets a person received was a measure of a team member's popularity with the montagnards. Ed Sprague led the bracelet contest, with more than twenty on his right arm. He eventually limited his wearing to only one bracelet at a time because he would otherwise be heavier on his right side. The Jarai and Bahnar loved him, including the King of Fire.

Dr. Gerald Hickey was an anthropologist working for the Rand Corporation and living at the MACV team in Cheo Reo. One day, Doctor Hickey brought the King of Fire to Mai Linh. Immediately, all work stopped, and the montagnards began arranging a ceremony for the king, which was held the following day. But then there was a problem on how to house the King of Fire overnight.

The King of Fire is like a grand shaman or pope. There are also lesser kings of Wind and Water who are never allowed to meet each other, perhaps because that would be too much spiritual power in one place. But because of the perceived aura of these kings, they are never invited into a village or a montagnard longhouse. They conduct their ceremonies outside of montagnard villages, and the villagers build temporary quarters for the king. With the King of Fire at Mai Linh, the CIDG built him a temporary lean-to on the camp parade field.

The next day, a water buffalo was ritually slaughtered on behalf of the King of Fire and there was the usual rice wine ceremony. Many of the CIDG had been converted by missionaries and were nominally Catholic or Lutheran, but the animistic tradition never quite went away. The King of Fire was respected by all tribes, regardless of other religious affiliation. We learned that local custom could never be disregarded.

The spring monsoon was late in 1966, and the Jarai were sure they knew why. In March 1966, Joe Simino had come upon a cache of old Cham figurines in the jungle northwest of Mai Linh. He picked a few and brought them back to Mai Linh. When the rains didn't come, Joe was asked to return his souvenirs, and a shaman accompanied a CIDG company back to the Cham site. A religious ceremony was conducted to appease the ancient Cham spirits, the figurines were replaced, and within days, the spring monsoon started, and the rice fields were flooded. We preserved our relations with the Jarai, but our relations with others were not so ideal.

MACV Team 31 was located at the province headquarters in Cheo Reo. Also in Cheo Reo were Lutheran missionaries, a Korean medical team, and a French Catholic priest. The missionaries liked us, the Koreans and MACV team were neutral toward us, and the French priest hated us. At one point, we considered assassinating the priest because his anti-Americanism was getting out of hand, and we had evidence that he was a Viet Cong agent; but we restrained ourselves. We were both competing for the same audience, the montagnards, and we won.

The missionaries would visit Mai Linh about once a month and scrounge things from us. In return, they taught us more Jarai than we were picking up on our own. At one point, Roger Knight was bringing them in once a week to give us language lessons.

Winning friendship with the MACV team was not easy. Under the administrative rules at the time, our team commander was rated or indorsed by the MACV commander, but our operations were controlled by Special Forces. Muddying the waters even more was that the ARVN had a battalion of the 22d Division sitting in Cheo Reo, with U.S. advisers, and doing nothing.

We sent and received mail through the MACV team and used their small PX to buy cigarettes and toiletries, but other than that, we kept our distance from each other. Once, they hung a sign in their compound barring SF vehicles from parking there. They didn't seem to care about us very much, and we probably gave them sufficient reason.

Although we were only a few miles away and drove in daily, when MACV people visited us, they considered it a combat operation and armed themselves accordingly. Once, two U.S. captains drove out to pick up one of our CIDG company commanders as a VC suspect to turn over to the ARVN for interrogation. Roger Knight refused to release the individual, and the captains became belligerent so Roger drew his M-16 on them, and Ed Sprague backed him up. The two captains left as they came. Another time the ARVN sent us a message to send a montagnard school teacher we employed to Cheo Reo for interrogation. We again refused to cooperate. We grew to see MACV as meddlers rather than helpers. They often tried to emulate us but didn't succeed very well.

We began to send a monthly convoy through the Chu Tse Pass to Pleiku and on to Qui Nhon for supplies. We always used at least three vehicles, with a platoon of CIDG as security, and a Bird Dog aircraft flying overhead for cover and communications relay. After we had made two runs with MACV going along with us, the MACV team tried the run by themselves. They took two trucks, a platoon of ARVN, and went without air cover. Of course they were ambushed, the platoon wiped out, and the lone American hid in the jungle for four hours until a relief force arrived.

In the summer of 1966, we were visited by one of the civilian spooks assigned to the MACV team. Ostensibly the province police and safety adviser, he brought us a device to take on operations. The device was an infrared light and battery pack which we could use to see if a suspect had fired a weapon within the past twenty-four hours. The system is common in police work nowadays, but we had to explain why we didn't want to use his device: It weighed thirty pounds, which was a considerable weight to be humping out in the woods. More important we didn't need to find out if a suspect had fired a weapon recently. The mere presence of a military-age male out in Indian country was enough to get him shot or captured.

The MACV team had plenty of toys like the infrared light that we could play with, and they wanted us to use them. They had an ARVN battalion of the 22d Infantry Division that never went on operation, so they couldn't use their own toys. Since they never used their own toys, MACV didn't understand how cumbersome some of those toys could be.

But we did tend to rely on MACV. Their greater creature comforts also helped to make our lives a little easier. We could borrow 16mm Hollywood movies from MACV, which we showed outside in the evenings at Mai Linh. The montagnards loved the movies, particularly westerns. They identified with the Indians and cheered when the Indians attacked the cavalry or a wagon train. Aside from that, the movies showed a side of U.S. culture that everyone wanted to emulate. The VC/NVA had nothing positive to give that could equate to what we showed in our nightly movies.

Doctor Hickey was an interesting person. One afternoon, I listened to a conversation between him and Ed Sprague about the "bandit" incidents in the Central Highlands. It seems that before the advent of the VC there were numerous bandit attacks and robberies (usually initiated by montagnards against ethnic Vietnamese), but as the VC became more active, the bandit incidents fell off. What was suspected was that the bandit incidents didn't really decline, but that banditry episodes were included in the VC statistics.

Gerald Hickey made Cheo Reo the base for his study of the montagnards, and he eventually became a major writer on the various tribes and their culture. But it is not generally well known that Ed Sprague was a primary source of information, particularly in his subsequent tenure in Vietnam.

Probably no one person makes more of an impact on an A-team than the team sergeant. Ed Sprague had such an impact on A-226. Ed has to be looked at in a bit more detail to fully understand how and why A-226 developed so well.

Edmund Walcott Sprague was born on 16 January 1930 in Boston, Massachusetts. The youngest boy in a family of eight children, he outgrew an impoverished childhood, became one of the legends of the U.S. Army Special Forces, and later went on to a distinguished career in the State Department. Along the way, he became famous for his efforts on behalf of the montagnards of Vietnam, particularly during the fall of the Central Highlands in 1975 and the aborted rescue of thousands of those same highlanders. Awareness of his importance is spreading among journalists and historians. But no one has come close to capturing the real Ed Sprague.

In our popular culture, he would probably be portrayed as a John Wayne from Boston. Since he's slightly built and less than six feet tall, that image would be inaccurate. Perhaps Clint Eastwood, in his role in *Unforgiven*, comes closer to the real man. But any cinematic portrayal would be unable to capture the complex personality and exploits of this remarkable man.

With his full head of white hair and gracious manner, Ed Sprague today could be described as patrician, avuncular, and aloof. But the same man is also tenacious, caring, and brave. He is full of heart and compassion to most, but he also directed the war in the heart of the Central Highlands for more than seven years, killing hundreds of Viet Cong and North Vietnamese army troops before Vietnam fell to the Communists in 1975.

To say that Ed Sprague is a complicated person is only the beginning of understanding. Jim Morris, in his book *The Devil's Secret Name*, called Sprague "a crotchety old fart" and a "Far East addict with a serious montagnard fixation." Other authors describe Sprague as "soft-spoken" or as "overidentifying" (with) and "oversensitive" in reference to the montagnards. Who is he then? Finding the answer can tell us a lot about the uniqueness of Special Forces and about those who do best in that demanding organization.

Growing up on the east side of Boston during the Depression had a formative effect. Ed Sprague still remembers the horse-drawn wagons of his youth in the mixed ethnic neighborhood where he grew up. Mafia shootings occurred periodically, and to survive, you had to be tough. Sprague's father worked as a printer, kept the family fed and together, and taught the family values common to the 1930s. The family itself was multiethnic, with American Indian, Scotch, German, and English ancestors. The senior Sprague came to Boston from Maine, having left home at the age of thirteen.

During World War II, Ed Sprague worked for a dairy company, helping to deliver milk products. While butter was rationed throughout the United States, Sprague had access to a plentiful supply, and his family ate well. On the other hand, Sprague also tells the story about seeing the plentiful food available (Spam and beans) in his first army mess hall and being amazed at the diversity and quantity, and thinking what a good deal the army was. Perhaps the first identifying factor that can be said of Sprague is that he was a product of the Depression and World War II—Spartan times that shaped many of his generation.

Sprague was a bright and intelligent youngster but indifferent toward school. And although he has read throughout his lifetime, he quit high school at the age of fifteen. But then, he had mostly been on his own since age thirteen. He lied about his age and joined the army. Too late to serve in World War II, Sprague entered the army in January 1946. He took basic training at Fort Dix, New Jersey, and was sent to Fort Sam Houston, Texas, for training as a medical aidman. Then he was sent to Fitzsimmons Army Medical Center in Denver, Colorado.

In the racially segregated army of the forties, Ed Sprague became the head of black wards for tubercular and psychological patients. As the ward master, he was responsible for sanitation of the wards, delivery of medications, and the myriad of administrative tasks connected with army medical care. Another important job was keeping the peace in his ward. He proved adept, was accepted by the black patients, and was rapidly promoted. He also met and married Eve, his wife of almost fifty years and mother of his seven children.

Eve's family had lived in Colorado for generations. Although she can also show a fiery temperament at times, Eve Sprague, for the most part, is a calm, level-headed individual. She balances her husband quite well, and their children reflect their bright, assertive father and their quiet but strong mother.

Wanting more for himself and his new bride, Sprague left the army and returned to Boston. He enrolled in a preparatory school to finish his high-school education. Although at eighteen still a teenager, Sprague had been living and working in an adult world for more than three years. While taking a break one day at school, he lit up a cigarette. A teacher, more used to dealing with teenagers than adults, slapped it out of Sprague's mouth. Sprague hit the teacher back and was promptly expelled.

In the 1940s, graduation from high school was still more the exception than the rule. Ed Sprague's father only had three years of high school, and his mother only completed two years. So following in the family tradition, Ed was also now not a graduate.

With no job prospects, a pregnant wife, and no chance to obtain a high-school diploma, Ed Sprague reenlisted in the army and was assigned to Fort Jay, New York. Since he had been out of service more than ninety days, he lost his sergeant's rank and had to reenter as a private first class.

Assigned to the medical detachment at Fort Jay and working in the Fort Jay hospital, Sprague was assigned as the ward master of the prison ward, a challenging position for a young soldier. Later, he trained as an X-ray technician and also met Capt. Francis J. Kelly, who was to become the commander of 5th Special Forces Group in Vietnam in 1966.

When the Korean War broke out in 1950, Ed Sprague expected to be sent to Korea as a medic in a rifle platoon. Instead, he was given orders to the Panama Canal Zone and assigned to the army hospital at Fort Clayton. At that point in his life, fortune played a part: Ed Sprague met Bob "Sam" Bass, another legend in Special Forces, and he became a mentor to Ed Sprague. Bass was serving as the first sergeant of the hospital unit that Sprague was assigned to, and recognizing the potential in Sprague, Bass counseled him to transfer to a combat-arms unit. Both Bass and Sprague transferred to the 33d Regimental Combat Team. Sprague was assigned to the regimental medical company and rapidly promoted to staff sergeant. He was made a medical platoon sergeant, with additional duty as an operations and training NCO.

Although they were assigned to different companies in the 33d RCT, Bass stayed in touch with Sprague and advised Sprague to attend jump school, become a paratrooper, and join a more elite part of the army. Bass explained to Sprague that the majority of the army was composed of ordinary units and ordinary people, but that Sprague wasn't ordinary and ought to be doing more challenging things in extraordinary units.

After he left Panama, Sprague followed Sam Bass's advice. He served briefly at Fort Knox, Kentucky, then went to jump school at Fort Bragg, joined the medical company of the 504th Parachute Infantry Regiment, part of the 82d Airborne Division, and was again a platoon sergeant.

Service in the 504th Infantry probably did more to mold Sprague than any earlier event. He learned the fast (sometimes frenzied) pace of a typical Airborne unit, the frequent field exercises, absences from family, parachute jumps and subsequent hikes back to garrison, the everyday physical training, alert and readiness exercises, and the required spit and polish.

During the decade of the fifties, the Cold War competition with the Soviet Union was at its peak, the draft was in effect for every able-bodied male from eighteen to twenty-seven, and the United States was as close to wartime mobilization as it had been in 1940. The Korean War revealed our unreadiness, and the military chiefs vowed not to be caught unprepared again. Every military unit had to be ready for war, but the Airborne units had to be more ready than most. That caused a training and readiness posture that put family life a distant second to the needs of the army.

But Ed Sprague thrived. He enjoyed the fast pace, the obligation to train his platoon, the attachment to infantry companies, and continuous field exercises. In training his troops, he continued to train himself. He stressed anatomy and the usual medical subjects. He insured that his soldiers periodically served in the local dispensaries and the base hospital, training that couldn't be taught within the platoon. The payoff was that all of his eligible troops passed their annual proficiency tests and subsequently received additional proficiency pay.

A battlegroup of the 504th Infantry was eventually transferred to Mainz, Germany, and Sprague's medical platoon went along. There, it was business as usual except that Sprague was in an environment where he was part of the U.S. forces facing the Soviet Union and the Iron Curtain less than sixty miles distant. Consequently, the readiness posture increased, and the pace became more demanding. Sprague adapted and continued to thrive. He was in an environment that was meant for him: He was a leader, leading men in an infantry support role, in an elite unit. Then Ed Sprague volunteered for Special Forces and was accepted.

Ed Sprague did well in Special Forces. He was soon promoted to master sergeant (E-8) and assigned as a team sergeant. None of us knew it at the time, but Sprague would become one of the historic figures of the Vietnam War. In 1966, all we knew was that Ed Sprague ran one of the best A-teams in Vietnam.

Because of the one-year tours in Vietnam and the individual-replacement policy, there was a gradual phase out of the original team members while new replacements arrived. Over the course of a year, the original team dwindled to four: Joe Simino, Ed Sprague, Henry Caesar, and John McFadden. Mike Dooley had begun his extension leave and would remain in Vietnam until his death. I had left three weeks earlier to be commissioned in Nha Trang.

Replacement team members began arriving about two

months after we arrived in country. Arnold Sims was transferred out, and our new demo sergeant was SFC Premond "Bob" Bowen. Bowen had previously been at B-22, and was most impressive. He had a natural gift for languages and was an outstanding engineer. Most of the real improvements at Mai Linh could be traced to him. I've met demo sergeants before and since Mai Linh, but Premond Bowen has always stood out in my mind as what a demo sergeant ought to be.

Ed Sprague had returned to the United States in November on a TDY trip to escort the remains of Dave Boyd home and then had returned to Mai Linh. Dave Boyd wasn't on our team but was the commander of airboats in IV Corps. Dave was killed on November 14 while reconning by fire at suspected enemy ambush positions. One of the positions was live, returned fire, and killed Dave. Ed Sprague received word that afternoon and packed for a short trip to the States. It was a sad day at Mai Linh because Dave had been a friend to us all.

We all met again during out-processing, drank beer, told war stories, and reminisced. Nobody had to tell us that we were one of the better A-teams; we knew it. But we were leaving our montagnard friends behind, and we worried how they would fare, caught between the South and North Vietnamese.

CHAPTER 5

Second Lieutenant Dooley

On the morning of January 18, 1967, I woke up in the senior NCO transient quarters at SFOB in Nha Trang. My instructions the previous day from the group adjutant were to cut off my stripes and tape them back on with tape underneath so the group commander could pull them off when I was commissioned a second lieutenant. I was also told to put the crossed rifles of infantry branch on my left collar.

As I went through the required cutting and pasting, I looked around at my roommates. They'd occasionally glance at me, then look away. There was little conversation. I thought at the time, what's wrong? Have I done something wrong? Maybe they were embarrassed for me. It surely couldn't be living in close proximity with officers; hell, my roommate at Mai Linh was the team leader. Officers and NCOs on A-teams lived together as a matter of course. Maybe they thought that I was crossing a forbidden trail. It didn't matter, though, I was going through with it.

I had started on that path a couple of months before. Captain Jim Zachary was my team leader when I talked to him about getting a direct commission. He told me to go ahead, and wrote a glowing recommendation. Ed Sprague supported me and told me to go for it.

When I filled out the application, I thought, Is this how Audie Murphy did it? Audie Murphy was the most decorated soldier of World War II and received a battlefield commission in Europe. Audie eventually received the Medal of Honor and went on to become a movie star. I knew that I wasn't in his league.

Still, I was a terribly young twenty-five-year-old sergeant first class (E-7). I knew that by the way things were going I'd be a master sergeant (E-8) in two or three more years. Then after that, I'd be a sergeant major (E-9) for the rest of my time in the army. Was that what I really wanted? In enlisted terms, I was a fast burner; but could I keep the pace? I knew that if I stayed in the enlisted ranks, I'd advance, but to be an officer? I had doubts, because like many NCOs, I didn't think very highly of, or trust, officers.

Sure, there were some great officers so far in SF: Simino, Knight, Kvederas, and Zachary. But as good as those guys were, there weren't very many of them. So far in the army, I had met many more careerist officers than people that I could admire. It seemed to me that West Point specialized in turning out officers intent on advancing only themselves (and they weren't in SF). The people that I still admired were Sergeant Major Price, First Sergeant Childress, and Master Sergeant Sprague.

Life is full of decisions. So I decided to see what I could become as an officer. The worst thing that could happen to me would be that at some time I might be sent back to my permanent rank of staff sergeant (E-6). No guts, no glory.

I had to go to Nha Trang once to take a physical examination to see if I was physically fit to be commissioned. Then, I had to appear before a precommissioning board in Nha Trang. So there I was, a sergeant first class (E-7) drawing proficiency pay, with a Combat Infantryman's Badge, answering questions about my enlisted background to a group of captains with considerably less combat time than I had.

When the precommissioning board president announced that it was recommending that I be commissioned, but as an adjutant general corps (AGC) officer, I silently accepted their finding. Then I went to find Bob Kvederas who was, at that time, assigned to the S-3 (operations and planning) shop. I asked him if he knew the board president. Bob said yes; in fact, the man was his roommate. I told him then to please prevent any embarrassment to all concerned, and that I would not accept an AGC commission. If I wasn't good enough to become an infantry officer, I'd stay an NCO. I'm still sure Audie Murphy didn't do it that way. I wasn't ashamed of my administrative background, I just wanted to move on and do other things. Being in the woods was fun for me! Bob Kvederas has never told me what happened, but the board changed its finding and recommended me for an infantry commission.

Sgt. Maj. George Dunaway was the group sergeant major at the time. We talked idly about our time in the 101st, Sergeant Major Price (a friend of Dunaway's), and the casualty board in the foyer of group headquarters, before I was admitted to the group morning staff briefing. There, Col. Francis J. Kelly, the group commander, pinned on my new gold bar, making me a second lieutenant. I wasn't aware at the time that Colonel Kelly was an old friend of Ed Sprague, but I knew that it was a small army and that many people knew other folks in common.

I had arranged ahead of time that my first salute would be given by Sgt. Ran Haggard, the junior medic from Mai Linh, then visiting SFOB. I gave Ran the ritual ten dollars for the first salute and haven't seen him since.

Then, I reported into Headquarters and Headquarters Company, 5th Group, as the executive officer. But first I had to move my stuff from the enlisted quarters to lesser quarters in the bachelor officer quarters (BOQ). It was a lonely trip.

The BOQ was more crowded and less nice than my previous NCO quarters. I guessed that transient officers didn't notice the differences very much.

Unlike the dining situation at an A-team, where the food was free, SFOB had a mess association that everyone had to join and pay for each month. The monthly fee was used to buy rations and pay the cooks, KPs, and servers in the separate officer and enlisted dining facilities. I went to join the mess association and again met my old first sergeant from 326th Medical Company, Wilbur Childress. Childress was a sergeant major (E-9) and was head of the mess association. I had heard that Childress and Sprague had made master sergeant (E-8) together in the 10th Group in Germany, but didn't know that Childress had come to the 5th. But it was typical of Childress to work at SFOB, near the seat of power, rather than at a B-team somewhere. Perhaps I was unfair in my judgment though, as Childress almost always had an evening job running one of the enlisted clubs at Fort Campbell. Probably, his experience running clubs qualified him admirably for running the SFOB mess association. I joined the association, paid my monthly dues, and then we talked about old times and friends. But there was now a distance between us. Sergeant Major Childress wasn't going to get too close to any officer. Well, I was learning and would have to get used to it.

As executive officer of Headquarters Company, 5th Group, my duties were terribly mundane. I had to do the jobs that the company commander didn't want to do. Okay, I understood that. The army had to keep me busy until I went back to the States. Supposedly, I was to rotate home by February 5, 1967. So I only had to wait a little more than two weeks.

One of my first time-absorbing jobs was to inventory the narcotics in the 5th Group dispensary. So I reported in, counted the morphine, codeine, etc. While doing that, I jokingly told the NCO accompanying me that if any was missing, I could go to any A-team around and cover the loss. My remark was taken wrong, and the NCO assured me that the group dispensary took its accountability for narcotics seriously. I began to realize the vast difference between an A-team and SFOB. SFOB was composed of mostly non-SF qualified people, and most people there had no concept of what went on in an A-team other than they didn't want to do that stuff.

At an A-team, the medics usually had a complete pharmacy. If opiates or controlled drugs were needed, then they were used, and no attempt was made to account for them. No team member would use or abuse drugs. It just wasn't done. In fact, every team member carried an IV (intravenous) blood expander kit and a packet of morphine syrettes, and some carried other pain medications. When I was on patrol, I limited myself to an IV kit, morphine, and dextroamphetamine. I didn't have enough experience to administer other drugs, and didn't want to hurt someone through my lack of training. Although I had been trained to do a "cut down" to find a vein and start an IV, I never looked forward to trying it. Thankfully, I never had to.

There were definite differences between SFOB people and the people on A-teams. I once met a supply clerk who bragged how he took captured weapons and mailed them home for himself. At the time, 5th Group had a policy that captured weapons had to be forwarded to SFOB for "intelligence" purposes. In reality, that meant souvenirs of combat weren't reported and the capturing person (such as myself) didn't send the weapon to SFOB to be confiscated by some clerk. Everyone I knew who wanted to get weapons back to the States did so.

My worst job as executive officer was to visit the sick and wounded in the hospital in Nha Trang. Normally, the job would have been done by the company commander, but he didn't want to do it. So I went and visited people I didn't know, talked to them, and wished them well from their company commander. I suspected that sort of thing wasn't what the leadership committee at Fort Benning taught, but I was only a brand-new second lieutenant.

As they say, it all flows downhill; and I had the law on my side, the law of gravity that is.

My DEROS (date of expected return from overseas) passed as Ed Sprague and all the others came through Nha Trang and returned home without me. Sure, we partied and raised hell, especially with the guys from the original team who had been transferred elsewhere. We mourned common friends, particularly Dave Boyd, but my friends were leaving without me. My family for almost a year was leaving me behind.

Most people, civilian or military, can seldom understand the bonding that goes on through training and on an operational A-team. Even now, more than thirty years later, the members of A-226 who served together in 1966 keep in touch. We've lost contact with a few people, but most remain close. I still consider Ed Sprague the best friend that I have.

After all my friends had gone home and my DEROS had passed, I decided that if I was going to leave Vietnam, I'd have to take matters into my own hands. So I went to talk to the 5th Group personnel sergeant, who told me that messages had been sent requesting orders, but if I called infantry branch in Washington, I could get orders over the telephone. Notice that I went for advice to the personnel sergeant and not the personnel officer. Mrs. Dooley's little boy didn't get dumber just because he was commissioned.

The following evening, after 2000 hours (8:00 P.M. local time), I began calling Washington. I had to call Saigon switch (switchboard), ask for Manila switch, get connected, ask for Hawaii switch, get connected, ask for Washington switch, get connected, and then ask for the telephone number that I had been given for infantry branch. I called for six hours, until 0200 (2:00 A.M. local time), before I was connected. Many times, I almost got through, then was disconnected and had to start all over again. It wasn't like direct dialing nowadays.

Finally, I reached Major Somebody, and I told him that I was newly commissioned in Vietnam, past my DEROS, and wanted to go home. The good major gave me an authorization and an assignment to Fort Benning and the Army Training Center, with an initial stop at the Officers Basic Course, which was basic training for officers at Fort Benning. I tried to get an assignment back to SF at Fort Bragg, but the major was doing me a favor getting me out of country, and I was willing to take any assignment just to leave. I figured that I'd find a way back to SF when I came home.

I knew that SF hated second lieutenants, and normally wouldn't accept them. But I also knew that I had been an SF senior NCO before I became an officer and that *that* ought to count for something. The first mission was to get back home. I didn't realize that my past was behind me and that my officer career was a brand-new slate. Supposedly, I forgot everything I ever knew when I was commissioned.

Later that day (since I had gotten authorization in the very early morning), I had orders to leave Vietnam. I hopped a flight to Saigon and reported into the 5th Group liaison detachment on Pasteur Street. I still wasn't home.

Saigon was brand new to me; I had never been there before. But in February 1967, that city wasn't like anything that I had seen elsewhere in Vietnam. Other than a curfew, I don't think that those folks knew a war was going on. Sure, the reporters could sit at their hotel rooftop bars and watch the flares and artillery fire for miles out, but they weren't experiencing war; it was more like watching a live-action play.

I had to wait three or four days in Saigon before I could get a flight out of Bien Hoa, about twenty miles to the northeast. So I decided to wander. Saigon was a beautiful city, but the place still seemed surreal to me. It was too artificial for a war zone.

I was driven to Bien Hoa by way of Camp Goodman. At Bien Hoa, I boarded a plane to the United States; unfortunately, one landing on the East Coast, at McGuire Air Force Base, next to Fort Dix. Oh well, I didn't care as long as I was back in the States.

At McGuire, the passengers were herded into a large reception hall and given a half-hour briefing. At the time, I had no idea why anyone would want to delay soldiers just passing through, but someone felt it was necessary. One of the reasons was soon apparent: The First Army commander didn't want anyone traveling through his area in a summer khaki uniform. Since that amounted to most of the manifest, we were all supposed to travel to Fort Dix and buy winter uniforms that would have to be altered and have the proper patches sewn on. I could expect to spend the next two days at Dix waiting. The First Army commander had a very small point; it was February 1967, and it was winter in New Jersey, but I wasn't about to be slowed down by stupidity.

A Fort Dix drill sergeant asked me to get on the buses heading to the main post. I told the drill sergeant that I wasn't going to travel in uniform, but was changing into civilian clothes. So I headed for a latrine and waited for the buses to leave. Then, still in a khaki uniform, I caught a cab for the airport in Philadelphia. I figured that at 2:00 A.M. on a Sunday morning the drill sergeant wasn't too enthusiastic to enforce an obviously stupid policy. Besides, if I traveled by commercial airline in civilian clothes, I had to pay for a full-fare ticket; in uniform, I could travel for half fare.

Back home in Chicago, I returned as a combat veteran, keeping the family tradition. Although the war wasn't won yet, things were looking up in early 1967. American divisions were operating throughout the four corps areas, engaging the VC/NVA, and generally kicking ass and taking names. Most people still felt good about Vietnam. Although I heard and read about war protesters, I didn't see any. Besides, I didn't think that we would bother each other. But there was one family tradition that I was about to break; I didn't want to join the American Legion.

Not very subtly, my father asked if I cared to join his post of the Legion. I told him that I'd like to wait a while because of the Legion's attitude toward Vietnam vets. In the recent past, one of the officials of the Legion compared Vietnam veterans to a bunch of crybabies. The Legion was still dominated by the World War II crowd, and those folks weren't sympathetic toward us. I'm not sure why since we were mostly the sons of their membership. We had continued the tradition of going off to war for our country, and then the premier veterans' organization didn't really want us. Maybe that was the first part of the rejection that my generation came to feel. Today, I still refuse to join any veterans' organization, although I later tried the Veterans of Foreign Wars and quit after a year. But there was still more adjusting to do.

Traveling from west to east has a terrible effect on the body clock. It took me about three weeks to adjust to time in the Midwest. I'd walk for miles through my parents' Gage Park neighborhood at 3:00 A.M., hoping to get sleepy. Another adjustment that I've never totally made is to stop evaluating the people and terrain around me in military terms. For the next few years, I always picked out possible ambush spots where danger might wait, and watched while I walked or drove on by. Today, I still look at terrain for armor approaches and places of concealment. I suspect that the habit isn't going to go away.

After a thirty-day leave, I headed my new 1967 Buick toward Washington, D.C., where I hoped to get shed of my Fort Benning assignment and return to Fort Bragg and Special Forces. Infantry branch was located at Fort McNair, which I found by way of stopping at the Pentagon and asking folks, "Where is infantry branch located?" I was naive but ballsy.

There wasn't a lot of time given to second lieutenants trying to change their first assignment. I was told to go to Benning and that I'd stay there until I made captain and then I could expect another tour in Vietnam. I really wanted to go back to SF, but I reconciled myself to being a "leg" (a derisive Airborne term for non-Airborne units and people) for the next two years. So I headed for Fort Benning by way of Fort Bragg. All my real friends in the army were either in Vietnam or at Bragg, so I decided to visit. It was good to see Ed Sprague and his family, and a few other friends still serving in the 82d Airborne Division.

When I reported to Benning, I rapidly learned how unimportant a second lieutenant is. At post headquarters, I was told that orders would be cut that afternoon assigning me to a student officer training company and to report to that unit. When I reported, the acting first sergeant (a fat, leg admin type) told me that I could not sign in at his unit without orders. I patiently explained that I was told by post headquarters to report here, that orders were forthcoming, and that he could pick me up on his morning report as attached pending assignment. The sergeant first class admin type still refused to allow me to report and we were heatedly discussing the issue when a fat, leg artillery captain stood me at attention and explained that he was the company commander, that I was a second lieutenant, and that I had better listen to his first sergeant. I went back to post headquarters and waited for publication of orders before taking them back to my training company.

By the time that I returned, the first sergeant and I realized that we had a common enlisted background, and he offered me a deal. I could have the next week and a half off until all the students reported in, and I wouldn't be placed on the *company* duty officer roster if I agreed to pull *battalion* duty officer that next weekend. I agreed. During the next eight weeks, I expected the first sergeant to renege on the deal, but he didn't. There was honor within the NCO corps.

In early 1967, Fort Benning was geared up to grind out lieutenants for the Vietnam War. There were multiple OCS battalions churning out officers, as well as bunches of newly commissioned ROTC graduates. The core curriculum was based on Vietnam and jungle operations. I thought that what they were teaching at the time didn't really mirror the Vietnam experience, but my thoughts weren't pertinent. We did have enough direct commissioned officers in the class to occasionally challenge some of the instruction, but the effort wasn't worth it. If the new lieutenants didn't have enough sense to listen to their platoon sergeants and heed their advice, then the lieutenant could expect to become a casualty, and a new lieutenant would take his place. War tends to be wasteful.

I was one of five oddities in my basic officer class: I had a direct commission. I also was Airborne and SF qualified and had a Combat Infantryman's Badge (CIB). I had no great message about Vietnam for my contemporaries. After all, the war was fought differently, depending where you were and who you were with. When asked, I could only say, Listen to your NCOs. They have experience that you don't have, and they can keep you alive.

Comparing officer status with enlisted status was amusing to me. With enlisted men, the army went to great lengths to measure their intelligence and capabilities. The Army Classification Battery (ACB) was a full-day set of examinations to measure this. But there was no comparable measurement of officers. Early in the first week of training, everyone was given the Graduate Record Examination (GRE) which measures aptitude, but nobody received his score. Along with everyone else, I took the GRE although my educational level was that of a freshman. I suspect that the army used the GRE results for officers much as they used the GT (General Technical) score for enlisted, except that enlisted had all their scores on their field records, and officers didn't. Maybe the GRE was an initial step to identify dumb officers. I sure hoped so.

After eight not very challenging weeks, I finished the basic course and reported in to the training center across the post.

The U.S. Army Training Center, Infantry, at Fort Benning consisted of three brigades conducting basic training for newly inducted enlisted men. One brigade was at the Sand Hill area, and the other two were in the Harmony Church area. The reception station was also located in Harmony Church.

The headquarters for the training center was in Sand Hill and was commanded by a brigadier general.

When I reported, I was sent to interview with the ACofS, G-3 (assistant chief of staff, G-3, or the staff officer responsible for training doctrine, plans, and operations). The incumbent at the time was a senior major who would shortly be replaced by a lieutenant colonel. I was asked the usual questions, my background, etc. At the end of the interview, I was told that I would be assigned as an assistant training officer in the G-3 shop. To hedge his options, the G-3 told me that I might later be assigned to one of the units within the training center.

I didn't care much either way. I learned very early that mostly they wanted a training inspector and someone to write lesson plans. Unlike most brand-new second lieutenants, I had been doing that sort of thing for a while. But if they wanted to assign me as a training officer in a Basic Combat Training (BCT) unit, I knew that I could turn out soldiers who would stay alive in Vietnam and still accomplish the mission.

My first real boss as a second lieutenant was Maj. Houston

Houser. Major Houser was a West Pointer, but one of the few really good ones that I met. Maybe it was because Houser was also SF and Ranger qualified. I can't say that Major Houser or subsequent bosses at the training center guided me, but they did turn me loose. Regardless, I enjoyed myself and my job, and helped my supervisors look good. In the meantime, medals that I won in Vietnam caught up with me, and I was promoted on time to first lieutenant, then to captain.

Major Houser started a Friday evening tradition where we all went to the Custer Terrace officers' club for happy hour. Now frowned upon within the army, happy hour used to be the end of the week ceremony where groups of officers could sit around, drink beer, eat oysters (a specialty of Custer Terrace), and discuss what we were doing and where we were going. It was during those gatherings that I slowly began to be steered toward a correct infantry career path.

It was explained to me that the first thing that I had to do was to get an RA (regular army) commission, get command time as early as possible, avoid flying helicopters, and stay away from Special Forces. I knew that I didn't want to fly helicopters, but staying away from SF required thought. I also knew that I wanted to command a rifle company because I could accomplish a mission and keep troops alive better than most. By the time that I made captain, I had ten years in the army, while most of my contemporaries had just two years' commissioned service. But Custer Terrace also had plenty of other facets.

I had stayed in touch with Ed Sprague at Fort Bragg. In 1967, his unit in the 6th Group was sent to the Ranger camp in Florida to pull duty as aggressors against the Ranger students. One day at Custer Terrace, I met a lieutenant from the 197th Infantry Brigade who had just returned from Florida. I asked him if he had met or knew Ed Sprague. He said no, and that SF didn't impress him that much. I asked him why, and he said that SF walked on trails (which was a Ranger School taboo). I knew immediately that not too many Ranger School cadre had ever read about Robert Rogers, the creator of the Rangers. But this was Infantry School doctrine poisoning real-world thought. Like any school, Infantry School developed doctrine. The key to success in the army was to observe the doctrine, and to sometimes consciously elect to ignore the dogma. SF would use trails in a denied area situation because they knew the trails. If introduced into a new and strange area, the right thing to do is to break brush (travel cross-country). But how do you teach intelligent thought?

In 1968, Ed called me one evening to tell me that his son was in Jump School at Benning, and he asked me to visit him. Well, when the team sergeant tells you to do something, the only response is to comply.

I was a first lieutenant at the time and went to the barracks at the Airborne School in uniform. I suppose that I surprised the charge of quarters (CQ) when I asked to see Mark Sprague. The staff sergeant (E-6) on duty called Mark to the orderly room. I asked if Mark could leave the area with me as I wanted to buy him a beer. Permission was granted, and Mark and I spent an uncomfortable hour together. We discussed his father and Vietnam. I hoped when I brought him back to his unit that he wasn't interrogated about what he was doing with officers.

Later, Mark went to Special Forces, trained as a medic and was assigned to the 10th Group in Bad Tölz. Mark and his soon bride-to-be were in Nha Trang when Vietnam began to fall in 1975.

But first we ought to go back to Ed Sprague.

Special Forces was formed in 1952 with the activation of the 10th Special Forces Group (Airborne) at Fort Bragg, North Carolina. In short order, the 10th Group was sent to Europe and established itself at Flint Kaserne, Bad Tölz, in the Alpine mountains of southern Bavaria, while a replacement unit, the 77th SF Group, formed at Fort Bragg and eventually became designated the 7th SF Group. The lineage of Special Forces is varied: It springs from the 1st Special Service Force, a joint U.S.-Canadian unit from World War II, the OSS, and various ranger units.

Regardless of the lineage, the concept of Special Forces was to operate behind enemy lines for extended periods of time, to train guerrilla forces, and to conduct unconventional warfare in support of U.S. objectives. As with the OSS, personnel selection would be most difficult. Some volunteers would be selected and trained, while others would be drafted because of their existing skills. Everyone, though, had to be able to infiltrate enemy territory by air (parachute), by sea (swim or small boat), or by land (walk in or stay behind by allowing the enemy to overrun). Ed Sprague was selected because he was a highly qualified medic, capable of teaching his specialty, and also because he was already Airborne qualified.

Ordinarily, Special Forces is a culture shock for a newly assigned noncommissioned officer. There are no longer any troops to do the things that you direct; now, you have to carry the aid kit, rig the demolitions, operate the radio and generator, or carry and man the mortar and ammunition. Most nonvolunteers don't adapt and are reassigned. But Ed Sprague had finally found what he was looking for in the army. He enjoyed the freedom to do his job within a small professional team, performing a job that was vital to the army and the country. And, he was heeding the advice of his old mentor, Sam Bass.

Throughout the fifties and sixties, Special Forces began to expand, and it attracted many top NCOs, Sam Bass among them. Ed Sprague met Sam Bass again in the 10th Group, along with many other highly motivated and skilled people. Working together, they taught each other while they trained. One humorous story of the time was told about an American army eastern European (selected for his language capability) who gave a class on Special Forces infiltration: "If you're not candlestein (sic, clandestine), you'll get *com*-promised (sic, compromised), and then you'll get *en*-ve-loped (sic, enveloped)."

Special Forces training was always varied and challenging. In the winter, there would be ski training and winter survival, perhaps in Norway. In the summer, mountaineering and scuba diving would be stressed, in the Alps and the

Mediterranean. Survival skills were developed and became as ordinary as breathing. Cross-training in the other skills present in an A-team was a constant. After a few years on an A-team, everyone was competent as a medic, radio operator, demolitions man, weapons sergeant, or as an operations and intelligence NCO.

Eventually, Ed Sprague was promoted to master sergeant and became a team sergeant. Now, he had the opportunity to lead his own team and put his personal stamp on an operational A-detachment. As with his medical platoons earlier, Sprague trained his team to be one of the best teams within 10th Special Forces Group. As a reward, his team got to go on more foreign missions, three of them to Greece.

Typically, a foreign mission would take the form of a mobile training team (MTT) to train a selected NATO force in various military proficiencies, such as small-boat handling or parachuting. During one of the missions to Greece, Sprague's MTT served as a cover to operate a real-world reception for an agent crossing over from Communist Yugoslavia. During the Cold War, that kind of thing was not an uncommon exercise along the borders of the Soviet Bloc.

Recently, the world was amazed to find out that the United States had cached thousands of weapons and large volumes of ammunition in Austria for use by guerrilla forces if Austria was ever to be overrun by the Soviet Bloc. But those buried caches were typical of the times and were what Special Forces did back during the Cold War in preparation for World War III. We should not be surprised when someday other journalists discover weapons caches in other countries.

Another aspect of Special Forces employment that was emphasized was the use of atomic demolition munitions (ADMs). ADMs are nothing more than nukes in a can that can be carried by one man to a desired location and employed to blow up a channeling terrain feature (such as a pass), an enemy staging area, or any other strategic target. But the most desirable thing about an ADM is that it can be emplaced ahead of time and detonated by a time delay or on demand without concern for air force delivery. Using ADMs doesn't necessarily give an A-team more firepower; on the contrary, it allows military planners to use an A-team as a natural delivery method for use of a tactical or strategic weapon.

In his years in 10th Group, Ed Sprague was exposed to more and more varied training than he had received previously in the army. That training further developed his unique background.

Ed Sprague returned to the United States in the early sixties as the Vietnam War was heating up. He was assigned to the 3d Special Forces Group at Fort Bragg, which had a mission orientation at the time covering the continent of Africa. Like the 10th Group in Europe, the 3d Group ran MTTs in Africa but had the additional responsibility for supporting the National Aeronautics and Space Administration (NASA) Gemini program.

The Gemini program was a prelude to the Apollo program, which later took astronauts to the moon. In the Gemini program, however, the basics were still being worked out in manned space flight. Earth orbits were planned to fly over water as much as possible and also over territory where U.S. recovery of the space capsule would be feasible. The 3d Group had the responsibility to recover Gemini capsules and crews that might accidentally land in Africa. That mission was accomplished by sending A-teams to Africa ahead of time, along with aviation assets and parachutes. Since these missions were funded by NASA, the usual thing for an A-team going to Africa was to find the most expensive hotel possible, spend NASA's money, and live the good life until the Gemini capsule came down at the intended ocean location. Ed Sprague's team didn't play that game.

In the spring of 1965, Sprague's team was sent to Kano, Nigeria, to await a Gemini shot and recovery. Since Kano was on the edge of the Sahara Desert, there were no real luxury facilities available; but that didn't matter to Ed Sprague, for he had no intention of staying at a hotel anyway.

Looking at the Gemini mission as another training opportunity, Sprague decided to camp his team along the runway at

Kano and eat field rations during the mission. His decision upset the assigned officers (including an attached major), but he would not be overruled. The team camped at Kano and trained during the day. Ed Sprague was hard-core.

"Hard-core" was an expression used in the sixties that derived in part from the term "hard-core Communist," which was then used to identify a particularly zealous or dedicated enemy soldier. Ed Sprague was considered hard-core and was proud of it. But the hard-core aspect of his personality resulted in exceptional A-teams that were always a cut above their contemporaries. The implicit message for a captain or lieutenant assigned to an A-team that Ed Sprague ran was to relax and let Sprague operate; the officer would get a good efficiency report because of Sprague's efforts and then would later move on to an assignment at the B- or C-team.

A-teams run by Ed Sprague were always good. There was little of the spit and polish found in other units, and everyone called each other by first name with no reference to rank, except for the officers. But there was always an unmatched professionalism, team camaraderie, and dedication to mission. If an individual—officer or NCO—didn't fit in, he would soon be transferred to another team. On a Sprague-run team, you had to want to be there, and you had to fit your personality into the team. No prima donnas were allowed, and everybody, regardless of rank, had to carry his load.

Ed Sprague was the consummate professional. But in 1969, he was getting old.

Throughout 1967 and 1968, Ed Sprague and I stayed in touch. I'm not sure who called first when we both watched on CBS News as Master Sergeant Boody, team sergeant at Duc Lap, told the world that Mike Dooley was killed on August 25, 1968. Mike was an original A-226 member and one of us. He stayed in Vietnam to work with the Mike Force, and then he was dead.

Ed Sprague kept me informed of the people we knew. Jim Stewart was finally in Vietnam (with a brief stop in Dom Rep), but ended up in MACSOG as one of the very first replacements. He wound up in the Hatchet Force in Kontum at Command and Control, Central (CCC), and later was the 1-0 (one-zero) or patrol leader of Recon Team Dakota. At the time, most people in SF knew that we were sending six-man teams into Laos, but everything about that mission was highly classified.

I've never understood why the army and government tend to overclassify everything. After all, the NVA knew that we had recon teams in Laos, so who were we keeping the secret from? Obviously, the American people and the media didn't know about SOG. But it was always amazing to me that monthly reports would come from USARV in Saigon about tonnages of supplies and numbers of people moving down the Ho Chi Minh trail, and nobody ever questioned the source of the data.

In January 1969, I made captain. It was time to go back to Vietnam. I wondered at the time why those little inept people from North Vietnam hadn't just quit. Surely, they had to realize that they couldn't defeat the might of the United States. Maybe somebody forgot to tell them. They lost tens of thousands in Tet of 1968, while also exposing their genocidal intent, particularly in Hue.

By early 1969 in the United States, it was obvious that there wasn't a lot of support for the war. Campuses across the nation were either rioting or closing down. Personally, I wasn't sure what was driving the antiwar movement other than fear of the draft. But I also wondered, didn't the rioting students understand what was going on in the two Vietnams?

South Vietnam was still a major rice exporter, along with other commodities, while North Vietnam was a major importer of goods, primarily weapons, ammunitions, and foodstuffs. As a more simple test, where did people want to live? Many more North Vietnamese chose to live in the South; few South Vietnamese ventured north. But objective evidence had no place in the propaganda war that occurred after 1968. Somehow, the vast majority of American people were led to believe that Vietnam was not a winning situation.

I remember a very dear aunt of mine visiting me before I

left for my second tour. Aunt Tillie was a Republican conservative her entire life. Yet, she asked, "George, when is this damn war going to end?" I didn't know how to answer. Most of the KIA/MIA that I knew were from SF or, at least, Airborne soldiers, and they totaled around forty friends and acquaintances. But still, in comparison with World War II and Korea, we weren't losing that many people, and the NVA were hurting.

Didn't anyone realize that it was just another phase of the Cold War?

CHAPTER 6

Second Tour

After I left Vietnam the first time, I visited infantry assignment branch in Washington. I wanted to get out of my assignment to the training center at Fort Benning, to return to Special Forces. Unhappily, I didn't succeed with either request, and I was told that I wouldn't go back to Vietnam until I made captain. So when I made captain in January 1969, I called infantry branch and told them I was ready. I was on my way in April.

Many of my friends thought that I was crazy for wanting to go back. By that time in the war, most career infantrymen had at least one tour and many had two. A few people had more than two tours. Some people resigned from the army rather than go back again. It was a time of turmoil in the United States, and the vocal antiwar sentiment led by a minority of students seemed to have influence far greater than the numbers of people involved actually deserved.

Perhaps I was weird, but I thought of Vietnam as the only war that we had, and the role of infantrymen was to go to war if they could. After all, why train forever if you're going to miss the chance to use the skills you've developed? Besides, most of my friends were then on second tours or getting ready to go back. And there were still the majority of us that believed that Vietnam was worth fighting for. I was still one of the believers.

From my own experiences on my first tour, I couldn't imagine leaving my montagnard friends to communism. The montagnards didn't like the South Vietnamese very much, but they hated the North Vietnamese even more. By then, I knew, FULRO had quieted down and had even made peace with the government of the Republic of Vietnam.

In return for the FULRO peace, the Vietnamese government had allowed montagnards into the legislative branch and had created the Office of Ethnic Minority Affairs. The Vietnamese were glad to allow the montagnards to fight for the Central Highlands, while the ARVN concentrated their forces elsewhere. With only two ARVN divisions in II Corps, the highlands was almost an entirely montagnard/American show (the two Korean divisions were located along the II Corps coast). But Tet of 1968 had changed the mood of the war.

Like many others at the time, I watched the Tet television war on the evening news and watched more of my friends come home in boxes. We attended the memorials and medal ceremonies, consoled the widows, and ached to get even. I was sad when Walter Cronkite said that he thought that we couldn't win and ought to get out, but then, I also thought that it was stupid to fight a war with one hand tied behind your back. I wondered why we refused to show the same resolve that the NVA had. After all, we never tried to bomb the Red River dikes, which would have flooded much of North Vietnam and disrupted its economy. For political reasons, the Haiphong Harbor was off limits and wasn't mined until President Nixon forced the issue in 1973. Fighting without the will to win was just plain stupid in my eyes. Perhaps I think in simplistic terms, but if we weren't fighting to win, then the government was just wasting American lives, and that's criminal.

Once again, I left my family with my parents in Chicago and flew by commercial jet to Seattle. I doubted that I would return to Special Forces and didn't even think that I would get an Airborne assignment. Special Forces and the Airborne units had become too glamorous, and the regular army officers would get first pick. So instead of reading a novel, I read army field manuals while flying to the West Coast, hopeful that I could at least command a rifle company in the 1st or 4th Infantry Divisions. I also knew that as an individual replacement and a reserve officer, I was on the bottom of the list; I would be sent wherever the army might need me.

Instead of a C-130, my transportation to Vietnam was a chartered commercial jet aircraft that lifted off from McChord Air Force Base, adjacent to Fort Lewis, Washington. Everyone on the plane was an individual replacement, and there were about thirty new officer graduates out of the SF officer course at Fort Bragg. They all had orders to 5th Special Forces Group, and I envied them. I still hoped that I could get an Airborne assignment or at least be assigned to the 4th Division in the Central Highlands.

We landed at Cam Ranh Bay, in-processed, and spent a couple days in the replacement depot. We were issued field gear, and everyone was antsy about assignments. Of course, rumors were everywhere. It seemed that the Central Highlands fighting was taking on almost a mythic aspect, with Mike Force battalions and U.S. infantry units getting into heavy fights everywhere. The NVA there usually operated in multiple-regiment size, and the war seemed to have changed drastically from what I had known in 1966. But then, rumors in replacement detachments have probably always been historically bigger than the facts. I shudder to think what the rumors were in the replacement depots in Normandy during the Battle of the Bulge in late 1944.

When assignments were announced, I was the only one to be assigned to 5th Special Forces Group. The people I had envied on the way over hated me; they ended up going to the assignments that I had expected to get. I suppose somebody in USARV or MACV must have realized that my SF qualification and experience would better qualify me for an SF assignment. Regardless, I wasn't about to question my good fortune. If I couldn't command a U.S. rifle company, I'd get an A-team.

I was told that I had to turn in all my field gear, as "Special Forces wasn't funded by the army." So I did so and recognized something that everyone always suspected: Special Forces in Vietnam was funded by the CIA. Everyone always knew that the CIA was involved with assignment of SF missions and that the other dynamic was that the army never really wanted to let Special Forces out from under its control. Of course, the army was proud that the majority of intelligence generated in Vietnam came from Special Forces, but the army also didn't want to hear about the less seemly side such as agents, assassinations, and the other aspects of unconventional warfare. Maybe that helps to explain the love-hate relationship between the army and SF. Regardless of who commanded or controlled SF, I didn't care as long as I was back in it.

Without field gear, but with a beret on, I flew a short hop the next day from Cam Ranh to Nha Trang. I in-processed into the 5th Special Forces Group, drew field gear again, and had to haggle with the group adjutant for an assignment. The adjutant wanted to assign me to III Corps, and I asked for II Corps, with the explanation that I spoke Jarai better than most and that my ability would be little used in III Corps. I even demonstrated my Jarai language ability with some short phrases, hoping to impress him. The adjutant relented and after refresher/orientation training, I was on my way to the C-team in Pleiku.

Refresher training was on Hon Tre Island in Nha Trang Harbor. For a week, we climbed the mountain on the island, with sandbags in our rucksacks, as our version of physical training. After two years in a staff job, I was glad that I was once again training to be a grunt in the field. During the rest of the day, we went over first aid, immediate-action drills, radio procedures, calls for fire, and everything else considered important to keep people alive and functioning in 1969.

The C-team was more formally known as Company B, and it was commanded by a lieutenant colonel. In contrast to what I had known of the C-team in 1966, a lot had changed. Company B was immensely bigger, there were two Mike Force battalions nearby, and it seemed to operate as a miniature SFOB (Special Forces operational base). But then, both Company B and SFOB were different from before.

* * *

By 1969, the war in Vietnam had imposed drastic changes on Special Forces worldwide. Almost every SF NCO had at least one Vietnam tour by then, and most were on second or third tours. Still, there weren't enough people to go around, so SF qualification standards were dropped, SF reservists were called to active duty, and many personnel spaces were filled by people not SF qualified. To make matters worse, some of the younger people assigned to SF used drugs, particularly at SFOB.

Fortunately, SF still didn't have the problems prevalent in other units, such as fraggings. But problems existed that hadn't been there before. To counter them, SF reacted logically and in a conventional military manner. Standards were set and enforced with the usual mechanisms of military units. Inspector-general inspections were staged; combat readiness inspection teams were founded and toured. Then to keep USARV happy, property books and hand receipts were maintained in accordance with conventional military wisdom. Of course, missing items could still be written off as combat losses, but at least the supply procedures were kept sacrosanct. I suspect that if someone went back through the records, they would find that many, many tons of equipment were lost on river-crossing operations. I also suspect that the volume of supplies said to have been lost in river crossings would dam the rivers of Vietnam and create new channels.

Perhaps I'm not the best person to testify about supply accountability; I believed that weapons and supplies were meant to be used. If I or someone else could use a million dollars' worth of something to save an American life, then I considered the trade worth it. But I was observing the world as a grunt and no longer as an admin person.

The accountability changes also lent more legitimacy to headquarters units, which grew larger and more ponderous. And when there are more headquarters personnel, such as clerks, the clerks feel left out that they can't get the awards and badges that the A-team people get. So to remedy that "morale" problem, clerks were allowed to go out on "local security" patrols leaving at 2300 and returning at 0100—two hours later—the next day. When a clerk got fifteen such "two-day patrols," he was entitled to a Combat Infantryman's Badge (CIB), meeting the criteria for thirty days in combat even though (most likely) hostile shots were never fired. Sometimes, instead of local security patrols, administrative personnel operated radio-relay sites. Later, we were doing the same in B-24 to CIB qualify our admin personnel.

The biggest change in the war, however, was that, for all intents and purposes, there were no more Viet Cong. Now, patrols in the jungle met regular North Vietnamese, often in large numbers and units. It was almost axiomatic that when less well-trained U.S. troops met a tougher and larger enemy, friendly casualties would increase. And so they did.

I have always maintained that the NVA were never very good, but when they massed and threw enough ammunition at you, people were going to get hurt. Conversely, because they were massed, the gunships and air force would come in and cause a whole lot of NVA casualties.

Another variable in the equation was the stated U.S. policy to pull units out of Vietnam and to "Vietnamize" the war, which caused most people to think twice before doing anything daring. After all, who wanted to be the last person to die in Vietnam? And the handwriting was on the wall. America was pulling back from the war.

SF had changed, and so had the rest of the army. But for an NCO turned officer and a captain, it was still the only war we had, and one might as well make the best of it.

Aside from the usual meeting-engagement contacts, the Central Highlands big war had almost turned into a measurable cycle. In the early part of the year, a provisional NVA division (often consisting of the 66th NVA Infantry, 28th NVA Infantry, and 40th NVA Artillery regiments) would form and lay siege for about two months to one of the A-camps in northern II Corps. Then the NVA would withdraw back into Laos or Cambodia, refit and retrain, march south and lay siege to one of the A-camps in southern II Corps. In May

1969, Camp Ban Het* was under siege when I reported to Company B.

Ban Het was located in Kontum Province, the most north-west province in II Corps, and directly opposite where the borders of Laos and Cambodia met that of Vietnam. There had always been an SF camp in that area, but earlier sites had been at Dak To, which was four miles east of the new camp at Ban Het. Regardless of where the camp was located, the geography of the area always made any camp located there an obstacle to the NVA. Ban Het/Dak To sat astride the east-west route between the Ho Chi Minh trail to the west and Binh Dinh Province on the east. Dak To lay at the entrance to the Tu Mrong Valley, long an NVA redoubt, while Ban Het occupied controlling access to the Dak Poko and Plei Trap valleys. North of Ban Het were the SF camps at Dak Seang and Dak Pek; to the southeast was the camp at Polei Kleng. Two other non-border SF camps were located at Plateau Gi and Mang Buk.

Kontum Province was densely forested and had rugged, towering mountains. It was one of the first provinces con-trolled by the Viet Minh during the French war in Indochina, and the NVA wanted the province back during the U.S. tenure of the war. Many fierce battles had been fought in Kontum Province, with the most notable at Hill 875 in November 1967.

Hill 875 was southwest of Ban Het, about six kilometers east of the Cambodian border. It was one of many areas of NVA activity when elements of the 173d Airborne Brigade arrived at Dak To in June 1967. Eventually, most of the rest of the brigade would arrive at Dak To. Also operating in the area was a brigade of the 4th Infantry Division, various Mike Force battalions, a number of ARVN battalions, and CIDG companies.

Throughout the summer and fall of 1967, it was obvious that the NVA wanted to take Dak To. The 173d Airborne Brigade proved to be the primary spoiler of the NVA plans, and they ended up taking the brunt of the casualties. Over two

*Through common usage over the years, Ban Het has been spelled and pro-nounced Ben Het. The official and Vietnamese proper noun was Ban Het.

hundred paratroopers of the 173d died during the fighting, and at Hill 875, the dead were so numerous that they were evacuated by Chinook helicopter sling loads to the airfield at Dak To.

The NVA hadn't gotten tougher, just more numerous. The guerrilla war had become more conventional. These guys died just as well (or badly?) as their earlier counterparts. Our mission was to send as many of them on to Buddha or Marx (depending on their ideologies) as could be accommodated.

The adjutant in Company B gave me my choice of going to B-23 in Ban Me Thuot or B-24 in Kontum. Since most of the action seemed to be in Kontum, I asked to go there. The 4th Infantry Division still kept a brigade south of Kontum City, and there was always a Mike Force battalion on operation somewhere within the province.

The B-24 compound was adjacent to the province MACV team compound and both shared a helicopter landing pad. When I arrived, I thought that the compound was too plush for a war zone. The buildings were all concrete block, finished over, and painted white. There were two bars, an excellent dining facility, and all the amenities common to a Stateside garrison unit. I expected something more Spartan, but couldn't complain about what others had built before I arrived. The engineer sergeant who met the helicopter pointed out that the field north of the compound contained the bones of hundreds of NVA* who had tried to take the compound during Tet (February) 1968. I had to admit to myself that maybe these B-team folks lived good, but they could still earn their living fighting. I soon found that I was to become one of them.

To my dismay, the B-team commander, Lt. Col. Andrew Marquis, told me that I was going to be a staff officer, specifically the S-1 or adjutant. I told him that I wanted to command

*Most of the graves were shallowly prepared by a bulldozer. During the monsoon season, which was starting, some of the dirt would wash away, exposing femurs and other bones.

an A-team, but he was adamant that I had to be a staff officer first. Hell, I thought to myself, I could have stayed in the States and pushed paper! I resolved to be a good little captain and do what the boss wanted but to push for an A-team whenever I could. But as I looked around at some of my teammates, I recognized that I might not be too happy at B-24. First Lieutenant Colonel Marquis had a reputation as something of a martinet. He was on his only tour in Vietnam, and he specialized in threatening his subordinates. I suspect that Marquis thought that the tour was his pathway to a promotion to colonel. But that was not to be. In fairness, however, B-24 was probably the most difficult B-team to command. The four border camps were the northernmost in country, the NVA were running rampant in I Corps to the immediate north, and they wanted Kontum.

I have never before or since met a commander as disliked as Lieutenant Colonel Marquis. He threatened every commander with relief to the point that few cared anymore. His staff officers were mere minions with the mission of making him look good. My favorite remembrance of Marquis is of him recounting his achievements to me (all legitimate) and directing me to recommend him for a Legion of Merit award based on those achievements.

It has always been my personal practice never to say bad things about fellow SF soldiers. Lieutenant Colonel Marquis is the exception. But supposedly, he is now retired in Florida and has stated that he doesn't remember anything about his Vietnam tour. That statement was offered in answer to a request that he correct another soldier's record. So be it.

Many of the officers and NCOs enjoyed their assignment at B-24. Some demonstrated that happiness by continually extending their tours of duty to stay in Vietnam and in Kontum. Yet there didn't seem to be much enthusiasm for serving on an A-team. But to be fair, those folks who gravitate to B- or C-teams are better off there than at an A-camp. Most were too old or complacent to be operating in the woods and would actually be a burden to an A-team. Many were not Special

Forces qualified and had transferred in from other U.S. units. But there were more than just homesteaders at Kontum.

To the east of the B-24 compound was a small compound occupied by a Mike Force battalion, actually an indigenous montagnard battalion with an A-team as the leadership cadre. SF NCOs served as the company commanders, and the A-team commander was the battalion commander. If there was any one good concept to come out of the Vietnam War, in my opinion it was the Mike Forces. Those battalions were light infantry, but they were better trained (and led) than the majority of U.S. and ARVN battalions. They also had long experience in the war, stayed active in the field for three weeks out of every four, and could still operate without the long logistical tail needed by conventional units. Dollar for dollar, the Mike Force battalions were the best investment we made in Vietnam.

Located within the B-24 compound and attached to 5th Group was a unit of the 403d Radio Research Special Operations Detachment, an Army Security Agency element that monitored and located the sources of NVA radio traffic. In the south side of Kontum City was FOB-2 (otherwise known as Command and Control, Central) of MACSOG. These units were significant to B-24 in their interaction (or sometimes lack thereof) with B-24 and its A-teams. What the two units did and the classified missions that they had were an open secret. Sometimes they helped, and other times they didn't.

Our relations with the 403d SOD were a good example. We fed them, provided them security, and gave them billets at the B-team and at the A-camps that they worked out of. But because of the rules that they worked under, they couldn't tell us information that we needed to know. Everything that they gathered was classified as special intelligence (SI), which nobody on the B-team was cleared to receive. So later on in my tour, I tried to get the B-team commander cleared for access to SI. Company B and the SOD folks told me that the B-team commander couldn't be cleared for SI because he was too far forward in the combat zone. When I replied that the SOD

Roger Knight and pet civet cat.

Capt. Roger Knight
presenting the Army
Commendation Medal to
S.Sgt. Jean Uszakow. To
Uszakow's right are SFC
Henry Caesar and
Lt. Joe Simino.

Capt. Bob Kvederas, A-226
commander after Roger Knight.

John McFadden.

George Dooley.

Bahnar refugees recaptured from the NVA. The NVA used the Bahnar as slave labor in the Central Highlands. George Dooley is at the left foreground. Note that SF didn't shave or bathe while on operation.

Ed Sprague determining his location on the map. With his shirt off, he could cool down and allow the garment to dry. In the oppressive heat of Vietnam, staying cool (and healthy) was important.

A CIDG Jarai tribesman. The dense jungle will make him invisible from another ten meters away.

A CIDG Jarai tribesman carries the radio while an LLDB (Vietnamese SF) reports their location. Note the absence of jungle.

Trail squad of a returning CIDG company. Notice that, although close to their home at Mai Linh, only one tribesman has slung his carbine. Unseen are the left- and right-flank security echelons.

Montagnard CIDG. The yellow scarves designate their unit.

CIDG company commander and his assistant.

CIDG on operation. The individual at right is using an HT-1 radio.

Jarai father and son with cattle.

George Dooley getting a bracelet from a local village chief. He's holding the bamboo straw from a rice-wine jug.

Inside an HU1B, flying above the highlands.

Ed Sprague on operation, ready for sleep.

Ed Sprague on an elephant. Some Jarai kept elephants as work animals. Having an elephant was a sign of wealth.

Mike Dooley. Later in the war, Mike was killed at Duc Lap.

LLDB team leader Lt. Siu Broai (Oai) with the Vietnamese team sergeant. Siu Broai was one of the first montagnards to be commissioned in the Vietnamese army. When Vietnam fell, Broai was a major and was sentenced to seven years of "reeducation."

George Dooley at Mai Linh.

Jarai child on a water buffalo. Although the animal was actually a caribou, U.S. troops throughout Vietnam called them water buffalo.

Ed Sprague sipping wine and getting another bracelet.

Mike Dooley, John McFadden, and Jim Zachary.

USSF participating in wapasat.

Jarai girls.

Ed Sprague in camp at Mai Linh.

John Mullins, Roger Knight, and Ed Sprague.

George Dooley.

General
Westmoreland
receiving his
first and only
montagnard
bracelet at Camp
Mai Linh in
1966. Capt. Jim
Zachary is sitting
at right.

Wife of Ksor Sung ("Mike"), our chief interpreter at Mai Linh.

The Vietnamese province chief with Bob Kvederas, A-226 commander.

Rear, left to right: John Mullins, Premond Bowen, Jean Uszakow, Mike Dooley. Front, left to right: Wayne Summers, John McFadden, Zane Osnoe, George Dooley, Ed Sprague.

Jarai tribesman.

Montagnards with a dead boa constrictor. There was meat in the pot that night.

Ed Sprague and the 5th Special Forces Group Catholic chaplain.

Ed Sprague and monkey, with Ed being "groomed."

Mike Dooley posing with a tiger that was killed on an operation.

Ed Sprague as a USAID civilian employee.

An old Jarai veteran of the first Indochina war, now serving in the second.

Ed Sprague on operation before settling into a night defense position.

Jarai canton chief with his shaman assistant, in a bracelet ceremony for Jim Zachary, commander of A-226. Front, left to right: Jim Zachary, the B-22 S-2 officer, and an unidentified individual.

A street in Cheo Reo.

Ed Sprague.

Near Mai Linh (left to right), Ed Sprague, the B-22 S-2 officer, the canton chief, and the unidentified individual who probably accompanied the B-22 S-2 officer.

LLDB team sergeant toasting Ed Sprague on being decorated with the Soldier's Medal.

George Dooley as a first lieutenant at Fort Benning, Georgia.

people were cleared for SI and were just as far forward, the catch-22 answer was that they were SOD and the B-team commander wasn't! I sometimes wonder whether we were destined to lose Vietnam because of our stupidity. Nevertheless, we somehow found a way to operate together.

Periodically, the SOD team leader would point to a coordinate on the map and say, "Mugwump (or some other code name) is here."

Then we'd play a question-and-answer game more suitable for a television game show than for a combat zone: "How big is Mugwump?"

"I can't tell you. That's classified SI."

"Well, if we sent a platoon from (name of camp closest to the plot), would that take care of Mugwump?"

"Oh no, Mugwump is too big for just a platoon."

Later in my tour as the S-3 (operations officer), I didn't want to gamble reacting to a radio plot with a small unit when the radio plot might be a regimental headquarters. The ground rules, being what they were, did not foster success.

We would carry on in that manner until we could figure out how to resolve the Mugwump issue. About six weeks later we would get a sanitized message from USARV that a specific NVA unit was at such and such a point and time; then we could correlate the code names with actual units and promptly (six weeks later) react against those units. Unfortunately, a lot of opportunities were lost along the way.

In *Green Berets at War*, Shelby Stanton, using formerly classified records, pointed out that the 28th NVA Infantry Regiment prepared the battlefield around Dak Seang for two months before the siege began. Yet, nobody at the camp or at B-24 had access to the information that the preparation was going on! There were sporadic contacts around Dak Seang and Dak Pek beforehand, but nobody cared to share the actual knowledge of what was going on with the people who had to fight the battle. Similar examples happened with MACSOG.

CCC might launch an across-border recon operation from one of our border camps, and often bring wounded back for immediate treatment, but we were not privy to the information that they acquired. If multiple NVA regiments were massing opposite one of our camps, we wouldn't find out until the first mortar rounds and rockets landed. Supposedly the army has learned to correct some of the mistakes from Vietnam. I hope so. Most times in Vietnam, the NVA knew more about what the spooks were doing than the people supported by the spooks.

It was mid-May when I began pushing paper as the S-1. Most of what had to be done was writing award recommendations, reporting casualties, and preparing efficiency reports. It was boring, but it kept Lieutenant Colonel Marquis happy. Normally, a B-team would have been commanded by a major, but there were more lieutenant colonels available for command positions than there were available majors. So oftentimes, a lieutenant colonel on his first Vietnam combat tour would be commanding a B-team, and he might have an executive officer who was a major with two or more combat tours. Even with lieutenant colonels filling nominal major positions, there was still intense competition for the "right" B-team. Because of all the NVA activity in Kontum Province, B-24 was regarded as a prime catch.

Ban Het had come under siege on 05 May 1969. But Ban Het had been a target for the NVA since it was constructed in 1968. Throughout its construction, the camp was a magnet for NVA mortar, artillery, and rocket fire. But because the NVA wanted its destruction, the camp was heavily augmented. Mike Force and 4th Infantry Division troops continually patrolled within the Ban Het operational area and two U.S. heavy artillery batteries were stationed there, along with World War II–vintage Duster twin-barreled antiaircraft weapons employed in the ground-defense role. Much later in life I would meet Steve Leopold, who was captured while assigned to Ban Het. Initially listed as missing in action (MIA) in 1968, Leopold was captured when the NVA overran his position west of Ban Het.

During the evening of 03 March 1969, a unit of NVA along

with at least three PT-76* tanks approached Ban Het along the road from the west. The defenders at Ban Het could hear the tanks coming, and the NVA walked and drove into a kill zone laced with mines and registered artillery fire. Also awaiting the tanks were 106mm recoilless rifles, U.S. tanks, helicopter gunships, and air force jet aircraft. Everybody claimed credit for the tank kills; but overlooked was the new extent that the NVA would go to in trying to destroy Ban Het.

I visited Ban Het twice during the siege. In their usual fashion (learned from the Dien Bien Phu manual for siege warfare), the NVA had dug zigzag trenches through the defensive wire in a number of places, but they never completed the trenches to the perimeter bunker lines. There were also trenches south of the east-west airfield, and mortar concentrations were plotted on the helicopter landing pad. When you landed by helicopter at Ban Het, you knew that mortar rounds would begin impacting within ten seconds of your arrival. Your choice was either to take cover behind one of the ARVN tanks at the helicopter landing pad or to run one hundred meters uphill to the camp. When the helicopter left, the mortar rounds at the landing pad quit falling. Amazingly, the NVA never got their fire accurately adjusted onto the landing pad.

On one visit to Ban Het, I accompanied Richard Threlkeld of CBS and his two-man camera crew. I watched as he stood in a trench and described outgoing U.S. artillery fire as NVA incoming; but then the folks back home who would watch his report didn't know the difference. After all, television news is about showmanship, not news. CBS got to film an Arc Light (B-52 strike) up close and also the devastation that Ban Het had been subjected to. When we left for the day, the helicopter took a couple of hits on the way out, and we stopped in Dak To to check the damage. Before we left Ban Het,

*Depending on the source, the PT-76s ranged from three to as many as ten. Probably only the NVA know for sure how many were involved. But after the battle, one relatively intact PT-76 was removed for display purposes, and there were two identifiable hulks left on the road.

the wounded were being loaded first on the right side of the helicopter and the CBS crew was throwing them off (until they were stopped) on the left side so they would have room on the trip out. To work with the media does not encourage respect for them.

During the sieges in northern II Corps, Dak To would become a forward operational base (FOB) for everybody involved in the siege. USARV would establish an advanced command post (CP), an aid station, and a minilogistics depot for the supporting aviation and armor. With all the resources made available for the Ban Het affair, there was no doubt that the camp would hold until the NVA got tired of absorbing casualties and crept back across the border. That happened, and the siege was lifted at the end of June.

When the team commander left Ban Het, I expected to be his replacement. That was not to be. SFOB, through Company B, sent a specifically named captain to assume command of Detachment A-244. Oh well, I knew that if I was persistent enough that I would eventually get an A-team.

Col. Robert B. Rheault assumed command of 5th Special Forces Group on 29 May 1969. After less than sixty days in command, he would be relieved, and he and some of his intelligence staff were actually jailed. And Gen. Creighton Abrams, commander of all military forces in Vietnam, would use the matter to get Special Forces out of Vietnam. But then, General Abrams didn't realize how much he relied upon SF for intelligence in Cambodia, Laos, and North Vietnam, and that he would have to bring some SF people back (covertly, of course; generals don't make mistakes). It all started with Thai Khac Chuyen.

Thai Khac Chuyen worked as an agent for Project GAMMA, Detachment B-57, which was a cross-border intelligence-gathering operation targeted on Cambodia. Unfortunately for Mister Chuyen, his photograph was found on a roll of film captured in Cambodia. More unfortunate for Mister Chuyen was the presence of NVA intelligence people in the picture. This information, when correlated with other information indicating a compromise in GAMMA, led people to conclude that Mister Chuyen was a double agent.

So after interrogations and polygraph examinations, the question arose as to what to do with Mister Chuyen. The Nha Trang CIA liaison was queried, and his reply was to eliminate Chuyen. Asking the CIA representative was probably amateurish enough, but then the GAMMA people (most of whom were trained in military intelligence but were not SF qualified) decided to involve Colonel Rheault. A cover story was created, and Chuyen was killed on 20 June 1969 and fed to the fish in Nha Trang Harbor. Then an involved military intelligence sergeant had second thoughts and confessed to the assassination of Chuyen. The cover story unraveled, but Colonel Rheault gave the cover story to General Abrams, not knowing that Abrams already knew the facts and that Rheault was lying to him.

General Abrams was no fan of Special Forces, and he leaped at the opportunity to get Colonel Rheault and to eventually throw 5th Special Forces Group out of Vietnam. Colonel Rheault and the GAMMA participants were jailed at USARV in Long Binh, but later released when the CIA would not testify about the incident. The damage was done, however. Colonel Rheault returned to the States, his career ruined.

Colonel Rheault had followed the normal rotation in assuming command of 5th Group; he had first commanded 1st Group on Okinawa. When people on Okinawa in 1st Group heard about the jailing of Colonel Rheault, some said they could break him out of Long Binh Jail (LBJ). In Bangkok, some folks in 46th Company planned to sabotage Abrams's rest and recreation (R&R) villa there. These were not happy times, and Abrams was universally disliked.

But General Abrams wasn't through yet. He assigned a non-Airborne, non–Special Forces officer to command 5th Special Forces Group. Some suspect that he probably giggled when he assigned Col. Alexander Lemberes as the new SFOB commander. But General Abrams's silliness was revealed when Lemberes broke his leg going through jump school at Dong Ba Thin, which was cadred by 5th Group. Finally, General Abrams recovered enough sense to assign Col. Michael Healy to command the group.

One has to wonder about General Abrams's actions in all this. He had an illustrious career behind him. He was the tank commander who broke through the siege of Bastogne, linking up with the 101st Airborne Division during the Battle of the Bulge. Did he not know that the 101st was infamous in World War II for not taking prisoners? But then, the blame doesn't rest with General Abrams alone.

If blame is to be assigned, it most logically rests with the GAMMA participants and the SFOB Group S-2 who allowed Colonel Rheault to be informed about the matter. Colonel Rheault was not left with any plausible deniability. After the decision was made to assassinate Chuyen, it should have been done and been forgotten. However, almost all the participants in the Chuyen affair were not SF qualified; most were military intelligence (MI) types trying to play with the big boys. Unfortunately, assassination is a product of unconventional warfare. The OSS did it in World War II and Special Forces did it before and after Chuyen. And, of course, the VC/NVA had been doing it for years.

As distasteful as assassination is, the American attitude toward it is more amazing. We accept other nationalities and races doing it, but we consider it beneath us. Yet in this age of political correctness, there, of course, ought to be just one standard. Our attitude seems to say that we Americans are morally superior to the rest of the world because it's acceptable for all the rest of the world to assassinate but not us. But then, the rest of the world sees us as terribly naive. We undoubtedly are. One can only wonder, would the world have been any better if Hitler, Stalin, Mao, or Castro had been assassinated early in their careers?

Putting my personal prejudices aside, however, the Rheault incident gave General Abrams the opportunity that the MACV/USARV staff had always looked for. SF was gone from Vietnam by March 1971. The projects were closed down, the CIDG program turned over to the ARVN, and MACSOG operations turned over to the Vietnamese, temporarily. But Colonel Rheault's brief effect on 5th Special Forces Group was not to be denied because he had brought along many of his protégés to Vietnam, and they remained after Rheault left. One of them was Lt. Col. John R. Hennigan.

It's axiomatic that A-team people don't like B-team people, even though SF people serve on both and move back and forth. When we got a second monkey at Mai Linh in 1966, he was named "B-team" because he was "fucked up and crazy." Yet, when Lieutenant Colonel Hennigan replaced Lieutenant Colonel Marquis, the A-teams of B-24 almost thought nice things about the B-team. Hennigan was deemed as fair and loyal as a B-team commander comes and was truly admired and respected. But he soon began to have run-ins with Colonel Healy.

Colonel Healy inspected B-24 in September 1969, shortly after Lieutenant Colonel Hennigan arrived. Colonel Healy had a long history with Special Operations, particularly with Ranger units during the Korean War*, but he also had a very large ego and tended to make snap judgments. Colonel Healy's briefing at B-24 went fairly well, but he intended to make his mark on 5th Group. After the usual token minor ravings, he would accept the explanations of what his most actively engaged B-team was doing. In later months, he relieved Lieutenant Colonel Hennigan from command twice, and each time Lieutenant Colonel Hennigan packed up, bid farewell to B-24, and then returned the following day after explaining and making peace with Colonel Healy. It was truly a strange war; but then there was no doubt that General Abrams** had told Colonel Healy to shake up 5th Group.

Throughout the summer and fall of 1969, B-24 made a lot

---

*Colonel Healy was known as "Blind Mike" because of the very thick glasses that he wore. When he was promoted to general officer, the sobriquet became "Iron Mike." In addition to never being wrong, general officers can't have wimpy-sounding nicknames.

**General Abrams was chief of staff of the army when he died of lung cancer in the 1970s. But in the interim, he mentored Mike Healy through the rank of major general.

of progress in Kontum Province. A U.S. engineer battalion totally rebuilt Ban Het, and NVA contacts were relatively small, usually only battalion, company, or platoon encounters. But we had also received word that the CIDG camps were closing out and that they would either be converted to border Ranger camps, or RF/PF sites. Significantly, the camps in Kontum Province were the last to be closed or converted, and Ban Het was the last border camp to convert on 31 December 1970. B-24 was converted on 31 January 1971.

During 1969, everyone watched the effects of Vietnamization. The brigade of the 4th Infantry Division pulled out of Kontum, and the 173d Airborne Brigade moved into the old 1st Cavalry Division base camp at An Khe. B-24, MACV, and an aviation company were the only Americans left in Kontum City. We periodically received mortar or 122mm rocket attacks, but there was no noticeable increase in activity. Dak Pek captured a 140mm rocket intact, and we thought that the war might be escalating and that we weren't the ones doing the escalating. Polei Kleng found an old NVA 140mm howitzer battery site, and we recognized that the NVA had gone much beyond guerrilla warfare. But we still had some problems with our LLDB (Vietnamese Special Forces) counterparts.

The LLDB still tried to sell rides to CIDG dependents on our daily work helicopter, and we had to closely watch the LLDB S-4 sergeant. We knew that there was some minor smuggling of cigarettes and other commodities to the A-camps, but we looked at that as a cost of doing business. Then one day, the LLDB S-4 sergeant offered his U.S. counterpart one thousand dollars if he would get the LLDB a Caribou aircraft to use for a day. The offer was refused, but we began to wonder about the extent of LLDB corruption.

There was an old LLDB warrant officer (or third lieutenant) assigned to the LLDB B-team, whose innocuous title was "finance officer." But *we* were paying the CIDG, so we didn't know what his job really was. Eventually, we found out that he was the LLDB bagman. Every week, he'd visit each A-camp and pick up the profits from the LLDB enterprises at each camp. Ah, you might ask, what were those LLDB enterprises?

Each camp had an LLDB-sponsored canteen and convenience store (and sometimes a brothel). Under LLDB auspices, a CIDG soldier could get a haircut, buy a beer or cigarettes, purchase the services of a prostitute, or buy additional food (often stolen from CIDG rations in the first place). Of course, if a CIDG member didn't have any cash, credit was available at 5 percent interest, repayable at the end of the month. Then there were the ghost payrollers.

Ghost payrollers were individuals who had quit the CIDG (or who had enlisted twice), but who were still on the payroll. Some camps had as many as an extra one hundred ghosts on the payroll. When payday rolled around, an individual would go through the pay line once for himself and then go around again under somebody else's name with the second pay allowance going to the LLDB. Of course, we tried to stop that with ID cards, fingerprinting, and photographs, but every control method was circumvented. The really bad thing about ghost payrollers was not the loss of money (a CIDG soldier made about twenty dollars per month), but the loss of available combat power.

Once, when I was at Polei Kleng, I scheduled an airmobile operation to the Plei Trap Valley and demanded that my counterpart, *Dai-uy* Ha, provide a minimum of 100 of the authorized 132-man company strength of a CIDG company. When only 80 people boarded the helicopters, I threatened to pull the Americans off the operation. To make the 100-man minimum, *Dai-uy* Ha pulled 20 people from a patrol that was just walking in the gate off an operation. The bottom line, of course, was money, and the money (with appropriate skims) was sent up the line. We'll come back to *Dai-uy* Ha later.

Corruption within the LLDB was endemic. But to be fair, corruption, skimming, and payoffs were (and are) as much a part of the Vietnamese culture* as voting Democratic or Republican is a part of the American culture. I suspect the reason that the Mike Force battalions were so effective was that they were directly commanded by SF, with no LLDB involved. The larger issue, however, was to get on with the war.

---

*I still correspond with montagnard friends back in Vietnam. Payoffs to Communist Vietnamese officials are as normal in 2000 as they were in 1969.

CHAPTER 7

Camp Polei Kleng

In October 1969, I finally had the chance to command an A-team. There were only four possibilities left (since Ban Het was already spoken for): Mang Buk, Dak Pek, Dak Seang, and Polei Kleng. I ended up at Polei Kleng, Detachment A-241. I might add that if Lieutenant Colonel Marquis had been around, I still wouldn't have gotten an A-team. Lieutenant Colonel Marquis's explanation for not assigning me to an A-team was that General of the Army George Marshall in World War II was always considered too valuable to be a commander and that a good staff officer didn't need a combat command. Translated, that meant that Marquis was content to use my writing talents but wouldn't look out for my career.

Polei Kleng was the first camp south of Ban Het, and generally due west of Kontum City. It was three *days'* march from the border, supposedly because an earlier Kontum Province chief wanted it sited to secure the western approach to Kontum City. Even with its disadvantageous location, it was still considered a border camp and had a border surveillance mission.

Polei Kleng had been the worst camp under B-24 for about six months. The LLDB team there refused to cooperate with the Americans, and in general things just weren't getting done. John Hennigan's solution was to replace the entire team with a new one, and try to start over. So we swapped people, and Capt. Jim Selders came out. On the plus side, a few of the veterans stayed. The most significant of these was the team sergeant, who was known as "Field Marshal" Carl Mayse.

Carl was cocky and assertive almost to the point of arrogance, which is probably why Bucky Smith, the B-24 operations sergeant (E-8), hung the nickname Field Marshal on him. Carl was also one of the best team sergeants (although still only a sergeant first class (E-7)) that I had ever met (other than Ed Sprague) and was a genuine SF character. Originally a non-Airborne tanker, Carl realized the error of his ways and applied for Airborne and Special Forces and then proceeded to live down his past. Unfortunately, in creating his legend he made some mistakes and enemies along the way. One result was that about fifty Cambodians at Camp Dak Seang wanted to kill him.

In September 1969, Carl Mayse was the team sergeant of A-245 at Dak Seang. Like all the other border A-camps of B-24, Dak Seang had two Cambodian recon platoons, the result of the various ethnic alliances made by FULRO with the other minorities in Vietnam. Unfortunately, the Cambodians were ill-suited to the mountainous terrain of the Central Highlands and had a tendency to take shortcuts. Some might even say that the Cambodians didn't belong in the highlands and couldn't be trusted outside their own area of interest.

One of the Cambodian recon platoons was on an operation to the northwest of Dak Seang, supposedly patrolling along the border. One day, a Bird Dog aircraft flying north of Dak Seang spotted human activity on a bald knoll seven kilometers due north of the camp. The aircraft pilot radioed the information back to Dak Seang, where Carl Mayse checked his maps and found that he didn't have any friendly operations within fifteen kilometers of the bald knoll. So he had the two 105mm howitzers in the camp shoot ten rounds onto the target. Within a minute after the artillery impacted, the Cambodians reported their true location as being on the bald knoll and that they had fifteen KIA, with the rest of the platoon being wounded. While helicopters were flying out to evacuate the dead and wounded, Mayse was evacuated to Kontum City to protect him from the wrath of the remaining Cambodians. Subsequently, he was shipped to Polei Kleng.

Carl had been at Polei Kleng for about a month, and I considered myself fortunate to have him as the team sergeant. Carl had already been butting his head up against the intransigent LLDB. Now it was my turn, and I met with *Dai-uy* Ha for about two hours the evening that I arrived.

I explained to *Dai-uy* Ha that we would work and cooperate with him, but that some things had to be improved immediately. I thought that we had an understanding, but in the days to come, I found that *Dai-uy* Ha was still reluctant to cooperate with us. The major issue was the perimeter grass and garbage within the perimeter. As a way of getting back at the Americans, *Dai-uy* Ha refused to provide labor to cut the perimeter grass. The result was that the grass had grown ten feet tall throughout the defensive wire and only by standing on top of a perimeter bunker could we see outside the camp. I offered to pay food rations to the montagnards living in the village down the western hill from the camp if they would cut the grass. But *Dai-uy* Ha always found a way to stymie my efforts. I figured that I would have to work around *Dai-uy* Ha.

When I had been at the camp a week and there was no notable progress on the perimeter grass problem, I walked out into the perimeter during the daily siesta period, which ran from noon to 3:00 P.M. each day, usually called *pak* time. I knelt down to see if the dry grass was flammable by lighting my cigarette lighter and found out that it was! Within ten minutes, there were flames twenty feet high along the south and west walls of the camp, and I thought that my first A-team command would be in a burned-down camp. Claymore mines were burning and popping all around, and *Dai-uy* Ha had the entire camp clearing the areas where the fire hadn't yet reached.

We eventually had to replace more than eighty claymores. I'm sure that *Dai-uy* Ha thought that I was crazy, but he did respond to my future requests. Thereafter, there were daily work parties in the perimeter. However, problems still remained, and the biggest of these was the usual LLDB corruption.

One day, a C-123 arrived with the weekly CIDG rations, a pallet of one hundred–kilogram bags of rice, some vegetables, and three live cows. Two of the cows were led away for future slaughter, while the LLDB executive officer took the third one and disappeared with it. I found later that he had sent a detail with the cow to Kontum City to sell it, and the LLDB pocketed the money. I reported the incident to B-24, and the LLDB lieutenant was pulled out of camp the next day. Officially, we were told that the lieutenant had been court-martialed and jailed. In reality, he was transferred to a southern II Corps camp under B-23 at Ban Me Thuot. Such were the games played by the LLDB.

Through the team's work, but mainly due to Carl Mayse, Polei Kleng passed a 5th SF Group combat-readiness inspection in early November, and things were looking up. But we failed two other inspections: The air force said that our airstrip needed work, and an artillery inspector said that our two 105mm howitzers were the "filthiest guns that he had ever seen." We fixed everything that was found to be at fault, but one might ask, Why is such emphasis being placed on relatively trivial garrison-type matters? The answer is that the army in Vietnam in the late sixties had degenerated that far. But the inane incidents didn't stop there.

One day, IFFV (I Field Force, Vietnam), the controlling U.S. corps command structure in II Corps, sent out a message that everyone had to have revetments for their vehicles and that the vehicles had to be "combat parked" within those revetments, meaning facing out so that vehicles could drive away quickly during mortar, artillery, or rocket attacks. All SF camps already had revetments, but we parked our vehicles with the fronts facing the far wall so that the radiators could be protected. During attacks, shrapnel might flatten our tires, but we could always fix a flat. But if shrapnel hit a radiator, we couldn't fix the radiator in camp. Our practical experience was meaningless to some antiquated colonel on the IFFV staff. It sometimes seemed that the staff at the various higher headquarters just didn't have a clue as to what the rest of the world was doing or experiencing.

I arrived at Polei Kleng right after the sensors of McNamara's wall had been emplaced. The sensor arrays had been conceived by the secretary of defense as a way to detect and pinpoint enemy movement along the border by sending a signal to an Airborne command post whenever a sensor was activated by a passing NVA soldier (or tiger, or water buffalo, or monkey). It was thought that the high-tech solution would be a great asset to the people on the ground and that we could react against this enemy infiltration. We would get about eight sensor messages per day from an air force headquarters located in Pleiku, and most reports were placed into the intelligence files without any action on our part.

Once, an angry air force major radioed me asking why I had ignored three days' worth of readings by sensor XYZ-56 (or some other code name). I explained that we were twenty-five miles away from sensor XYZ-56, that our artillery could only shoot half that far, and that it would take three days to walk a unit out to that location. Furthermore, I could only realistically react against that sensor (and all the others) if I had helicopters on standby at Polei Kleng or if Polei Kleng was moved closer to the border. My answer didn't please the AF major, but I think that he began to understand my dilemma. As much as I respect the air force and the support that they have always given me, I think that they were the most hidebound of the services in Vietnam.

During one operation close to the border, we had to establish a radio relay on a mountaintop to insure communications between the unit on the border and Polei Kleng. Since there weren't a lot of people available, I was forced to send the most junior person on the team to man the radio relay, along with a platoon of CIDG. When the radio relay got probed by the NVA on the second night, we called in a Spooky gunship to give supporting fire. Through an honest error and lack of experience, the radio operator brought the gunship too close to the perimeter on one pass, and two CIDG were killed by friendly fire. Two days later, an air force major arrived at Polei Kleng to conduct an investigation of the incident. He was told by Vietnamese and Americans that the incident was a simple accident of war, nobody (particularly the air force) was at fault and that we would rather have suffered two friendly fire casualties than to have the position overrun. Sadly, the war had gone on long enough for Stateside rules to catch up with us, and the fact that we were fighting a war didn't really matter much anymore.

Demolitions became one of the hallmarks of the Vietnam War and made our jobs easier in many ways. Everyone knows about the fast burning charges that can cut steel, such as C-4, but slower burning charges also had their uses. A forty-pound cratering charge is actually a shaped charge and burns relatively slowly, at eleven thousand feet per second, and digs a very good instant foxhole. Of course it can also be used for its main function of cratering a road. A more common use for that kind of charge was to provide sand for making concrete.

Most SF camps were located near fairly small streams, which were their main water supply. But since sand was needed for concrete construction, the stream also had to be used to provide sand. Typically, though, the streams had hard sand and gravel bottoms that didn't yield their sand easily. Blowing a forty-pound cratering charge in the middle of a shallow stream would create a five-foot-diameter hole that would fill with sand washed down by the stream. A daily supply of sand was thus provided.

Satchel charges and bangalore torpedoes were other explosive devices available, both manufactured and expedient. Unfortunately, most often those devices were used by the VC/NVA to blow bunkers and clear wire obstacles. Satchel charges were favored by sappers, but were not as effective against SF camps as against U.S. firebases and base camps. I don't personally know of an SF camp overrun by sappers, but know of many firebases successfully attacked. In April 1970, Camp Dak Pek was partially overrun by sappers, but most of the sappers were killed within the American perimeter.

Booby traps were the meat and potatoes of the Vietnam war.

A claymore mine could be rigged as a defensive weapon, a booby trap, or as a means to break contact. Strapped to the back of a rucksack of one of the members of a small recon patrol, the claymore was a wonderful expedient source of firepower. If the patrol met enemy to the front, the wearer of the claymore could remove his rucksack, turning the claymore to the front, while the forward people broke contact and ran to the rear. When everyone was clear, the claymore was detonated, giving everyone precious time to move to the last rally point.

"Sonja devices" were commercially made booby traps. They were only issued on written request after submitting a detailed plan for their use and a specification as to how long the device would be active. Once set, the device wouldn't arm for fifteen minutes, then would be active for however long it was set for before blowing itself up, typically thirty to sixty days. During the active period, anyone touching the device would cause it to detonate whatever explosives it might be attached to.

In late 1969, Carl Mayse requested permission to run a Sonja operation in the Plei Trap Valley, next to the Cambodian border. At that time, the Plei Trap was almost entirely owned by the NVA, and a patrol was guaranteed contact and trail followers if it operated there. The operation was approved, along with helicopters, and Field Marshal began his preparations. He took a CIDG rucksack, filled it with a quarter-roll of barbed wire with twelve pounds of C-4 filler and connected a Sonja device to it. After helicopter-assaulting a CIDG company into the Plei Trap, they moved out, took a ten-minute break, activated the device and left the rucksack behind. Thirty minutes away, there was a huge explosion in the area they had just left. Obviously, an NVA trail party came upon the rucksack, thought that some dumb montagnard had left his rucksack behind and that they could find food, cigarettes, and ammo. That's not what they found. Instead, Field Marshal had ruined their day (and all the rest of their days).

Chieu Hoi radios also made good booby traps. As part of the psychological-operations aspect of the war, someone conceived the idea to buy cheap Japanese pocket radios that were pretuned to a propaganda frequency broadcast from Pleiku. Vietnamese songs, interspersed with appeals for the

NVA to surrender, were broadcast twenty-four hours per day, and the radios were designed as an irresistible form of entertainment that the typical NVA soldier could not pass up. The radios probably cost two to three dollars to manufacture and were individually packed in a shockproof Styrofoam container. Then they were dumped along the Cambodian and Laotian borders by low-flying helicopters.

Unfortunately for the psychological operations folks, they staged their radio drops from Special Forces camps, which were also spotted along the borders. Many of the radios were given to the SF teams with the understanding that they would drop the radios throughout the jungle while they had operations out. It didn't take too long for someone to figure out that the Styrofoam container could be opened, the radio taken out, and its innards removed. With the battery and power switch in place in the housing, a blasting cap and a quarter-pound of plastic C-4 could be inserted into the radio case, and the "energized" radio could be replaced into the Styrofoam case. Then, when the psy ops package was left in the jungle, it really would convert an NVA soldier to a noncombatant.

It's easy to imagine the conversation between Nguyen and Tran, two NVA soldiers walking through the jungle.

NGUYEN: "Look, Tran, one of those imperialist capitalist running-dog American propaganda radios!"

TRAN: "You know, Nguyen, that comrade squad leader told us not to listen to those things."

NGUYEN: "But he'll never know, and besides the music is good. We don't have to listen to the propaganda, just the music. Give me your knife and help me get this plastic stuff off."

TRAN: "I don't know, Nguyen."

NGUYEN: "Don't worry, we'll play the radio low, close to our ears, so comrade squad leader won't hear it. Come close, and I'll turn it on."

Boom, there went Nguyen and Tran. Of course the psy ops folks didn't like that sort of misuse, but it was fundamental that our goals were different. Psychological operations missions were a distinct secondary function to our primary mission of pacification and defeat of the enemy. But then, the same dichotomy was at work at the national level. On the one hand, there was the "winning of the hearts and minds" mindset, which was promoted by the psychological warriors. The opposite view was that if you grab them by the balls, their hearts and minds will follow. That conflict of methodologies operated throughout the armed services all through the Vietnam War. Sometimes the ball grabbers were in the ascendancy.

When I got back in country in 1969, Armed Forces Network, Vietnam, the GI radio station, broadcast a public announcement about every two hours, something to the effect that nobody should fire enemy ammunition through their captured enemy rifles because the ammo was often faulty and could hurt the GI using it. I immediately thought that we were finally booby-trapping or doctoring the ammunition that the NVA uses. I was right. Years later, it was confirmed that MAC-SOG operations were dropping off doctored ammunition along the Ho Chi Minh trail and that the ammo was then being used by the NVA. I had often wondered during the war why we didn't plant Chicom grenades that didn't have delay fuses built in. Maybe we did.

An overcharged AK-47 rifle bullet could blow the receiver on a rifle, while an 82mm mortar round could blow away an entire mortar tube. Either way, the probable result was an injured or dead NVA soldier or crew. Of course, since the program proved very effective, the army decided to end it in February 1970.

I've since met special operation support folks who said that they were involved in doctoring the ammunition on Okinawa, but who knows if they're telling the truth? My own experience is that I usually only trust information from other Special Forces people. Jim Stewart said that the SOG recon teams were dropping AK-47 magazines along the trail in Laos in 1966.

Five days before Thanksgiving, SFOB sent every camp a frozen turkey for the holiday. Our cook at Polei Kleng was an old Jarai woman who had never seen a frozen turkey before. When she received the bird, she put it under a kitchen counter and forgot about it. The day before Thanksgiving, one of the team members went looking for the turkey. The heat had thawed it, and the meat had begun to rot. It was purple and didn't look very appetizing. Our medic, Andy Szeliga, said that it might not be safe to eat.

We called the B-team and asked them to buy another turkey and send it out by helicopter. Just in case that the purple turkey might be okay after all, we baked it Thanksgiving Day morning. Later that morning, a fresh thawed turkey arrived from the C-team in Pleiku, and we cooked that one too and celebrated Thanksgiving with it that afternoon. Since the questionable turkey didn't look too bad after it was cooked, we gave it to the LLDB team. The consensus was that the worst that could happen is that the turkey would poison all the LLDB and that they'd all be replaced. The LLDB didn't get sick so the situation turned out to be win-win all around.

A week after Thanksgiving, the C-team commander visited Polei Kleng along with Lieutenant Colonel Hennigan. After the obligatory briefing and reciprocated comments on the progress being made, *Dai-uy* Ha and I were walking out of the teamhouse with the C-team commander when he asked: "Hey, what did you ever do with that poisoned turkey?"

LTC Hennigan, who knew what had happened with the turkey, mumbled: "It got taken care of," as he hustled the commander out the door. *Dai-uy* Ha just looked perplexed.

Andy Szeliga, our medic, had a particular dislike of our Cambodians at Polei Kleng. The Cambodes were from the flatland areas of Vietnam and just weren't well adapted to the mountainous highlands. Once, Andy came into the teamhouse and said, "I've got a Cambode with cerebral malaria who's going to die in about two hours. He has a temperature of 104, and it's rising."

"Well, call a Dustoff helicopter and get him evacuated to Pleiku," I told Szeliga. "I'd rather he die at the CIDG hospital than here. Besides, that way the other Cambodes will see that we care and are still trying to help."

Andrew disliked the Cambodes because they had eaten the puppies of the dog that was our camp mascot. But he called the medical evacuation helicopter, and the sick Cambode was sent to Pleiku to die. Five days later, the recovered soldier returned to Polei Kleng. It was a good call on my part.

After only a little more than a month in command, Lieutenant Colonel Hennigan pulled me back to the B-team. This time I was to be the S-3 or operations officer. I wasn't happy about leaving Polei Kleng, but I knew that the camp was scheduled to be converted in nine months and that, increasingly, our work would be aimed at achieving that goal instead of combat operations. Mike Lewis was the executive officer, and he had recently made captain, so he assumed command of A-241. Mike had originally been commissioned a quartermaster officer and was very good in logistical matters. He would be ideal to begin the phaseout of Polei Kleng. Still, I was disappointed to leave A-241 and return to B-24.

Just days before I left Polei Kleng, Martha Raye visited. I hadn't seen her since 1966 at Mai Linh. Still, she remembered me. She said, "You're the guy with the monkey!" She was still a remarkable lady.

My disappointment at moving back to the B-team was relatively short lived. The next best thing to commanding an A-team for a Special Forces officer is to be the B-team S-3. I was now going to get a different view of the war and what we were contributing.

Still, leaving the cast of characters at Polei Kleng was a sad event for me. Carl Mayse would remain, as would the Cambodian-hating team medic, Andy Szeliga. But *Dai-uy* Ha would also remain to try and stymie the American team, along with the Vietnamese recon platoon leader that had once turned a .50-caliber machine gun on the Americans. Eventually, all the Americans on A-241 would survive to go on and do better things, while the Vietnamese later met their fate at the hands of the Communists.

CHAPTER 8

Dak Seang and Dak Pek

With Vietnamization well under way, the fall season of 1969 in Kontum Province was a busy time. We began to do more with less assets, while the Vietnamese tried to take over the war. Unhappily, we took some U.S. casualties along the way, with two Americans dying at Dak Pek in October and one from the B-team in December. Significantly, only one of the KIAs was an experienced Special Forces soldier. But then, the war wasn't an SF-type conflict anymore. Our CIDG were light infantry trained and equipped to engage VC guerrillas, but we were meeting NVA battalions. There was a lot of morbid humor around, like the day that the Chinese entered the war.

Toward late January, Dak Pek sent a message that one of their operations working west of the camp had just killed three Chinese soldiers. The dead looked Chinese, were taller than the average Vietnamese, and weighed considerably more than a typical Vietnamese. We all thought that Vietnam was going the way of Korea and that if the Chinese were helping the NVA, we had a whole new ballgame. There was a lot of concern about Dak Pek anyway.

Dak Pek was the northernmost border camp in Vietnam because there were no border camps left in I Corps. Kham Duc had been immediately north of Dak Pek but was taken by the NVA in May 1968, and there was always fear that the NVA intended to roll up as many more camps as they could. Besides, there was increasing NVA activity around Dak Pek, which was a sure indicator that bad things were in store for the camp.

The message was passed along to Pleiku, and we were told that ARVN II Corps headquarters would send an anthropologist out to identify the bodies. Dak Pek was asked to move the Chinese bodies back to the camp, which they did.

Our work chopper was busy delivering supplies and mail, so I couldn't get a helicopter ride to Dak Pek until about two hours after the first report. When I arrived, the bodies were at the helicopter pad, and the anthropologist had already been there and left. He had identified the Chinese as Nungs, a minority ethnic tribe that existed in North Vietnam and therefore made for proper NVA soldiers. We all breathed easier. Meanwhile, the fierce heat was rapidly decomposing the three bodies. Their facial fat had liquefied, and I could literally see beneath their skin. The swarms of flies on the bodies were not contributing to the pleasantness of the situation. I asked the LLDB camp commander to have the bodies buried, but he informed me that due to Vietnamese and montagnard customs, nobody would touch the dead. Removal of the bodies was an American problem.

I asked Gordon Strickler, the detachment commander, if he would give me three body bags. Captain Strickler agreed as long as I promised to replace them. I said that I would, and we had some CIDG bag the bodies. We loaded the bodies in the helicopter and made a "leaflet drop" over the Tu Mrong Valley, to the east of Dak Pek. I worried for a week thereafter about some news correspondent finding out the story of an SF captain (me) throwing North Vietnamese out of helicopters. The news people who were still in Vietnam were no longer trusted. In fact, I, and many others, made it a policy to never talk to any correspondent; talking to a correspondent might get your picture on television or your name in the newspaper, but no good ever would come of it.

One of the times that Colonel Healy relieved Lieutenant Colonel Hennigan was when John Hennigan had given an interview to a CBS correspondent. Of course, throughout the army in Vietnam, that was common. But it was either a matter of ego with Colonel Healy or a fear that General Abrams would notice that eventually made everyone paranoid about talking to the media. Thankfully, John Hennigan was reinstated.

The increase in NVA activity in Kontum Province meant that we were getting more B-52 strikes and Mike Force operations in our area. We also knew that the NVA were building up by the B-52 safety plots that we were getting for Laos and Cambodia that overlapped into Vietnam. A typical B-52 strike was one kilometer wide and three kilometers long. To insure the safety of friendly forces, a three-kilometer safety zone was added all around, and that took up a fair size chunk of ground. Supposedly, it was part of the secret bombing campaign going on outside Vietnam, but everyone who operated close to the borders knew about it, just as we knew about the MAC-SOG cross-border operations.

With Mike Force operations, however, we had different problems. Ordinarily, a Mike Force operation meant a battalion-size element on the ground, and that required support that often taxed everyone's capabilities. A dedicated helicopter was quite often necessary for resupply, evacuation, and control, but we couldn't always get an extra helicopter for the mission because the helicopter units were also phasing out of Vietnam. Usually, we ended up working our one daily assigned helicopter extra hard. If things didn't get done, the effect was felt at the A-camps.

None of that is meant as a criticism. When we were fortunate enough to have a Mike Force battalion operate in our area, it was a blessing, not a hindrance. A Mike Force battalion projected a lot of power into an area, and they were better equipped and trained than an NVA counterpart unit. But some Mike Force units could be excessively demanding.

I received a call one day from a Mike Force battalion operating five kilometers north of Ban Het. They had spotted three NVA soldiers five hundred meters to their front and wanted a pair of gunships. I recommended that they consider using some of the artillery at Ban Het, but the response to me was: "Are you questioning the commander on the ground?"

I said no, but that it would take me more than thirty minutes to get a pair of gunships on station from Kontum City, and I was concerned that they might lose their target by then. So that all egos were soothed, we scrambled gunships and shot the artillery. But the story points up a common deficiency developed in Vietnam.

All units became so dependent on using aircraft, both air force and army, that we grew away from using our mortars and artillery as much. With U.S. units, the problem wasn't so big because artillery and mortar liaison teams were assigned to maneuver units. SF didn't have that luxury; we tended to forget about our indirect-fire assets and underused them when they were available.

We understood the NVA intentions finally on 01 April 1970 when, at about 0700 hours, we received a message that Dak Seang (Detachment A-245) was taking heavy direct and indirect fire. I immediately notified Company B, requested gunships that by that time had to come from Pleiku, and asked for a forward air control aircraft. The first aircraft on the scene at Dak Seang was a Headhunter L-19, flown by a friend, Capt. Bill Ridgeway, out of Kontum.

John Hennigan told me to take the work chopper to Dak Seang and tell him what the situation was. As soon as it arrived, we attached the portable (and makeshift) antenna that the B-team commo sergeant had devised between the skids of the UH-1H aircraft and headed for Dak Seang. We arrived at 0800 hours, and Dak Seang didn't look good.

All the wooden structures in the camp were burning, the camp had already taken over five hundred mortar, artillery, and recoilless-rifle rounds, and the NVA had already completed about thirty yards of zigzag trenches under the wire on the east perimeter wall. There were already about thirty dead CIDG, and half the U.S. team had been wounded.

Bill Ridgeway was working like a traffic cop with all the air assets coming in. He had air force fast movers stacked up waiting for targets while he first put napalm into the southern wire, and had army gunships strafing the eastern wire and

NVA positions on the north of the airstrip. We tried to get medical evacuation aircraft into the camp landing zone but found that position already zeroed in by automatic weapons and recoilless rifle fire. It was obvious that the NVA had come to stay. They were "hugging" Dak Seang closely in an effort to avoid the air force and army aircraft.

I radioed Lieutenant Colonel Hennigan that Dak Seang was in more trouble than I had ever seen at Ban Het and that reinforcement was needed immediately. Lieutenant Colonel Hennigan began arranging for a CIDG company from Plateau Gi to move from that camp by CV-2 to stage at Ban Het. He also had a long conversation with the Company B commander, and arrangements were started to begin moving a Mike Force battalion. Operations had to be diverted, curtailed, and canceled to free Mike Force units for Dak Seang.

For the next few hours, we tried to plot all the NVA positions around Dak Seang, but there were just too many, and they were all close-in to the camp. The NVA figured that their greater safety was in hugging the camp so that air power could not be used as effectively as normal. It was a target-rich environment; no matter where the aircraft bombed or strafed, targets were available. The siege of Dak Seang was to become as near to close combat as ever occurred with any SF camp in Kontum.

Late in the afternoon, we had a Plateau Gi company at Ban Het and four helicopters to ferry them to Dak Seang. Since using the airstrip or helicopter pad wasn't practical, we picked an LZ about seventy-five meters northeast of the camp. At about 1800 hours, we had inserted the company. Rather than try to fight into the camp that night, the company dug in and waited for morning. One helicopter pilot was reluctant to take the mission, but he was convinced to do so. When he told me that he didn't want to fly, I passed it along to Lieutenant Colonel Wood, the Company B commander. I don't know what was said, but the pilot calmed down and flew the mission. A few days later, that same pilot was killed north of Dak Seang on another insertion.

After the sun went down, a C-130 Spectre stayed on station

throughout the night. An air force Caribou attempted to resupply Dak Seang that night by flying north up the Dak Poko Valley, but the NVA were expecting it and shot down the aircraft. The same scenario reoccurred on two subsequent nights, and we asked the air force to stop until we could get a better hold on the camp and the situation. Dak Seang was hurting.

The Caribou aircraft was originally purchased by the army as a logistics aircraft. I don't believe that anyone ever envisioned it flying in an intense antiaircraft weapon environment. Although the Caribou flew well on its two engines and could land and take off on extremely short runways, it couldn't fly on one engine alone. If one engine was hit, the aircraft was going to crash.

Back at B-24 that evening, we burned the midnight oil. We sent in B-52 bombing requests and planned for insertion of a USSF/Australian–led Mike Force battalion to go in on 03 April. Of much more concern, however, was whether Dak Seang could hang on that long. On the evening of the first day of the siege, it looked like the camp might be lost that night or the next morning. After the first full day of battle, the U.S. team was living underground, relying on battery-powered radios with a 292 antenna pushed up through the debris of the team house. Fortunately, they still had contact with the team at Ban Het and with the continuous air cover. Despite the NVA digging under the defensive wire and various probes, the camp held through the night.

The next day, 02 April 1970, the Plateau Gi company made it into the camp at first light. With the Plateau Gi company reinforcing, we were fairly certain that Dak Seang could hold out until the morning of 03 April when the first B-52 strikes were scheduled and a Mike Force battalion was to be inserted south of the camp.

Remarkably, the Plateau Gi company was an exceptional example of a unit led by Vietnamese Special Forces. Plateau Gi had been turned over entirely to the Vietnamese earlier and was operated without any Americans assigned or attached. It served as the premier model for the Vietnamization program, and the

LLDB staffed it accordingly. With or without American SF, the Plateau Gi CIDG were good. They were always considered as an instant reserve for use by B-24.

Captain Ridgeway was back over Dak Seang at first light, but he was having a problem because there was no closer resupply of marking rockets and fuel than the airfield at Kontum. He'd fly thirty minutes from Kontum to Dak Seang, mark and assign targets for about an hour, then have to fly back to Kontum for more rockets and fuel. He had done that all day on 01 April for about twelve hours, and he did it again on 02 April. A tactical emergency had been declared at Dak Seang, and there was an abundance of aircraft to deliver ordnance, but only one Headhunter (Captain Ridgeway's call sign).

I was back over Dak Seang in a helicopter at about 7:30 A.M. The NVA rocket, artillery, and mortar barrages hadn't let up, but by that time, there were no more viable targets in the camp. Everyone was in bunkers, waiting out the siege. Whenever anyone tried to move in the camp, NVA recoilless rifles took them under fire. Another day was passing that we couldn't get casualties out or resupplies in.

About 1400 hours that afternoon, John Hennigan called me back to Kontum. We now had assigned B-52 strike plots and times, along with an insertion point and time for the Mike Force battalion. Everything was going to happen between 0700 and 0900 hours the next morning, 03 April. I was selected to bring the news to Dak Seang and to make sure that the camp held through the night. There was still real worry that the NVA might take the camp, and we couldn't allow that to happen.

Before I left to prepare for a combat assault into Dak Seang, Lieutenant Colonel Hennigan talked to me. He told me that I was his direct representative on the ground and that if I felt it necessary, I could relieve the detachment commander and assume command myself. We agreed that I wouldn't tell the A-245 commander of my authority, but that if I had to assume command, Lieutenant Colonel Hennigan would back me up by radio. I thought that that would be the most serious step I could expect to take, but it could only be a last resort. Relieving the commander of a team that had been continually fighting for thirty-six hours would heavily impact morale. Thankfully, I never had to consider it.

About five other replacements went along, and we took extra commo gear and medical supplies. For the first time in two tours in Vietnam, I (and the others) wore helmets and took protective (gas) masks. The NVA had shot some tear gas into Dak Seang, and since that stuff was heavier than air, it tended to settle into bunkers. Late in the afternoon, as the helicopter was cranking for liftoff, Sergeant Major Campbell came running up with a message. Captain Ridgeway had just refueled and rearmed at the airfield and his aircraft stalled out while climbing on takeoff. He was killed in the crash, but his crew chief/observer in the backseat survived. All those hours of flying had caught up with Bill, and he became the first U.S. KIA of the battle.

I took the death of my friend rather stoically. I had already figured that my odds of surviving the helicopter insertion were minimal and that I was most likely going to die that evening. In case I lived and was able to get out of Dak Seang when it was overrun, I had selected my escape-and-evasion point to be the top of a hill, northeast across the Dak Poko about one thousand meters. I figured that the NVA would expect survivors to try to exfiltrate to Dak Pek or Dak To, and that I would take a route that wasn't obvious. But all of that was just planning ahead. If necessary, I knew that I could head east through the mountains and follow the Tu Mrong south to Dak To. I didn't tell anyone about my plans.

Dak Seang had another good thing going. There were no reports of NVA tanks, such as went against Ban Het and Lang Vei. I figured that without tanks, the NVA infantry would have to assault and that we could kill them in the wire. Regardless, I knew that we would hold that night, or we'd die. I also knew that if I was close to being captured, I'd kill myself. That decision wasn't for everybody, but I made a personal vow that I would not become a POW.

The helicopter pilot and his crew had an ingenious plan to

get into Dak Seang. They decided to make a normal flight to Dak To, fly below the trees along the Dak Poko, turn west when we were just opposite Dak Seang, fly over the NVA trenches and wire and land inside the camp. They would only hover for an instant, enabling us to jump out and the crew to take off to the west. So that the NVA wouldn't guess our intentions, the pilot decided to make the trip without a gunship escort.

It worked. We landed in Dak Seang without being hit. I wished later that I knew what aircraft it was so that I could write them up for decorations. The pilot was exceptionally brave, and his crew was, too. Unfortunately, in the press of other things at the time, I never got around to writing the recommendations. But war is often about unrecognized bravery and sacrifice.

When we made it into Dak Seang, I think we were off the helicopter in less than a second. Everyone knew about the recoilless rifles and machine guns around the camp. Since the sun was going down, I took the opportunity to look at the defenses before I went to the American bunker. I checked two mortar positions. Both tubes had broken sights. I spot-checked a couple of bunkers along the eastern perimeter and found the occupants alert and watching the trenches to their front. Maybe things weren't so bad after all.

When I made it to the American bunker, I found that my assessment was correct. The team was tired, living on C rations and amphetamines, and had only candles for light, but the men's morale was good. There was still concern about being overrun that night, so we decided that we'd defend the bunker, no matter what. I explained what a running password was, that it was used when you were running back to safety (in the bunker), that you shouted the password while running past the guard covering the doorway and that the guard would shoot anyone running by who didn't use the password. Our running password that night was motherfucker.

Although the CIDG were in fairly good shape, the same couldn't be said about the LLDB. Command of the camp had effectively been passed to the Americans, and the LLDB were working on digging an escape tunnel to the north under the camp runway. Aside from a minor courtesy visit in the early evening, the LLDB were left alone for the rest of the night. They didn't want to be bothered with the defense of the camp. They were concerned only with keeping themselves alive and digging their tunnel.

I explained to the team that Dak Seang had to hold throughout the night and that the night of 02–03 April would be the last worst time. At about 0700 on the morning of 03 April, the first B-52 strike was going to be dropped immediately south of the camp. I explained that, usually, the safety distance was 3,000 meters, which was sometimes waived to 1,500 meters in emergencies, but that the first strike going in was at 750 meters because of the closeness of the NVA and that everyone in the camp had to be in hardened bunkers when it hit. The Mike Force battalion would land about seven kilometers south of the camp and follow the Dak Poko north.

Throughout the previous two days, numerous aircraft had been hit, but Dak Seang was hanging on. All we had to do was get through the night. I guess that I acted like a rah-rah cheerleader. We had nowhere to go, so our only option was to hold on. Besides, we all knew that we were tougher than any skinny, runty, untrained NVA teenager.

An air force C-130 Spectre came on station when the army and air force aircraft pulled out at sundown. I asked the detachment commander to put one American on each of the four walls to warn of probes and attacks. Then we sat in the bunker and directed the Spectre for the rest of the night. After midnight, we were probed twice on the western wall, but Spectre broke up the assaults.

Around 0300 in the morning of 03 April, the C-130 Spectre said that he was running low on fuel and was just about out of ammo and flares and had to return to Da Nang. I asked him if he was going to be replaced, and he said no. I still remember my plaintive response: "Please don't leave me!" But he had to, and he did.

When I had left Kontum that afternoon, I made sure that I had the frequency of the artillery fire direction center (FDC) at Ban Het. When Spectre left, I went to the artillery frequency and asked for Red Leg because I didn't know their call sign. They answered as Red Leg, and I explained who I was, where I was, and that my identity could be verified by the team at Ban Het. Red Leg said that they knew who I was because they had been monitoring me all evening long talking to Spectre. I love the artillery!

With my bona fides established, I asked to register concentrations and final protective fires (FPFs) around Dak Seang. We spent the rest of the night doing that, with the biggest problem being the north wall, which faced the camp landing field.

Ban Het was to the south of us, almost at the maximum range for 175mm and 8-inch guns. That meant that every round fired over us on the north wall meant that we were on the gun-target line, and at maximum ranges, the long-axis dispersion pattern is quite large. Therefore, every target fired on the north wall was a "danger-close" fire mission. With that in mind, I cratered the hell out of the Dak Seang runway. Still, the main concern was that we hold the camp through the night. The airstrip could always be repaired later.

All the members of A-245 performed well that night. One soldier assigned to A-245 was not SF-qualified, and I found he had abandoned his wall-watch position to hide in the medical bunker. Previously, when we were both assigned to Polei Kleng, I had relieved the soldier and knew that he wasn't SF material, but Sergeant Major Campbell had decided to give him another chance at Dak Seang. The man was a transfer from the 101st who had extended his tour in Vietnam to serve six months with SF, but he was just as gutless at Dak Seang as he had been at Polei Kleng. I told him to get his sorry ass back to the wall position. I can't abide cowards. Damn, if you're not prepared to die, you don't belong in the combat arms.

At first light, the NVA quit shooting at us and an eerie lull came over the camp. The NVA knew, or suspected, that B-52 strikes were coming and they took as much cover as possible. At that point, we could have had a camp formation above

ground, and nobody would have fired a round at us. The helicopter gunships and air force jets showed up and began
shooting up the NVA. By then, many of the team had been
living on dextroamphetamine and were keyed up, but the
hardest part of the battle was behind us.

But dextroamphetamine has side effects, like hallucina-
tions. I was in the camp watchtower with a radio and field
glasses, talking with the approaching gunships, when one of
the people on the southern wall reported seeing NVA putting
boats into the water. I reported this target to the gunships and
was trying to get a grid reference when I realized that I was
passing on a hallucination from one of the very tired members of A-245. The only body of water was the Dak Poko to
the east, and the reported sighting was to the upland area to
the southwest. There weren't any NVA with boats, so I found
new targets.

I was in the emergency medical bunker when the first B-52
strike went in. I watched as the ground trembled enough for a
two-hundred-pound medicine cabinet to vibrate six inches
off the floor of the bunker. It looked like the law of gravity
was suspended, but it was only our high-flying friends pound-
ing the NVA. It was obvious why the B-52s terrified the NVA.
The NVA paid a price for hugging close to Dak Seang.

After the B-52 strike, Lieutenant Colonel Hennigan landed
in the center of the camp, and we used his helicopter to
evacuate some casualties. I earned another Purple Heart because of a minor shrapnel wound, but we evacuated the most
seriously wounded. The B-24 commander stayed for thirty
minutes until the helicopter came back for him, along with
a pair of gunships as an escort. I got on the helicopter with
Lieutenant Colonel Hennigan and four more wounded, and
we were taking off when one of the gunships was shot down
about five hundred meters south of us. Fortunately, the crew
survived and was picked up a few hours later.

We flew out east over the NVA trench lines, and seeing
some targets, I emptied a magazine of M-16 rounds into
them. The door gunner on the right side also opened up, and
the NVA returned fire. So we had an air-ground firefight

while the helicopter fought for speed and height. The helicopter took a few hits, and the usual red warning lights came on, but we limped into Ban Het.

Another helicopter took us into Kontum, where we met the IFFV commander, Lieutenant General Collins. We briefed him on the condition of Dak Seang, assured him that it would hold, and listened as various staff officers described what other forces were being diverted to the support of Dak Seang. John Hennigan and I had to be the dirtiest and raggediest people in the room. Perhaps that helped our credibility. The Vietnamese commander of the 24th Special Tactical Zone (STZ), which included the Dak Seang area, asked for American ground help, but General Collins refused. Aside from the Special Forces people involved, the affair was to be strictly a Vietnamese show. Toward the end of the meeting, General Collins pointed to Lieutenant Colonel Hennigan and said that he wanted one of the A-245 team members to be written up for the Medal of Honor. Eventually, Gary Beikirch, the A-245 medic, received the medal. Another Medal of Honor was received by an ARVN Ranger battalion adviser.

USARV set up a forward CP at Dak To, and the assistant B-24 S-3, Capt. Udo Walther, went there as a liaison. But that only lasted for a couple of days. When the detachment commander at Dak Seang was evacuated for wounds, Udo assumed temporary command at the camp. Later, Udo Walther achieved much more notoriety when he participated in the raid on Son Tay prison camp in North Vietnam in November 1970.

Eventually, a second Mike Force battalion was committed to the battle of Dak Seang, and some ARVN Ranger battalions also participated. Sadly, though, there was a major debacle on the bald knoll seven kilometers north of the camp where, months earlier, Field Marshal Carl Mayse had killed the fifteen Cambodians. We didn't know it at the time, but that bald knoll was the location of the NVA divisional headquarters waging the siege on the camp.

On 03 April, operational control of Dak Seang had passed to the ARVN 24th Special Tactical Zone, and B-24 lost command and control responsibility for the camp. Somebody made a decision to insert at least one small recon team, and that team went onto the bald knoll. The insertion helicopter was disabled, so the chase ship went in to evacuate the crew and the recon team, and it, too, was shot down. By the time that everything was over, there were five downed helicopters. In blind and glorious loyalty to their compatriots, subsequent helicopters continued to try to rescue their friends and were themselves shot down. More U.S. MIA and KIA resulted.

The 403d SOD passed on rumors that the NVA were using helicopters just to the west of Dak Seang, but we had no concrete sightings from the camp or the Mike Force units. Maybe the 403d had monitored NVA aircraft in the area, but there was nothing specific. If there were helicopters, they could only be for resupply and medevac.

B-52 strikes continued to go in around Dak Seang, and we knew that we were hurting the NVA, but we didn't know how much. Although Dak Pek to the north and Ban Het to the south received some harassing mortar fire during the Dak Seang siege, nobody expected the NVA to split their forces and attack Dak Pek. But they did.

Dak Pek, like Rome, was located on seven hills and situated on the west bank of the Dak Poko River, actually a twenty-foot wide stream, about eighteen inches deep. The area was unique for Vietnam because the soil was sandy, and there were numerous widely spaced pine trees in the area. The camp was one of the oldest of the Special Forces outposts in Vietnam, having been continuously occupied since April 1962. Although located in a very scenic area, the camp was extremely remote and only accessible by air. Fixed-wing aircraft had to take off and land on an extremely short runway with hills on both ends.

On the night of 11 and 12 April 1970, an NVA battalion attacked the American hill and what was called the 106 hill because of the 106mm recoilless rifle that commanded the only viable approach up the hill. The 106 hill was the highest hill in camp and commanded the other hills comprising the camp.

Infiltrating sappers rapidly took the 106 hill under cover of rocket, artillery, and mortar fire. The defending CIDG and their families were all killed, and the NVA took over the CIDG bunkers and the 106mm recoilless rifle; for one of the few times in the history of the Vietnam War, the NVA decided to defend the ground that they took. Or, more likely, they had to defend because once they seized the hill, they couldn't get away.

Meanwhile, the American hill was overrun at the same time, but the SF team (Detachment A-242) decided to stay and fight. More than thirty NVA were killed by the Americans, most at very close range. By dawn, the SF team was still in control of its portion of the camp. One of the team was stuck halfway outside his bunker when the bunker collapsed on his legs from an NVA sapper-thrown satchel charge, trapping him in position. He spent the rest of the night shooting sappers as they moved around in front of him.

There were no more spare CIDG units to shift to Dak Pek, so Company B provided a CIDG company from one of its subordinate A-camps and a Mike Force reconnaissance company. Army and air force aviation assets were diverted from the Dak Seang battle to attack 106 hill, but the rest of the camp was so close and the NVA so well dug in that the air strikes had little effect. After two days of attacks, the Mike Force recon company made it into the trench line at the top of the hill. Then they went bunker to bunker with grenades and rifle fire, killing all the defending NVA.

The U.S. Special Forces commander of the Mike Force recon company was a first lieutenant of Japanese heritage. He was wounded on the first day of the battle, along with some montagnards of his unit. As the casualties were being loaded into a helicopter bound for Pleiku, he pointedly kept repeating, "I'm a roundeye." As good as the CIDG hospital at Pleiku was, he preferred being brought to the U.S. evacuation hospital.

Dak Pek was much the worse for wear, but it was back in

friendly hands on 14 April. The NVA surrounding the camp continued to pound the camp well into May.

The sieges of Dak Seang and Dak Pek were broken by 08 and 09 May, respectively. Unlike earlier sieges at other camps in the highlands, the NVA decided to hug both camps and pound them with a previously unequalled amount of fire. But that meant that the NVA could not sustain the sieges as long as they previously had, and they had to withdraw sooner. Previous sieges were only two-thirds as long but much more intense. No matter, both camps held.

Among many other decorations, there were two Medals of Honor awarded for the battle of Dak Seang. Everyone else at Dak Seang received either a Distinguished Service Cross (DSC) or Silver Star (the second and third highest decorations awarded). Nobody saw everything or everybody during the battle, but from my viewpoint the decorations that everybody earned were all richly deserved. The guys at Dak Seang and Dak Pek and in the Mike Force units were all heroes. There were none better, and I'm proud to have known some of them. A unique chapter of Special Forces history was written in April and May 1970.

Buddha must have loved me. I was truly fortunate to serve two tours with the best soldiers in the world, the U.S. Army Special Forces. After I left Vietnam, I was not ever again privileged to go back to Special Forces. But to this day, more than twenty-five years later, I still relish my combat service with SF. We did things that other soldiers wouldn't think of doing, and we did them with distinction.

Until I retired in 1981, some of my fellow infantrymen would ask me why I would ever think of deserting the mainstream infantry career pattern and join SF. I'd usually answer their questions with questions of my own, such as: What rank were you when you commanded your first company? Your first battalion? They might respond that they commanded a company as a first lieutenant or captain. And if they ever commanded a battalion, it was as a major or lieutenant colonel. My response always was that I commanded my first company as a staff sergeant. As a sergeant first class, I was still running companies, but learning how to run larger units. As a captain, I commanded more than a battalion. Why would I ever want to miss that experience?

To be in Special Forces was to be outside the normal army. Those of us who served in SF were able to do things that others missed out on: we had the opportunity to do an often complicated and dangerous job with nobody looking over our shoulder. But that's the attraction of SF! Special Forces is not for everybody, just as a rifle company may not be suitable for everybody. But for those with a desire to serve in SF, the missions and requirements are always there. Hopefully, there will always be a Special Forces on the army roster.

The Vietnam War would continue until 1975.

CHAPTER 9

Europe

Early in 1970, I received a call in Kontum from Ed Sprague. He was back in Cheo Reo and needed my help in getting some CIDG uniforms. I sent him a couple of cases, and we stayed in touch. But I have to backtrack to bring the story up to date.

Ed Sprague didn't have to go to Vietnam. By the end of 1965, he was coming up on his twenty years in the army and could have retired. If he had not volunteered, he would not have been levied for Vietnam for at least two more years. But avoiding Vietnam duty was not part of Sprague's makeup.

In November 1965, Ed Sprague reported to Company B, 7th Special Forces Group, for Vietnam premission training. Four replacement A-teams were forming, and Sprague was selected as team sergeant of Detachment A-9. It was the first time that Sprague would have some say as to whom he wanted on his team, and he tried for many people whom he knew back in the 10th Group. John McFadden was his personal selection as the senior commo sergeant, but he missed on getting Dave Boyd as the light weapons sergeant. Although he tried to select people he knew previously, he had to take a number of people who were unknown quantities. Regardless, they would soon be Ed Sprague indoctrinated and trained.

There was no indication during premission training that Ed Sprague would develop an affinity for the montagnards. On the contrary, his gruff exterior gave the initial impression that he didn't care very much for anyone, particularly strangers and foreigners. But that gruff exterior masked a warm-hearted individual who did indeed care for people but was not a "people-person" in the conventional sense. Ed Sprague found his mission in life when he went to Vietnam and met the montagnards.

Today, there isn't a montagnard in Vietnam or the United States who has not heard of Ed Sprague. On meeting Sprague today, many remind him of when they first met previously. Of course, Sprague often doesn't remember but acts as if he does because he doesn't care to disappoint anyone. But this recognition by the montagnards didn't happen overnight. It began gradually in 1966.

When Ed Sprague first arrived at Camp Mai Linh in February 1966, the montagnards were not terribly impressive. They were primitive tribesmen with hygiene problems, smelled bad, and were not particularly attractive to look at. But that was only our first impression.

The Jarai seemed to be more civilized than their cousins, the Rhade. Both tribes, moreover, seemed more advanced than the surrounding Bahnar who were almost reclusive in their primitive living habits. Yet, the Rhade were presented in premission training as the preeminent tribe because Ban Me Thuot was a major Central Highlands city, and Y B'ham, a Rhade, was the leader of FULRO. What was not presented in premission training or, perhaps, was not known was that the Jarai were very content to allow the Rhade to appear to lead the montagnard movement. After all, Pleiku was the Jarai capital (and bigger than Ban Me Thuot) and Nay Luett (a Jarai revolutionary) was happy to allow Y B'ham to take the heat for leading the revolution. Those were the supposedly simple, unsophisticated mountain people that Ed Sprague was to deal with.

Among the other myths taught in premission training were that the montagnards were so primitive that they didn't know how to lie or dissemble. Even though everyone suspected that the last race with those characteristics was Neanderthal man (long extinct), everybody listened and believed. Ed Sprague didn't. Sprague accepted the montagnards as they were, and truly liked them. He recognized that they were natural warriors, yet fearful of the Vietnamese, and that they needed help.

Although he admired the montagnards, he ranked the CIDG companies at Mai Linh from good to not so good. Civilian Irregular Defense Group companies 236 to 240 were the companies assigned, with 237 Company generally considered to be the best; 240 and 239 companies brought up the rear. After evaluating the companies, Sprague assigned operations based on company capability. No unit was assigned a mission that would put it in over its head against any enemy that it might meet. But Sprague excelled most at what was always the primary SF mission: winning the people to his side.

Ed Sprague led the way in meeting people at the village level. He accompanied medical patrols, often helping as a medic himself. He was happy helping other people, and the montagnards responded in kind. Intelligence information flowed freely in the Mai Linh area of operations, and the team always knew where the VC/NVA were and what they were up to. Since FULRO also had to be watched after, Ed's efforts also helped us to learn what FULRO was planning or doing in the Mai Linh area.

It was natural for Ed Sprague to want to materially help the montagnards. Although help from international humanitarian agencies was already coming in, Ed personally organized his family back in Boston to send gifts. The montagnard recipients knew the impetus for that largesse was Ed Sprague, and his image grew.

Sprague's benevolence toward the montagnards was not conceptually limited. He won a Soldier's Medal for rescuing a drowning montagnard during a combat operation. The photograph of the presentation of that medal is the lead picture in the article "No Greater Loyalty" (*Vietnam* magazine, December 1991), where Sprague is wearing the medal, but no explanation is offered about how it was earned.

Some detractors have said that Ed Sprague began to "go native" in 1966, but those who served with him back then know differently. He did like and respect the montagnards, but he never lost sight of his American roots and family or that the main mission was defeating the VC/NVA and furthering U.S. interests. Later, when Ed Sprague returned to Vietnam in a civilian capacity, still others were sure that *that* was positive proof that Ed Sprague had become a montagnard; some later said that Sprague was the model for Colonel Kurtz in *Apocalypse Now*, not realizing that the model for that story had been written in the nineteenth century by Joseph Conrad. Stories about Sprague abound, but the simplest explanation is the true one: Ed Sprague liked the montagnards and tried to help them, never losing sight of the mission and never placing the montagnards ahead of that mission.

Sprague left Vietnam in February 1967, returning to Fort Bragg and an assignment with the 6th Special Forces Group. Vietnam and the war had changed him. He was not content to train the flood of volunteers into Special Forces that had arrived on the tails of Robin Moore's book and Barry Sadler's song. There were training exercises at the Florida Ranger camp, ambushing Ranger school students, and other exercises held on the familiar sandy terrain of Fort Bragg, but to Sprague a lot of the fun was gone.

Once, Ed Sprague was placed in charge of teaching smallboat training to a group of newly assigned officers, mostly lieutenants. When they failed to pay attention and began grabassing, Sprague canceled the class, put everybody onto the trucks, and took them back to the garrison, where he promptly reported them as immature and not qualified for assignment in SF. An older, calmer SF veteran advised Sprague to relax and to become more accepting. Sprague realized, however, that he had grown much beyond the army and SF and that it was time to look forward to doing something else. His assessment was confirmed during the nationwide riots after the assassination of Martin Luther King in April 1968.

After the assassination, federal troops were called up nationwide, including Special Forces. The 6th Group went to Baltimore, Maryland, to reinforce that city's police force. So as not to show that Green Berets were involved in riot control, the men had to cut off their SF shoulder patches and replace their berets with ordinary army baseball-type fatigue caps.

Sprague thought about what he was doing in Baltimore and realized that the U.S. Army had so mismanaged itself and the Vietnam War that there were few forces left in the U.S. to handle routine civil disturbances. Times were indeed bad when SF troops had to be sent on riot control duties. Ed decided to retire, but he wanted to see if he could work elsewhere in the federal government when he left the military. There was a CIA liaison office at Fort Bragg, and Ed went there first. With his background, he would have been a natural selection for that agency, but he was rejected. Undaunted, Ed Sprague applied to the Agency for International Development (USAID), a subsidiary element of the State Department. He was accepted after his military retirement, and he began training in 1969.

As a USAID representative, Sprague knew that he would undoubtedly be going back to Vietnam. He already spoke Vietnamese and was fluent in Jarai/Rhade. Besides, his army seniority was applied to the State Department job, and he would not have to start at the bottom of the pile.

Ed attended an orientation course in Washington, D.C., to find out what USAID was all about and what he would be expected to do overseas. He learned, in effect, that USAID did the nitty-gritty work of distributing humanitarian relief supplies, overseeing improvement projects, running psychological operations, and all the various things that came under the heading of nation building. Unlike the diplomatic corps, he would be at ground level and not attending diplomatic parties and functions. But it was also pointed out that intelligence gathering was an intrinsic duty, particularly in his case and because of his background. The last part of the orientation took place back at Fort Bragg.

Under the auspices of the JFK Center for Special Warfare, Ed Sprague was reintroduced to weapons and tactics, survival, evasion and escape, communications, demolitions, and the other skills needed by a new USAID representative. For

Ed's classmates, the instruction was new and interesting. But because the classes were being taught by Sprague's SF buddies, he skipped a lot. Sprague didn't have to be taught elementary skills to work in Vietnam. He was ready and looking forward to going back.

By May 1969, Ed Sprague was back in Vietnam and ready for further assignment. Unfortunately, the retired-major assignment person working at CORDS (Civil Operations and Revolutionary Development Support), the USAID acronym in Vietnam, wanted to assign Sprague to IV Corps, the southern delta area of Vietnam. When Sprague objected to that assignment, the assignment person patiently repeated the old bromide of assignments having to fit the needs of the service and that the needs were in IV Corps. After Ed explained his experience and fluency in Jarai, his desires were still rejected. Finally, in desperation, Sprague told the assignment person that he would return to the United States rather than be assigned to the delta. He went to the U.S. embassy and found more flexible people. He was told to report to CORDS headquarters in Nha Trang for assignment in the Central Highlands. As in the army, Sprague was developing a reputation for ignoring the bureaucracy and finding ways around roadblocks.

When Sprague arrived in Nha Trang, he explained his previous experience in the Central Highlands, his fluency in Jarai, and the affinity that he had for the montagnards. Nha Trang proved more pragmatic in assignment policy, and Sprague was attached to Military Assistance Command, Vietnam, Team 31 in Cheo Reo. Through manipulation and determination, Sprague managed to return to his old stomping grounds.

I was leaving Vietnam with orders to Germany. My outprocessing was through Pleiku and Nha Trang. On the way from Pleiku, I seriously considered stopping off to see Ed Sprague in Cheo Reo, but with the battles of Dak Seang and Dak Pek still raging, I didn't think I could spare the time to visit. Ed understood, and I stayed in Kontum until I had to leave to make my flight home.

It wasn't normal to receive an overseas assignment from another overseas area. By the summer of 1970, however, nothing was normal in the army anymore. Vietnam had received the lion's share of the assets for more than five years, and the army in the continental United States (CONUS) and elsewhere showed it. There were thousands of deserters and AWOLs throughout the army, and the effectiveness of the force was in jeopardy, particularly in Europe.

After a thirty-day leave back home in Chicago, I took my family to Europe. We drove to Philadelphia, shipped the car from there, and took a taxi to Fort Dix, New Jersey. From Dix, we flew by contract carrier (and an aircraft emergency and aborted takeoff) to Frankfurt, Germany. By the end of April 1970, I had reported in to Headquarters 3d Brigade, 3d Armored Division, in Friedberg, Germany.

I was told that there were less than fifty infantry captains in Seventh Army in Europe at the time. True or not, Seventh Army was in a shambles. Race riots were common, as were sit-down strikes in combat units! There were incidents of hand grenades being tossed into dining facilities, and drugs were everywhere, particularly hashish.

In my interview with the brigade adjutant, I asked to be assigned to the 1st battalion, 36th Infantry, the only infantry battalion in the 3d Brigade. Somebody decided that I could be of better use as the Headquarters Company commander of the brigade. I protested that the brigade headquarters slot was an armored position and that if infantry captains were really in short supply, then the logical place to put me was in an infantry unit. Logic didn't prevail. Besides, it was explained that I was an "old" soldier since I now had twelve years in the army and that my experience would better serve the army in a more complicated command. I realized years later that most "older" captains end up commanding headquarters companies. Ed Sprague's old commo man, John Southworth, ended up commanding a divisional headquarters company, which I considered a far worse assignment. The problem with commanding a headquarters company is that all your troops work for someone else, usually a primary staff officer who may be a senior captain or major. That means that it's harder to get training done, to assign work details, or to get maintenance taken care of on your assigned vehicles. And the headquarters company of an armored brigade has forty-five wheeled and tracked vehicles.

As the final part of my in-processing briefing, I was warned not to walk home to my quarters in the officers' housing area; off-duty troops had been mugging officers who walked home! I wondered who was responsible for letting the army get into that sorry situation. But I knew: It was the fault of everyone in the chain of command, from Secretary of Defense McNamara on down.

I had escaped the 82d Airborne Division because I didn't care for the spit and polish and discipline anymore and wanted to be a real soldier. Now, I found myself in a situation that required excess discipline to correct the laxness that had been allowed to build.

The first sergeant showed me around for the first few days, and I became more aware of my new surroundings. Most of the officers and NCOs in the unit were not Vietnam vets and were there in Germany precisely to avoid Vietnam duty. Okay, I could understand that. Not everyone wants to go to war, particularly tankers who would have been assigned as infantry if they had gone to Vietnam.

At my first meeting with the NCOs of the company, I explained my background. I told them I knew more about being an NCO than I did about being an officer since I had been an NCO longer. I also explained that I would rely on them to do their jobs and that if they felt it necessary to bring a soldier to me for discipline, that I would usually do whatever they wanted. But on the other hand, I wasn't going to do their discipline/training job for them. It seemed that we understood each other.

One of my first jobs was to try to decrease racial tension. I became an equal opportunity hardass. Many of the southern white soldiers had been flying miniature state flags on their vehicle antennas. That bothered the blacks because many of the flags included the Confederate Stars and Bars. I told the white soldiers that since the vehicles belonged to the United States Army, the only flag that could be flown was a miniature U.S. flag. Then I told the black soldiers that the black-power salute and slapping and dapping were out if they interfered at all with anything military. If slapping and dapping greetings between soldiers prevented a chow line from moving, then it was out. Soon, both races hated me, but there was no doubt as to who was in charge.

When my personal driver (who was black) went AWOL, I had him court-martialed and placed in confinement. The troops figured out that I wasn't playing. I had a druggie helicopter crew chief who used to tell me that I should try LSD. He knew that I couldn't do anything to him since he was just talking about drugs. I had to catch them in his possession before anything could be done. Anyway, the young man decided to give me a polite, indirect warning one day.

Jones (not his real name) said: "You know, sir, back in the Nam, you're the type of guy that the troops might frag."

I replied, "Jones, do you really think that officers didn't frag jerks like you first?"

The boy was truly perplexed, and sputtered about unfairness and things like that. But there were no more threats, implicit or otherwise.

The drug problem was the next most difficult issue. Hashish found its way into Germany, and the German police didn't much care at the time because it wasn't a German problem. Hashish was an "American problem" until the Germans began using it, but that came later. American soldiers could go to Frankfurt and buy hashish for one dollar per gram. LSD and heroin were also available, but the usual drug of choice was hashish.

Early in my tour, during a command information class, I told the troops my rules for smoking hash: "If you smoke it in my barracks and I catch you, I'll burn you. If you smoke it off the kaserne, downtown, I don't care. My rules are simple." Unfortunately, a number of troops didn't follow my rules and were burned. A maximum company-grade Article 15 was the usual result (one-grade reduction, fourteen days' extra duty, and fourteen days' restriction).

Contributing, however, to the discipline and drug problems was McNamara's Project 100,000, which was implemented to bring more draftees into the armed services. Since the college-student potential inductees all had deferments and kept going to school to the point of getting graduate degrees, the draft was expanded to take in Category IV and V people, those in the two lowest mental categories, which mainly consisted of school dropouts and functional illiterates. It was not a proud time for the armed services. Many of the Project 100,000 draftees proved to be good soldiers, but the statistical evidence proved that the majority were problems.

A related draft problem was the issue of drafting homosexuals. In the sixties and seventies many homosexuals were still "in the closet" and were reluctant to publicly expose their sexual orientation. When a homosexual was drafted and admitted his orientation, he was rejected for service, and his orientation became a public matter. On the other hand, a homosexual could conceal his orientation and accept being drafted and hope that he would never be caught and would eventually earn an honorable discharge.

I think that many others did as I did. We ignored the homosexuality issue unless the individual was caught in a compromising act, which forced the matter and caused action to release the offender from service. I reasoned that, after all, the government drafted the person against his will and put him into the army; if he could serve his time honorably and be discharged with good paper, then that's how it ought to be. But people were caught and administratively discharged.

The problems facing the army, and Europe in particular, began to be addressed in 1970. With the Vietnam War winding down, emphasis was placed on moving successful battalion and brigade commanders to Europe for back-to-back tours. The problems began to be solved. Europe went from being a haven for people avoiding the Vietnam War to a field army being staffed more and more with Vietnam veterans. Sure, it was hard for Vietnam returnees, but it put Seventh Army back in business.

Eventually, Col. Sidney Haszard took over 3d Brigade. Haszard had been in the 9th Infantry Division in Vietnam and had been a tanker since World War II. He had won the DSC for ramming a German tank in Nuremberg, 1945, then jumping out and killing the crew. Many of the Vietnam veteran commanders sent to Europe went on to become general officers. This didn't happen for Colonel Haszard, but that didn't make him less of a brigade commander. I was fortunate to learn from him.

Colonel Haszard would go to the divisional commander's conference in Frankfurt and then hold a conference of his own when he returned to Friedberg. As a commander, I got to sit in with the battalion commanders and listen to the latest directives from 3d Armored Division. I knew to keep quiet and listen, and it was all informative. I was learning how the army really worked.

Often the conferences were about maintenance of weapons systems and vehicles, which was always a big thing in an armored or mechanized division. Some of the problems and solutions seemed comical. As an example, in a tank platoon of five tanks, if four tanks were deadlined with one for main gun problems, another for track replacement, another for engine replacement, and another for radio problems, then only one tank was deadlined and unit readiness should be reported that way! The rationale was that if we went to war, we would cannibalize one tank for parts to make three others operable. Ergo, we went from one operable tank in a platoon to four.

We kept all our vehicles combat loaded with a basic supply of ammunition so that we could head to the Fulda Gap and fight the Soviets when they came across the West German border. Unfortunately, some troops were stealing the ammo to shoot at or blast other races; others used the weapons and ammo to hold up their German drug dealers. The alternative was to download all the ammo and store it, but since it took three days to upload a brigade, that wasn't a good choice. We had problems.

Early in Colonel Haszard's tenure as brigade commander, we had our monthly alert and had to move to our dispersal position east of Friedberg. We arrived at about 7:00 A.M., and I had the mess section break out C rations for the breakfast meal. Colonel Haszard called me to him after breakfast. The conversation went something like this:

"Dooley, you're an infantryman. Therefore, you think at 2.5 miles per hour (walking speed) and only plan to use what you can carry on your back."

Colonel Haszard continued: "Armor people are much more intelligent than infantrymen. They know that they go into combat in vehicles. And in those vehicles, they can carry creature comforts that infantrymen can't imagine. We can carry cots, food that can be cooked, and that sort of thing. Infantrymen need to suffer because it fits their psyche, tankers don't. Do you understand?"

"Yes, sir!" was the only answer. Thereafter, I had the mess sergeant stockpile "alert rations" in packets so we could at least cook a hot meal within thirty minutes after moving into an area. Powdered eggs and canned sausages with fried potatoes proved to be a better breakfast meal than C rations. Chili and rice could do the same thing at lunch. Creativity was the watchword, and nobody really much cared about the master menu. When we went on field exercises around Schotten and the Vogelsberg, I'd send a truck back to Friedberg each day to pick up Class A rations to cook and eat in the field. I learned that tankers *were* truly different than grunts. Sure, it was an imposition on the mess section, but it benefited the troops.

One day, Colonel Haszard called me into his office because I had four quarter-ton jeeps deadlined for maintenance problems. Two jeeps needed new engines, one needed a transmission, and another needed a rear differential. Colonel Haszard wasn't happy and asked me what I was doing about it. I explained that I had been pushing the direct support maintenance company, but that wasn't doing any good. Colonel Haszard leaned on me, expecting that I'd lean on the maintenance company. Instead, I reverted to how I got things done when I was an NCO. I bought two bottles of whiskey and got five pounds of coffee from the mess hall. Then, my supply sergeant and I got in my new 1970 Buick and tried to find the vehicle major assembly rebuild point in Germany. First we went to Hanau, but were told that the unit I was looking for was somewhere around Zweibrucken, near the Rhine in the Army Communications Zone. So we drove to Zweibrucken and finally found the rebuild unit.

The unit was staffed with German labor-service forces that were paramilitary. They wore uniforms and had the equivalent of a first sergeant. I spoke to the first sergeant and explained that I needed two engines, a transmission, and a differential. The coffee and whiskey helped, and I was soon driving my cargo the one hundred miles back to Friedberg. The next problem was my motor sergeant.

My motor sergeant said, "Sir, I can't put these assemblies into our vehicles! That's third echelon maintenance!"

I explained, "You have the tools, don't you? You have the knowledge to do it, don't you? So just do it."

By then the motor sergeant was convinced that I was crazy and tried again: "Sir, of course I can do it, but it's a violation of every maintenance and logistical regulation and procedure that we have."

Patiently, I explained, "Sarge, I don't care about rules. I care about having four jeeps that run. If the Russians come across the border this evening, they won't care about rules either. So just fix my vehicles."

The motor sergeant fixed the vehicles, and Colonel Haszard was delighted when I told him that all my jeeps were fixed. He wasn't so happy when I told him how I did it, but when he thought about it for a while, he changed his mind.

At the next brigade commander's conference, he chewed out all his battalion commanders who had deadlined vehicles and pointed out how one enterprising captain solved his maintenance problems. I was on cloud nine for about five minutes until Colonel Haszard volunteered me to procure major assemblies for the rest of the brigade. I delegated the responsibility to my motor sergeant and kept him supplied with coffee and whiskey. Our short circuit of the logistics system lasted for about a month until Colonel Haszard told the division commander what he was doing at the next meeting. The logisticians immediately closed my contact down and demanded that the German rebuild point not deal directly with any combat units. I began to wonder if support personnel really cared about the rest of the army that they were tasked to support.

I don't know why, but when 3d Armored Division headquarters mandated that each brigade establish a drug awareness council, Colonel Haszard appointed me as one of the members for 3d Brigade. My own attitudes toward drugs were nebulous. I didn't care who used (or didn't) as long as he could do his job and fight when necessary. Colonel Haszard appointed himself president of the council.

Within a month, the division drug awareness council came to visit us in Friedberg. The division council consisted of the division G-1 (personnel and morale), the division surgeon, and the division psychiatrist, and a few others.

The division folks made a well-rehearsed pitch for controlling drugs within 3d Armored Division. As they spoke, periodically Colonel Haszard would nod and say, "The Chinese solution would apply here." Then they'd go on with their pitch. Periodically, Colonel Haszard would say, "Yep, the Chinese solution is the definite answer here."

Finally, after about twenty minutes of the "Chinese solution," one of the division staff members said: "Colonel, perhaps I'm ill-informed, but I don't know what the Chinese solution is."

Colonel Haszard was in rare form and waiting for the question. "Well when the Chinese Communists came to power in China, they executed every social deviate and misfit. I propose the same solution here. I can eliminate every drug user in my brigade and make it combat ineffective, or accept that I have a drug problem and deal with it as I keep my tank crews and infantry squads as they are, drugs and all. Will you support me in my proposal to kill all drug users in 3d Brigade?"

The immediate response was that the division people couldn't support that solution. So Colonel Haszard said: "Well then, I guess I just have to continue to deal with the problem as best as I know how."

The division drug awareness council returned to Frankfurt with its tail between its legs.

Drugs were still a problem in the early seventies in Europe, but there were no easy solutions. Once, a team came from Frankfurt to do random urinalysis tests in the 3d Brigade. The officers and men from Headquarters Company (including the staff) were assembled in the brigade gym. The brigade executive officer told the enlisted men that the tests were mandatory. Then, he said that the tests were voluntary for company-grade officers. All my fellow captains and lieutenants went off and urinated in bottles. The XO asked me why I wasn't cooperating. I responded: "Sir, I don't do drugs. If these tests detect good German beer, then so be it. But are officers now suspect by their grade? Why are field-grade officers being left out? I'll take the test if you tell me to, but I won't do it otherwise. I'm an officer, the same as you!"

The XO declined to push the issue, but I began to think differently about the army. Perhaps that was the first indication that the army was changing, and I was still holding on to different standards. After all, in SF I had access to whatever drugs I might have wanted. There was no control of drugs at an A-team; amphetamines, opiates, and other drugs were there for the taking, but nobody ever abused the access. We knew that drugs were mind altering, but nobody wanted his mind altered.

However, this was only the first change that I began to notice in the army, that officers and EM were both suspect. There were also more women coming into the army, and we had to accommodate them. One of the infantry NCOs in the 1/36th Infantry had a pregnant WAC wife, and she became a typist at brigade headquarters, even though at the time she wasn't authorized to be assigned at brigade level. But the army was changing, and I was still wondering.

However, I must have pleased Colonel Haszard. He strongly recommended that I receive a regular army (RA) commission, which I attained in 1971. I knew that with an RA, the same commission that West Pointers had, I would probably be safe from the reductions in force (RIF) that were beginning. As Vietnam continued to close down, reductions in personnel strength had to take place. That meant that thousands of officers had to be RIFd. As usual, many good people were asked to leave, along with some others who didn't belong in a peacetime army. RIF was the army equivalent to corporate downsizing. But I began to notice many more similarities between the army and civilian corporations. Supposedly, in managing organizations, theory says that we reward success and punish failure. Overwhelmingly, what I saw in the army was that mediocrity was rewarded, and success was punished. Don't believe it?

If a manager (battalion or brigade commander) has three or four supposedly equal units working for him, an outsize proportion of assets will be given to the least achieving manager. After all, "We have to bring Joe/Pete/Jim along and help him get back on track." Nobody ever thinks about it, but when that is done, a leveling process is going on, and failure is being rewarded, success is being punished. Mediocrity is the goal. Thought is seldom given to what heights could be achieved if additional assets were given to the proven winners.

I knew that even if I had an RA commission I would not remain competitive with my contemporaries if I didn't get a college degree. It didn't matter that I had been doing okay without a degree; the army required its officers to be college educated, and I had to get one. Except for my last Vietnam tour, I had been taking college courses in the evening since I was commissioned in 1967. Studying and writing in the evenings and on weekends had become a habit. In Germany, whenever I wasn't in the field at one of the training centers (Hohenfels or Grafenwöhr), I was going to school in the evenings.

Even in Germany, Vietnam and Special Forces were never very far away. My first sergeant, Lorenzo Perea, had a program where a young soldier would accompany him throughout the day to see what a first sergeant did and why. It was an extremely effective human-relations program, and it worked well to increase understanding between the troops and "lifers."

Well, First Sergeant Perea's program was written about in *Stars and Stripes* for his "First Sergeant for a Day" program, and there was a very brief mention that the commander of Headquarters Company, 3d Brigade, was Captain George Dooley. Carl Mayse saw the write-up and called me and asked me if Perea was as good as he (Mayse) was. I told Carl that Perea was better. With that, Carl said, "I know you're lying now, 'cause nobody is better than me." Carl was still his usual humble self; the Field Marshal had never changed since he had made master sergeant (E-8). We talked, and I found that John McFadden was back in the 10th, and we visited the next time that I made it to southern Bavaria.

In 1973, I was able to attend a presentation given at V Corps headquarters in Frankfurt on the NVA introduction of tanks into Vietnam. The U.S. response was to ship helicopter TOW antitank missiles to Vietnam. The Airborne TOW missiles were remarkably effective as tank killers. From a hidden point three thousand meters away, those missiles could defeat any armor that the NVA—or just about anyone else—could bring onto the battlefield. Since most of the tank fighting had taken place in Kontum Province, I asked the major presenting the briefing about the SF camps there. Apparently, only Ban Het had held. All the rest, including Polei Kleng, had fallen to the NVA. At Polei Kleng, the NVA armor attacked from the south, across the runway into the camp. I wondered how *Dai-uy* Ha had fared and how many of the LLDB had been killed or captured.

After commanding for twenty-two months, I was moved to brigade staff in April 1972. Colonel Haszard wanted to make me the brigade S-4 (logistics) officer, but I told him that I didn't know enough about logistics to be effective. Sure, I could work around the system and make it work for me, but I just wasn't a logistics type. I was made the assistant S-3 (operations and training) instead.

Since I had been a B-team S-3, I knew how to write plans and maneuver troops, only now I was playing with American units. Emphasis was on training and recovering from Vietnam. Vietnam was to haunt us for years.

We had one lieutenant tank platoon leader who actually told his platoon that they should purposely fail tank gunnery qualification that year to protest the Vietnam War. "Boloing for peace" is how the lieutenant phrased it. When you don't qualify on your individual weapon or your crew-served weapon, you have "boloed." The lieutenant was a college graduate and saw no connection with Vietnam, the Cold War, and what we were doing in Germany. The fact that there two (plus) Soviet combined arms armies to our immediate east meant nothing to him. I have often maintained that stupidity is common through all ranks in the army; but it hurts to see stupidity in action.

A brigade staff job in Europe was professionally rewarding. Each year, our brigade stayed four months out of the year in the field or at various training centers. I was able to watch tank units in action and absorb some of the armor mentality. Of course, tankers looked down on mere infantrymen as grunts and as "lubrication" for their tracks when they proposed to roll over them. Friendly infantrymen riding on the outside of tanks were considered "standoff," protection against enemy antitank projectiles.

During my tour in Europe, Brigadier General Patton was assigned as an assistant division commander in Nuremberg. General Patton was the son of Gen. George S. Patton, commander of Third Army in World War II. As such, he was looked upon as a minor deity by armor officers throughout the army, particularly to West Point tankers who had served as cadets when Major Patton was a tactical officer at West Point. One day, Patton was admitted to the Nuremberg hospital, and there was an exodus of armor officers from the

Frankfurt area to Nuremberg so that they could worship around his hospital bed.

I watched most of the back-to-back battalion commanders turn poor units into good ones. I also watched some poor West Point officers with connections later make general officer while their more outstanding contemporaries didn't. But hey, nobody ever said that life was fair. Eventually, in 1972, Colonel Haszard was replaced by Col. Daniel French. Colonel Haszard went to Frankfurt to become the division chief of staff.

Dan French was a fast mover in the army and eventually retired as a major general. He was lucky to take a brigade from Sidney Haszard. Almost everything was already in place for him.

I had about a year as the assistant S-3, and I enjoyed the job. When we were on a training exercise, we might get a frag order in, that is, a change in operation, and that would require a whole new operations order. While the S-3 and other staff, the executive officer and maybe Colonel French would study the map and do "what-ifs" to develop a maneuver plan and argue, I'd sit back at a typewriter and task-organize the brigade and write a plan. At the end of half an hour, I'd be the only one with a written plan. Different things work for different people. Invariably, my plan would be accepted and sent to the subordinate battalions.

My parents visited me in 1971 and 1972 in Germany. I'd usually take a week's leave and drive them around Germany. My father enjoyed touring his old combat sites from World War II. After their last visit, my parents returned home, and my father went to the doctor one day because of lack of coordination. The doctor said that my father had suffered a minor stroke but ordered further tests. He was found to have a brain tumor, and I requested an emergency leave, which was denied.

I decided to fly home to Chicago on commercial airlines on ordinary leave and was at the airport in Frankfurt when my boss arrived. Maj. William Balfanz, along with Colonel French, had pushed the division surgeon to approve an emergency leave for me, which he was reluctant to do. Finally, the division surgeon relented and recommended emergency leave. Major Balfanz had the approved emergency leave and took me to the military side of the airport and put me on a plane home to the States. I owe Major Balfanz.

When I arrived home, my father was being prepped for surgery. It wasn't a good time, and when it was announced that the tumor was malignant, the family nominated me to break the news. I've wondered why I've always gotten the hard jobs. My father lasted less than eighteen months.

I returned to Germany and applied for a curtailment of my tour. I wanted my children to spend some time with their grandfather while he still had some good time left. The curtailment was granted, and we came home in May 1973. Before I left, Colonel French offered me command of a rifle company if I extended my tour. I'm sure that he meant well, but it was an offer made too late.

As much as Germany and the U.S. Army in Germany wanted to disassociate from the Vietnam War in the 1970s, it was impossible. Vietnam was only one aspect of the Cold War that had been going on since the end of World War II. The Vietnam War was used to spur radicalism throughout the world, all with an agenda to advance a cause. West Germany's radicals were known as the Red Army or Baader-Meinhof gang. When the Baader-Meinhof gang blew up the V Corps officers' club in Frankfurt, everyone began paying attention. Within an hour after the explosion, the 1st battalion, 36th Infantry was pulled from Friedberg to guard the V Corps complex, which was centered on the old I. G. Farben building in Frankfurt. Simultaneously, security was increased by both the Germans and Americans.

American kasernes and housing areas throughout Germany were locked up as much as possible, and soldiers and their families were warned to decrease their travel and to be wary. The German police began securing transportation facilities and started vehicle inspections at checkpoints.

After another bombing, at a Seventh Army computer center

in Heidleberg, the German police put enough pressure on so that they eventually caught a few members of the Baader-Meinhof gang. But the Soviet Union had upped the stakes in the Cold War, and everyone knew it. It's axiomatic that no revolutionary or terrorist group can long survive without outside assistance, normally furnished by a sponsoring country.

Baader-Meinhof, and later the Red Army Brigades in Italy, made the Europeans take notice. It was during the turmoil caused by the Baader-Meinhof gang that I left Germany in the late spring of 1973. My family and I were flying home commercially, on a Pan American 747, and we were surprised that we had to go through a body search before we could board the aircraft. The German army was doing the searching, and I was surprised to find that I was allowed to skip through the search because I was traveling in uniform. By that time in the army, I doubted if my own army would have shown me that professional courtesy.

CHAPTER 10

Land of the Big PX

After three years in Europe, it was good to be home again. My father's health was deteriorating, however, and everyone knew it was just a matter of time before he died. Nevertheless, we had thirty days' leave together before we had to drive to Fort Benning. But other things were also happening in the world.

After the Christmas bombing in 1972, the North Vietnamese came back to the negotiating table in Paris, and an end to U.S. involvement in the Vietnam War was worked out. Supposedly, the United States would get out of Vietnam with some face-saving honor. The major benefit, however, was the release of the POWs from Hanoi in early 1973. I would soon meet some of these folks at Benning.

But the return of the POWs wasn't universally joyful. It was announced shortly after the POWs had returned to U.S. control that some of the prisoners had not acted honorably and had sought favors from their captors by informing on fellow prisoners. I was saddened to learn that some SF soldiers were in that group. I rationalized, however, that it was a result of allowing younger soldiers into SF.

Years later, in a conversation with Steve Leopold, a former POW, I learned that the Vietnam POWs had formed an organization and had annual reunions. He told me of the SF collaborators and that they were not welcome at the yearly reunion. Most people don't understand how important it is that soldiers keep the faith with their fellow servicemen as they are the soldier's support group. Torture, starvation, and mind games are a given in a POW situation and are to be expected; turning on your own kind is not.

Many of the army POWs were in Special Forces when captured. After all, SF duty had the greatest exposure to possible capture. Many of the former POWs proved to have been very heroic in trying to avoid capture. Nevertheless, becoming a POW was not considered a distinction. I was always one of those who knew I would rather be killed than be captured. Sure, there are situations where capture isn't avoidable, but I always trained myself to avoid the possibility of capture. Evasion and escape (E & E) courses were an example.

In the basic and advanced courses at Benning, there was a night E & E course built into the curriculum. Small groups of five soldiers were formed, "ambushed" in enemy-held territory and had to evade back to friendly lines. If anyone was captured, they were made most uncomfortable until they could again attempt to escape and evade. I always lost my group and traveled by myself throughout the course. Being alone in the woods at night never troubled me; traveling with a noisy group of people did. I always made the first group of trucks returning to garrison when I moved alone.

In May 1973, Fort Benning hadn't changed very much. The pace was slower because the Infantry School was no longer charged with putting out large numbers of officers for Vietnam. In 1973, the mission of the school was to help bring down the strength of the officer corps by identifying officers for the reduction-in-force (RIF) program. Consequently, there were several make-break points in the Infantry Officer Advanced Course (IOAC) curriculum. One of those was the land navigation course.

Since I had reported to Benning early because of my curtailment of my European tour, I was given an innocuous job in the company operations committee of the Infantry School until my class was to start in July. I had a lot of time on my hands and met some of my new classmates when they also reported in early. To help the aviators in our class, some of my friends and I began walking the land navigation course in the evenings and on weekends.

During the bad old days of Vietnam, infantrymen were encouraged to go to flight school and learn how to fly helicopters. But once an aviator was qualified, he wasn't able to serve ground time in an infantry unit. The infantry aviator usually served multiple tours flying in Vietnam. While navigating in a helicopter above the jungle and through mountains is fairly easy, the typical aviator never honed the skills needed for navigating on the ground. So infantry branch began to use the land navigation course as a discriminator to identify captains for RIF. If it doesn't sound fair, it wasn't. The post-Vietnam RIFs were especially hard on aviators. It seemed to many of us that armor and artillery branch valued their aviation qualified people, but infantry branch didn't value people who went outside the mainstream. Infantry aviators were disproportionately RIFd. So we tried to help the folks who had helped us years before in Vietnam.

Terrain appreciation is difficult to teach, particularly in hilly, scrub-pine south Georgia. You stop and explain, "Look, to the left and right the ground is sloping down steeply, yet we're walking northeast down a gentle slope. Maybe we're walking down a finger. Check the map and contour lines and see if it confirms the terrain." Maybe we saved the careers of some infantry aviators. I'd like to think we did.

I was assigned to IOAC class 1-74 when it started in July 1973. The class was one of the last to have a full complement of two hundred captains; most Vietnam-era infantry captains had already been through the advanced course. I ran across some old friends, including Mike Lewis, my XO at Polei Kleng. Mike had stayed in SF and become diver qualified. He had also participated in a reenactment of the Lewis and Clark expedition, scouting the Missouri River. Mark Smith, a Special Forces vet who had been captured northwest of Saigon, was one of the newly released POWs. Mark was made executive officer (XO) for our class. Staying with my operations background, I was appointed the class S-3. Among the two-hundred-man student body, we had eight allied officers. Most would return to countries that would later undergo socialist revolutions. The world was still a perilous place.

During the course, the Arab-Israeli 1973 war erupted. Egypt attacked across the Sinai Desert, while Syria attacked from the Golan Heights. Unlike its other wars in the Middle East, Israel began to suffer heavy casualties and use up its war stocks. A large supply of TOW antitank reserves based in Europe were flown to Israel and a group of Israeli soldiers flew to Benning for a quick course in TOW gunnery. They had some minor disputes with Arab students, also at Benning, but nothing major. As usual, liaisons from the Infantry School flew to Israel to observe the war and report back later.

A major benefit of going to the advanced course was that senior generals and officials came to visit and brief about what was going on in their sphere of influence. Army chief of staff Creighton Abrams came to talk about two months before he died of lung cancer. Al Haig also visited and talked about his job. This was the beginning of the grooming process for future assignments. When assignments were handed out at the halfway point of the nine-month course, I received the assignment that I expected to get: fifteen months at Columbus College to complete my degree.

As soon as the course had started, I went to the Columbus College liaison at Benning to see if I could enter the degree completion course there. My transcripts were reviewed and showed all those tedious nights and weekends previously spent reading, studying, and writing for the previous six years. I was assured that I could get a degree within fifteen months, but that I would have to take another foreign language. I used the acceptance to apply for the degree completion program, to start after the advanced course. If I'd been smarter back then, I would have explored getting a degree at Harvard or University of Chicago, but I wasn't that bright.

Since Vietnam had wound down, the Infantry School had returned to its earlier emphasis, a potential World War III in Europe. The majority of the study was devoted to defending

West Germany from attack by the Soviet Union. But the doctrine was straight out of World War II. There was less than four hours of instruction on special operations and psychological operations. No mention was made of the OSS in World War II. I began to see why Colonel Haszard had accused the infantry of a 2.5-miles-per-hour mentality.

Infantry school doctrine can be summed up quite succinctly: Two up, one back, occupy the high ground, feed the troops a hot meal. It seemed that nobody was figuring out that the world was changing and that technology could do wondrous things for us. I remembered back to Vietnam when the 101st took horrific casualties in I Corps, at what they called Hamburger Hill. Later, a Hollywood movie would be made about Hamburger Hill and the gallant ways that soldiers died fighting *up* a hill. When I read about it, I wondered: Didn't anybody consider assaulting the crest of the hill and fighting *down* it? Of course not. That would be too simple. Besides, it would not be in accordance with the school solution, which is a sacred concept at Fort Benning.

It was at Benning when I was first exposed to the game scenarios called Lost in _____ (you can fill in the names: Yukon, space, the desert, the arctic, etc.). Generally, the scenarios described a situation for a group: An aircraft went down at a location, carrying these people and/or this equipment. The solution had to be derived by group consensus, and generally two solutions emerged: walkers and stayers. Usually, the walkers had the ideal solution; it was better to walk away from an aircraft wreck than to stay with it. The scenarios were developed by people we were told were experts and quite often had the imprimatur of other such experts (such as the Louisiana Fish and Wildlife Service).

I'd talk with my aviator colleagues: "I've always been taught that you stay with the wreck, that you're easier to find that way. Is there a better way?" The aviators would usually agree, which coincided with army doctrine for establishing E & E nets for downed aviators. About this time, one might wonder what is the author talking about? On the one hand he challenges doctrine, and on the other he obeys doctrine. Well, it's easy: The proper solution is to do the thing that works best. I still maintain that my destiny in World War III is to be with a guerrilla band in the Urals.

What was really being taught was group consensus and how to achieve it. Management theory from the civilian world was pervasive. Group consensus was ideal; making decisions that didn't account for consensus was not good. But military leadership quite often hinges on making rapid decisions with little information, and making those decisions work. Somewhere along the way, the army was forgetting leadership in favor of management, slowly moving to consensus and committee decision making. I wonder what Sheridan, Sherman, Pershing, Patton, and other fighting generals might think about the army of today?

Largely, I kept my mouth shut and graduated. I made the commandant's list by graduating in the top 10 percent of my class and looked forward to doing something different.

I had a spare month before school started for me at Columbus College, so I asked to attend the "Prefix 5" course, nuclear and chemical weapons target analysis. An explanation is necessary.

The army puts prefix numbers on an officer's MOS (military occupational specialty) code. My basic MOS was 1542, infantry officer. But prefixes in descending order are attached to show qualifications. A prefix of "8" meant instructor qualification, a prefix of "7" designated Airborne qualification. I had already earned those qualifications, but the lowest prefix that I had was "3," which stood for Special Forces officer, so my MOS was 31542, or SF infantry officer. The lowest prefix was considered the most important and took precedence. Nuclear weapons (or prefix 5) wouldn't change my MOS, but it would give me a further skill that I thought I'd like to have.

For three weeks, I learned about high, low, and surface bursts, tree blowdown, residual and downwind contamination, and all the other facets of nuclear and chemical warfare. Most of the course was and is still classified. What was significant, at least to me, was that chemical weapons were not nearly as effective as conventional weapons. Chemical weapons work well as a first strike, but their effectiveness is immediately degraded thereafter.

A casualty rate of 30 percent is considered to make a unit combat ineffective, but that didn't make too much sense to me. Almost all the Americans at Dak Seang were wounded, but that didn't make them combat ineffective. Maybe different rules apply to different units.

I became prefix 5 qualified, then traded in my uniforms for civilian clothes and went to college. Columbus College later became Columbus University, but it was still part of the University of Georgia system. When I went there, it had just advanced from a community college to a four-year school. It was a small school in a small town in the South.

For my application to school, I'd decided that a degree in political science would get me through college to a BA as quickly as possible. My language study was to be German. I wished at the time that I could get credit for Vietnamese and/or Jarai, but that was not to be. So I went to school. As a working adult, I was going to college with teenagers and young adults. Goodness, I had a full scholarship with expenses, and a full-time salary.

Early on, I decided to get straight As. After all, the army was sending me to school for two or three hours a day, and I figured that I ought to show a good result. I did, and eventually graduated Summa Cum Laude, and was named the political science student of the year for 1975. I regretted later that the school I selected didn't have a Phi Beta Kappa chapter. But aside from German and statistics, I didn't learn all that much that I didn't already know.

I'd usually go to school in the morning, run three or four miles in the afternoon, and study or write for the rest of the day. I made it a practice to type my notes each day. Eventually, people began to ask me if they could buy my notes. I didn't sell them, but gave them away. Still, some folks gave me money for what I wasn't selling. Maybe those notes are still floating around today. Xerox machines are wonderful devices.

One day, I ran across a young student who was speaking great things about matriarchal societies. I asked him: "What matriarchal societies actually exist today?" He replied the montagnards of Vietnam.

I responded something to the effect that I had lived and fought with the montagnards for two years on two different tours in Vietnam, and matriarchal societies were grossly mislabeled in academia. To be sure, the montagnards practice passing birth names from the mother, and the women own all the property. But when the tribal/village judges and leadership are all men, are things really different? Besides, when property is nebulous in a nomadic society, ownership of property is meaningless. There was no doubt that I didn't change his mind, but my thoughts were still on Vietnam, particularly the Central Highlands. The years were 1974 and 1975, and I was still watching the drama unfold on nightly television. Ed Sprague was still out there.

As the events of April and May 1975 occurred, I thought back to Ed Sprague. As the head of CORDS in Cheo Reo, Ed Sprague was able to implement the rural development programs that the montagnards really needed. He gave out agricultural supplies and tools, provided improved breeding stock of cattle, swine, and rabbits, and started meaningful medical aid and education projects. Montagnard refugees, primarily Bahnar, were coming into Phu Bon Province at a rapid rate, but the Jarai were reluctant to share their land with their ancient enemy.

In response, Sprague opened a refugee camp at the site of the former Special Forces camp at Mai Linh. He got the Jarai elders to cede some unused jungle north of Mai Linh to the Bahnar, and new tribal villages were established. Of course, the new villages needed nurturing and supplies until they could become self-sufficient; so Sprague continually created more projects.

He also reestablished his contacts with the Jarai village chiefs in the area, and they, in turn, introduced him to Nay Luett and Ksor Rot. Nay Luett was a member of the ruling cabinet under President Thieu and served as the minister for Ethnic Minority Development. Ksor Rot was a senator in the national assembly and represented the people of the highlands. Both, however, were former revolutionaries, active in BaJaRaKa and FULRO.

Nay Luett was a charismatic leader who was the original founder of BaJaRaKa. Educated by the French in Europe, Nay Luett spoke six languages. When he returned to Vietnam, he was unwilling to take a subservient role as a second-class citizen under the Vietnamese. Quite naturally, as with most revolutionaries, Nay Luett served extensive time in prison for his activities. Only with the downfall and assassination of President Diem in 1963 was Luett released. He then returned to the highlands and linked up with Y B'ham and helped to form FULRO. There were some who said that Nay Luett was the true head of FULRO, while Y B'ham was only the nominal leader. But by early 1970, the argument was academic. Y B'ham remained in exile in Cambodia, and Nay Luett held the highest position of any montagnard in Vietnam. Most fortunate for Ed Sprague, Nay Luett came to like and trust him. The feeling was mutual.

Nay Luett began to confide in Sprague to the point that he was giving him the minutes of every Vietnamese cabinet meeting. Sprague passed these along to his superiors, and they in turn were pleased with the rapport that had developed between Nay Luett and Sprague. Frequently, they traveled together in Vietnam and shared some of their thoughts.

It was always Nay Luett's goal that the Central Highlands achieve as much autonomy as possible from the Vietnamese. The ultimate goal was for the highlands to become a separate country. If that was ever to occur, Luett wanted Sprague to be the leader of his armed forces. Unfortunately, Luett's dream was never to become reality. But the dream shows the confidence that Luett had in Ed Sprague and says enough about their relationship.

With Nay Luett in his corner, Sprague was on a success path. But with success comes jealousy, and Sprague's route was not always smooth. Many times throughout his career in the State Department, colleagues bad-mouthed him as an ex-Green Beret cowboy and worse. But that was still to come.

When Nay Luett accepted him, Ed Sprague gained entry into Jarai culture and society unequalled by any western anthropologist. Unfortunately, he was not a scholar and couldn't publish his findings, so many of the myths and misperceptions about the montagnards have prevailed. One such myth is that some montagnards are cannibals, an allegation that derives from the Vietnamese centuries-old campaign to portray the montagnards as savages. Obviously, if a tribe of people practices cannibalism, then they must be savages. But there is no proof of cannibalism among the montagnards, and Sprague never found any evidence to support the premise.

Another little known fact about the montagnards is that they keep slaves. Although it is relatively rare, some Jarai villages did keep one or two Bahnar or Jarai tribesmen as slaves. But this practice was dying, even in the seventies. Bahnar captured in village raids might become slaves; but so would Jarai owing debts to another family, or children without relatives taken as foster children.

A favorite misperception that has been seized upon by some western feminists is the matriarchal aspect of montagnard society. The montagnards are one of the very few matriarchal cultures in the world. Children receive the mother's family name and property ownership rests with the women. But in a society where there is very little property to own, the matriarchal factor is meaningless. Men still control the village courts and the village chief and elder positions, while the women work morning to night in the fields and also cook and clean. To be a montagnard woman is not a good thing. Yet many feminists glorify matriarchal societies as the ideal model.

Ed Sprague's increasing knowledge of the montagnards made him more effective in dealing with the insurgency.

The NVA continually tried to subvert the Jarai and Bahnar. Usually, the Jarai ignored the NVA efforts, but this wasn't always true with the Bahnar. Some Bahnar did help the NVA, perhaps as a result of their animosities with the Vietnamese and Jarai. Ed Sprague, however, vowed to win the Bahnar over to the government side. His efforts were both conventional and unique.

The Bahnar under government control were actively recruited into the paramilitary self-defense organizations, and they proved to be able and fierce fighters. Sprague promoted cooperation between the tribes even to the point of recommending intermarriage. He did have a lot of success, and Phu Bon Province again became pacified.

Another innovation that Sprague implemented was the creation of a cultural drama team and band, and a rock band. In this endeavor, he was fortunate to meet Ksor Hip, a former radio announcer and singer at the station in Ban Me Thuot. Hip became leader of the team and soon began writing propaganda songs that were accompanied by guitars, gongs, and drums. They were so successful that the Rhade began to copy some of the songs in their own, slightly different dialect.

Sprague's success, however, resulted mostly from his day-to-day activity. As the CORDS province representative, he had the leeway to stay on the road and visit villages continually. Once, he pulled into a village that was preparing for the imminent death of the village chief. The chief had severe dysentery and decided that he was going to die, which in a montagnard is a self-fulfilling prophecy. Sprague reverted to his former persona as a medic, administered morphine to stop the wave action of the chief's intestines, thus halting the dysentery. He then started an IV to rehydrate the chief, and administered antibiotics. The chief recovered, and the legend of Ed Sprague grew further. But Sprague could not as easily cure the distrust between the montagnards and the Vietnamese.

Even though there had been a nominal peace with FULRO, Nay Luett was serving in President Thieu's cabinet, the montagnards had representation within the government, and the majority of all montagnard men were armed, individual Vietnamese soldiers continued to harass the montagnards. Typically, a drunk Vietnamese soldier would enter a Jarai village and try to rape a woman or steal something. The drunk soldier was usually beaten or shot, but incidents of that sort continued. Finally, Sprague advised the village chiefs not to worry anymore about Vietnamese soldiers coming into their villages and just to kill them. That hard-line tactic worked, and more civility ensued.

Once, while Sprague was visiting in Nay Luett's house, a drunk Vietnamese soldier entered the house and compared Luett's daughter to a pig. Sprague physically and violently subdued the soldier while Luett called the province chief on the radio and ordered the soldier removed and punished. But the incident reflects the disdain of the Vietnamese for the montagnards, even for a cabinet-level national political leader.

The war continued to change as the U.S. military drew down in Vietnam. More and more, the war began to be run by the State Department, and military direction of the war passed to civilian control.

The Phoenix program was initiated by Bill Colby of the CIA, and it resulted in the virtual elimination of the remaining Viet Cong infrastructure. With a Phoenix team operating within every province, and advised by Special Forces soldiers loaned to the program, most remaining VC officials were either captured or killed. Perhaps the most significant aspect of the civilianization of the war in the highlands was the assignment of John Paul Vann in May 1971 as the senior American adviser in II Corps, effectively filling the position of a major general.

Like Sprague, Vann was retired military who returned to Vietnam working for USAID. But Vann would be more than Sprague's USAID boss; Vann was a retired lieutenant colonel and a staunch critic of how the war was waged. Vann was later chronicled in Neil Sheehan's book *A Bright Shining Lie,* as a manipulative self-promoter, liar, sex offender, and delusional fraud. But Vann fought the war in the highlands with massive airpower and showed the NVA that airpower could inflict decisive casualties. Vann pounded the NVA with B-52 strikes, but never forgot that, regardless of the NVA incursion, the war would be won with the people.

Sprague enjoyed working for Vann. Their backgrounds were similar, except that Vann probably suffered from satyriasis, excessive sexual craving. Vann had multiple mistresses and partners, yet he proved a friend to Sprague and backed all of Sprague's efforts in Phu Bon Province. When Vann died in a helicopter crash on 09 June 1972, the military resumed temporary control. Eventually, Mike Healy, by then a brigadier general, assumed the role of senior adviser in II Corps.

The senior adviser at MACV Team 31 was an army lieutenant colonel, and he received a message one day that General Healy was going to arrive for a briefing the next day. The lieutenant colonel began rehearsing his staff and organized a dog and pony show for General Healy, but didn't know how to fit Ed Sprague into the presentation. Since Sprague was a civilian, he was hard to direct, and besides, most military people really don't like civilians anyway; so he ignored Sprague and just glossed over the USAID role in Phu Bon Province.

The next day when General Healy arrived, the lieutenant colonel had his staff in formation to greet him while Sprague loitered next to his CORDS Bronco, twenty yards away. When Healy exited his aircraft, he saw Sprague and went to greet him, ignoring the MACV commander and staff. The lieutenant colonel didn't know that Healy and Sprague were old friends. From that time on, the lieutenant colonel warily eyed Sprague and treated him with deference.

Sprague's success in Phu Bon Province had resulted in a number of rapid promotions, so in January 1973 he was made the senior adviser in Quang Duc, the southernmost border province in II Corps. It was directly south of Darlac Province, whose capital was Ban Me Thuot and the center for the Rhade tribe. But Quang Duc was important for other reasons: It was the southern back door into the Central Highlands, and the NVA wanted to take it. Ironically, the old SF camp at Duc

Lap, where Mike Dooley died, was just outside of Gia Nghia. The civilian CORDS adviser refused to stay in Quang Duc, and no other civilian wanted the job. Somebody with military experience was needed to become the senior province adviser, and Ed Sprague was the natural pick.

Ed Sprague assumed his new post at Gia Nghia, the province capital. There were not so many montagnards as at Cheo Reo and significantly more Vietnamese, both friendly and unfriendly. Supposedly, the Paris peace treaty was in effect, and there was a cease-fire between the South and North Vietnamese. Yet, NVA tanks were in the province, and there were sporadic contacts and incidents. The only way in or out was by air, and aircraft were reluctant to brave the antiaircraft fire to land there. Sprague's main link with the outside world was single-side-band radio.

Once, as he was driving along a rural road near the border, an NVA tank fired at him. Fortunately, it missed. Sprague set the world's record in turning a four-wheel-drive vehicle around and disappearing.

In Quang Duc, Ed Sprague initiated the same programs that had served him so well with the Jarai in Phu Bon, but because of the heavy Vietnamese influence in the area, they were hard to implement. Still, he had his successes, and he was the subject of newspaper articles by the Associated Press and the *Washington Post*. But Quang Duc was only a training ground in preparation for Ed Sprague to return to Cheo Reo as the senior adviser in Phu Bon Province. Besides, Nay Luett wanted him back and lobbied hard with the U.S. embassy for his return.

When he returned to Cheo Reo, the size of the MACV team had been reduced considerably, and the team would soon be phased out entirely. In the interim, he had to deal with an army lieutenant colonel who refused to work for a retired master sergeant. Sprague talked to the officer and explained that he (Sprague) used to be a master sergeant but that now he outranked the colonel and that the choice was clear: the

colonel could work for Sprague, or the colonel could be relieved. The colonel refused to put his damaged ego into check
and would not work for Sprague, so he left. Fortunately, the
incident was not an omen; everywhere else, Sprague was
heartily welcomed back, and he resumed his efforts on behalf
of the montagnards.

In 1973, the International Control Commission (ICC) had
moved in and was monitoring the cease-fire and peace in
Vietnam. There was an ICC team in each province, and each
team consisted of a Communist-bloc member (usually Polish),
a pro-West member (Canadian), and a neutralist member
(Indian). However, the ICC team in Cheo Reo had little effect
as the Phu Bon Province populace was uniformly in favor of
the government of Vietnam (GVN). Nobody realized that
they were only experiencing a lull in the fighting and that the
Communist North Vietnamese would take over the country
in 1975.

One day in 1973, Jim Morris showed up in Cheo Reo,
where he met Ed Sprague. He recounted the visit in the first
chapter of *The Devil's Secret Name*. But at that same time, Ed
Sprague's family had come to visit, including his wife Eve
and his son Mark. Mark was himself a former Special Forces
NCO who had joined the 10th Group in Europe in 1969.
Sprague was able to host Morris and his family at a Jarai village, and of course, the ever-present rice wine was produced.

Ed Sprague had difficulty convincing other USAID contemporaries in the highlands of the importance of drinking
rice wine with the villagers when you visited. To the montagnards, drinking rice wine was a normal custom of greeting,
but to many Americans the taste of rice wine was akin to
kerosene. Besides, when a rice-wine jug was opened and its
leaf covering taken off, a flurry of roaches usually scurried
out. As awful as the stuff looked and tasted, to refuse the offer
of rice wine was to commit an unpardonable breach of eti-
quette. Yet, many Americans did refuse and were not ever accepted by the montagnards. Through his good deeds on their
behalf and his understanding of the importance of ritual in

the lives of the montagnards, Sprague had gained an un-equalled standing with them, but the end was in sight.

The lull in fighting eventually ended, and by late 1973 con-tacts and combat were on the upswing. By the end of the year, fighting raged all along the border, and the artificial peace in the highlands was ending. On 11 March 1975, Ban Me Thuot fell to the Communists. Kontum City quickly followed, and the GVN decided to abandon Pleiku when Gen. Pham Van Phu surrendered the highlands. With Route 19 between Pleiku and Qui Nhon on the coast cut by the NVA, the only way out for the remaining GVN forces was down Route 7, southeast through Cheo Reo, and eventually through Phu Yen to Tuy Hoa on the coast north of Nha Trang.

There was an uneasy lull in Cheo Reo. The inhabitants knew what was happening all around them, but they could see no signs of retreat. All of that soon changed. By Thursday, 13 March, all of the province officials had fled except for the province chief and one other staff member. The following day, the Vietnamese inhabitants of Cheo Reo began to feel uneasy and to make preparations to move to the coast. Their worst fears were realized on Saturday.

At 4:00 P.M. on Saturday, an organized military advance unit arrived on the northern outskirts of Cheo Reo from Pleiku. This unit consisted of tanks, armored personnel car-riers, and ARVN Rangers. As the unit passed through Cheo Reo, the vehicle commanders began selling rides to the Viet-namese civilians. Panic ensued, and soon every vehicle in the town was loaded and heading south behind the ARVN convoy. Soon, other civilian trucks, taxis, motorbikes, and buses arrived from Pleiku and followed the convoy south. The parade of fleeing vehicles kept up until late in the eve-ning and gasoline supplies in Cheo Reo were gone by the end of the first day of the exodus. The Phu Bon Province military units began destroying their weapons, including four 105mm artillery howitzers, and deserted south.

Sunday, 16 March, the stream of vehicles from Pleiku continued moving south through Cheo Reo. By that time, military and civilian vehicles were intermixed without any organization. The Vietnamese army in the Central Highlands was in a southbound rout to the coast! Then the Phu Bon police deserted, and there was no more traffic control. Vietnamese soldiers and police began forcibly confiscating vehicles from civilians, and soldiers were looting stores and warehouses for whatever supplies they could find. The ARVN deserters began shooting and raping montagnards and taking whatever they wanted. Paradoxically, most of the montagnard men who could have defended their fellow tribesmen were still fighting the NVA, thereby giving the Vietnamese deserters the opportunity not only to flee but to rape, kill, and pillage.

Ed Sprague began organizing the montagnards most closely identified with the American effort and told them to move through the jungle to the coast and that he would arrange ships to rescue them. In all, more than two thousand Jarai and Bahnar began moving southeast. Following Sprague's instructions, they stayed off the roads to avoid the rampaging Vietnamese, some of whose vehicles began to run out of gas and block those behind.

The anarchy reached a peak on Monday, 17 March. Vehicles continued to stream south, but fuel and food were not to be had. ARVN soldiers fired into stores, tossed in hand grenades, and took what they could. Ed Sprague watched adults and children gunned down by the berserk troops. Police and soldiers began shooting at each other for available loot and transportation. Walking refugees were hit by moving vehicles and run over.

Ed Sprague evacuated 16 million piasters that were still in the Phu Bon treasury. The money was taken to Nha Trang by Air America helicopter. In the meantime, the province chief told the remaining ARVN soldiers to abandon their posts and to flee south. He then told the remaining montagnard forces that they were responsible for defending Cheo Reo under penalty of death. Then the province chief fled. Four trucks from the Border Ranger group dropped off rifles, machine guns, and radios to the montagnards, then left to load the trucks with loot from stores and homes.

By nightfall on Monday, the only secure compound in Cheo Reo belonged to Ed Sprague, but he was in danger because he had the only available gasoline left. The montagnards were the last to desert, but two montagnard aides stayed with Sprague to the end.

Toward midnight, ARVN Rangers tried to break into the USAID compound. Sprague and the aides fended off the attack. Later, a national police captain and eight other policemen came to Sprague's compound asking for gas. When Sprague refused, the captain threatened to kill him; one of Sprague's aides told the captain that he would die in the process, and the captain began walking away then turned and fired at Sprague. In the brief firefight ensuing, all the police in his party were killed. The police and Rangers joined forces and laid siege to the compound throughout the night. By daylight, there were more than thirty Ranger and police bodies around the compound.

Tuesday morning, the American consul general in Nha Trang, Moncrieff Spear, sent two Air America helicopters to evacuate Sprague and his remaining staff. ARVN soldiers attempted to hijack the helicopters, but Sprague and his party managed to fly away on a promise that Sprague would send helicopters back for the hijackers. Since the promise was made under duress—an M-16 was pointed at him—Sprague felt no obligation to keep the vow.

As soon as Sprague was in the air, his compound was looted and his vehicles stolen. The helicopters then flew southeast along Route 7, where thousands of vehicles were stalled north and south of Cheo Reo. Farther south, the NVA had cut the road, and there were more than twenty dead and wounded Vietnamese lying along the road.

By noon, Sprague was briefing Moncrieff Spear on the debacle in the highlands, and they both attempted to salvage the situation. But by then it was too late, and everybody evacuated to Saigon. On 01 April, Sprague briefed the U.S.

ambassador, Graham Martin, on the situation, and possible solutions were war-gamed. Nay Luett offered to create a montagnard guerrilla insurgency in the NVA-held highlands, but the United States refused to provide tangible support other than to ask FULRO to harass and fight the NVA occupiers. Promises were made but never kept.

When the highlands fell, South Vietnam was fighting for its life. Ed Sprague remained in Saigon to help Nay Luett with montagnard refugees, but he soon found that the two thousand Montagnards that he had helped to escape to the coast were not picked up and that the U.S. ships never came. We had abandoned our allies, and nobody other than Sprague seemed to feel any shame over it.

Ed Sprague evacuated to Thailand in late April, just before the fall of Vietnam to the Communists. Although he was then a civilian employee of the government, he was the last Special Forces soldier out of Vietnam. He later flew to Camp Chaffee, Arkansas, and helped head the Vietnamese refugee resettlement project there. Later, as he processed thousands of bar girls and Saigon cowboys, he sadly remembered the truly brave and dedicated montagnards that we left behind. But there were many favorable sides to the massive resettlement project. Communities throughout the United States offered to take in refugees. More than five hundred homosexual Vietnamese were sponsored by the gay community in San Francisco.

Ed's son, Mark, was there with his soon-to-be wife Kathleen when things began to fall apart. These two are also part of history, although it isn't generally well known. Mark was an SF medic in 10th Group in Germany in 1970. He had spent his teenage years in the same area while his dad served in the 10th in the early sixties. Unlike his father, Mark served one tour in SF and got out.

I was close to graduation from college in August of 1975 when I called Infantry branch asking for my next assignment. I was told that I had a choice between Fort Polk, Louisiana, and Fort Carson, Colorado. "Was there any possibility of going back to Special Forces or, at least, an Airborne assignment at Fort Bragg?" The reply was that it was out of the question. Oh well, I recognized that I was still one of the plodders in the army. I had to go wherever they assigned me.

Soon, I would have eighteen years in the army, but I still didn't have enough clout to ask for and get an assignment that I wanted. I was sure that I would make major when I was scheduled for promotion, but I hadn't been selected for promotion in the secondary zone. Well, since I was close to twenty years' retirement at half pay, it was time to consider what I was going to do outside of the army. For an old intelligence sergeant, every indication was that I was not going to be a fast mover. At best, I could count on rising to full colonel (O-6), but I would never become a general officer. Therefore, I would plan on retiring as soon as I could and see if I could do better in civilian life. Mrs. Dooley's little boy knew better than to hang around if there was little future for him. I vowed to get an MBA or other graduate degree as soon as possible and to start writing a resume.

When orders came, I was assigned to Recruiting Command at Fort Sheridan, Illinois. So much for forts Polk or Carson. The army didn't care enough about me even to follow through where they said that they were going to send me.

In the spring of 1975, I watched the news and the fall of Vietnam. I watched as air force cargo C-141s attempted to evacuate orphans out of Vietnam, and as a C-5 crashed outside of Long Binh. It was painful to watch the helicopter evacuation off the roof of the American embassy in Saigon. After eight years of combat and fifty thousand American lives, that was what it came down to. I was ashamed to have participated because I knew that it didn't have to be that way.

I felt worse when the *Mayaguez* incident happened off Cambodia, and the Marines and air force didn't know for days what their casualties were. I thought at the time that we had forgotten all the lessons of Vietnam and previous wars: squad leaders always keep track of their people and know who is a casualty, and so on up the chain. Even though the army hadn't participated in the incident, I knew that my army had forgotten how to fight.

I left Columbus, Georgia, figuring that I'd spend two more years in the army and retire.

CHAPTER 11

Recruiting Command

My new home for almost two years was to be the headquarters of Midwest Regional Recruiting Command (MWRRC) at Fort Sheridan, Illinois. MWRRC at the time was colocated with Recruiting Command, its higher headquarters at Fort Sheridan.

The draft had been ended after Vietnam, and the armed services had to fill their ranks with volunteer enlistees. In good economic years, the army was an impossible sell; in bad economic times, the army still had a difficult job. Of all the services, the army has always had the most difficult recruiting job.

When I reported, the major I was soon to work for asked me, "Before you sign in, how would you like to be assigned as a recruiting area commander in Fargo, North Dakota?"

"No," I replied. I went on to explain that my family and many of my friends were from the Chicago area and that I looked forward to being close to my extended family for a while. I didn't add that I was thinking of retiring near Chicago, anyway, and that Fort Sheridan might be my last army assignment.

My new assignment was chief of the special actions branch. Although the title sounded exotic, it was nothing more than assigning and processing the investigations of suspect recruiters in the thirteen midwestern states. An additional duty involved processing recruiters who had been relieved and getting them reassigned outside of Recruiting Command.

For headquarters people, Recruiting Command was a good assignment. There was little pressure, and everything could usually be accomplished in an eight-hour day. For the individual NCO recruiter, depending where the assignment was, life could be pure hell. In some places like Iron Mountain, Michigan, virtually the entire high school graduating class would enlist in the armed services. On the other hand, affluent communities such as Highland Park, Illinois, would send almost nobody into the service.

Similar to the successful back-to-back tours for commanders in Seventh Army in Europe, Recruiting Command had a program for lieutenant colonels commanding district recruiting commands (DRC). Each DRC was commanded by a lieutenant colonel who had usually just completed a successful battalion-command tour. Usually, there was one DRC per state, although some populous states had multiple DRCs. MWRRC had fifteen DRCs.

Unlike a battalion command tour, however, a DRC commander could draw on almost unlimited resources. There was plenty of money for advertising, training teams, high-school lists, vehicles, and whatever else was needed to fulfill the recruiting mission. Unlike commanding a typical army unit, recruiting was a sales function, and many military people had little experience and aptitude for it. But since there were ever-present weekly quotas to be met, rules tended to get broken and promises made to applicants that couldn't be met.

Shortly before I arrived at MWRRC, over half of the DRC commanders were relieved on a one-day fly-around by the midwest commander. Within my short tour at MWRRC, I watched three more DRC commanders get relieved. One DRC commander committed suicide, and another DRC commander was killed when his wife committed suicide. The wife sat in her car in the attached garage, with the engine running, eventually killing herself and the rest of the family as the engine fumes crept through the house.

Recruiting duty was hard duty, and the pressure increased

as the chain of command went down. At the individual recruiter level, the pressure could be unbearable. Some recruiters falsified police checks to show no criminal record for an applicant, while other recruiters manufactured phony GED (general education development) certificates to qualify an applicant with a high-school equivalency. Other recruiters falsified test results or provided test questions and answers. Some recruiters joined with recruiters from other states and services in trading applicants back and forth to circumvent application policies.

In one case, two DRC commanders proved ingenious in meeting quotas. At one point, Recruiting Command not only set overall quotas but established quotas by mental category. Applicants could only be enlisted in the top three mental categories (of five), but DRC commanders were faced not with meeting total numbers but a breakdown by category. The commander at DRC Minneapolis could meet his total number with category 1 people, but he couldn't meet his category 2 and 3 quotas. The commander at DRC Miami had the opposite problem: He could meet his total quota, but he couldn't meet the category 1 quota. In good logical fashion, DRC Minneapolis began to send category 1 personnel by bus to Miami to enlist, while DRC Miami sent category 2 and 3 people to Minneapolis for enlistment processing. The taxpayer paid for meals and transportation for months until someone at Recruiting Command realized what was going on and eliminated the category quotas.

But not all recruiters had difficulty meeting their quotas. Many overachieved and were given plaques and medals for their efforts, along with exceptional ratings and promotions. At the time, a good recruiter could stay in recruiting indefinitely if he brought in the numbers.

Some recruiters found the unstructured civilian lifestyle to be too much, and other problems resulted. Some drank too much, some womanized too much. Some took advantage of female applicants. Usually reports of these problems and irregularities made it to the regional recruiting headquarters, and every allegation had to be investigated.

Less than 10 percent of recruiter malpractice investigations ever found the recruiter at fault, which would have caused automatic relief from recruiting duty. But the mere fact of an investigation was usually sufficient to deter future incidents. However, the recruiter who paid to have phony GED certificates typeset and printed was more prone to get caught as he would accrue multiple allegations and would draw attention to his operation.

After a while, I somehow caught the attention of the MWRRC chief of staff and was given a sixty-day detail to be the chief of the accounting branch in the comptroller's office. More amazing at the time was that I had never taken an accounting course in my life and didn't know the difference between a debit and a credit! Colonel Barry explained that the job that I was being given would normally be filled by a GS-11 civilian, but there was nobody else available who could take the job or who wanted it. That should have told me something. Furthermore, I was to supervise fifteen civilian women who had a four-month backlog in their work. It was also intimated that many of the employees were motivated mainly by drawing overtime pay and didn't care to eliminate the backlog.

I explained to Colonel Barry that I was an SF officer and an infantryman, that I could shoot people and break things. I wasn't sure how fifteen civilian women would react to me. My assessment was correct: Most of the women hated me from the first instant. Nevertheless, the job got done, the backlog was cleared, and overtime was virtually eliminated. I won't bore anyone with the details, however.

Before I got to supervise fifteen women, I always thought that women and men were pretty much the same and would react similarly. Perhaps I was an early feminist. After all, women had been around the army since World War II, and many of the uniformed women were better soldiers than the men. But my observations had been from afar and didn't involve civilian women. I found that supervising women was very different. With young men, I could criticize and correct, and they would usually respond immediately. If a young man felt hurt or nursed a grudge, it usually would go away within hours. It was not so with the women of the accounting branch. I'm sure that some of those women still harbor a dislike for me. Any particular woman would have no problem telling me what she perceived my deficiencies to be, but she would not ever treat another woman the same. An example: If woman A thought woman B was playing her radio too loud, she'd tell woman C, who would tell woman B. As with any experience, I found the situation to be educational. I learned to temper my infantry persona in dealing with women.

As a reward for my accounting branch efforts, Colonel Barry made me the headquarters commandant. The job was similar to my earlier job as a brigade headquarters company commander, but this time it was better.

Almost everyone assigned to Recruiting Command, officer and enlisted, was rated at the top of his peer group. Discipline problems were virtually nonexistent, and the NCOs and officers were exceptional people. At the time, Recruiting Command had the right to refuse personnel if they weren't up to standards. In effect, the cream of the crop was being skimmed, and it was all okay as long as the enlistment quotas were being met. This was not always the case. In the days of the draft, recruiting duty was looked upon as a dead-end assignment. After all, the army didn't really need to recruit as it could rely on the draft for manpower. But when the volunteer army (VOLAR) came about, all that changed. The army had to compete to attract enlistees, and the competition was fierce. The result was that Recruiting Command had almost a blank check. As a result, my job was simple. If someone in MWRRC wanted a piece of equipment that wasn't available in the army supply system, I could just go buy it. We still had to abide by the pro forma rules that the army perpetuated, but a way around the rules could always be found. One such rule said that a person could have a typewriter if more than 50 percent of his/her activity involved typing; on the other hand, that person could not have an adding machine/calculator because the same more than 50 percent rule applied. Ways were found, and some people had both typewriters and calculators.

Any problems that MWRRC had usually came from the Fort Sheridan garrison. It was to be expected that Fort Sheridan envied the resources allocated to us, but they didn't have to like it. They got even by dragging their feet on supply requests, not transferring problem recruiters out, and in myriad other ways. But we were still in the army and had to accept some difficulty.

In mid-1976 I learned that I was on the major's list and could expect to make major in the late spring of 1977. That would incur a two-year service obligation into 1979. I figured that I couldn't retire until early 1979 anyway, so the promotion would help my final retirement pay level, and I'd have twenty plus years when I retired. Then in the early part of 1977, while still waiting to make major, the 1977–78 Command and General Staff College (CGSC) list was announced, and I was on it. I had a problem.

CGSC was a good, career-enhancing step. After CGSC, I could go on to lieutenant colonel and colonel and get better assignments and jobs. But I still doubted that I wanted to stay in much beyond twenty years. Every additional year that I stayed in the army made me that much less employable as a civilian. Besides, the army wasn't that much fun anymore. Infantry branch wouldn't let me go back to SF, but SF would be the only reason that I might hang around. SF, however, had fallen on hard times. Special Forces was a shell of what it had been and was withering away. Nobody seemed to care anymore about SF, and still-promotable people were being warned to stay away from it.

After considering everything, I decided to go to CGSC. CGSC would give me a two-year service obligation, but my service obligations would overlap and the longest one would pertain. So I'd have to serve until 1980 before I could retire. Besides, I knew that if I didn't accept CGSC, the army just might assign me to Korea to finish out my time. The army could be petty if it wanted to be.

In June 1977, I made major and left for Fort Leavenworth, Kansas, the following month. Fort Leavenworth is an old frontier post, originally built in the nineteenth century. It is situated on the Kansas side of the Missouri River, across from Missouri. It is best known as the home of CGSC and the military prison. CGSC proved to be the best instruction that I've ever had, military or civilian. The instruction was at the graduate school level and aimed at developing officers for division-level staff or higher. Nobody could expect command of a battalion or higher level unit without getting the CGSC ticket punched.

The curriculum at the time was centered around defeating the Warsaw Pact in Europe, with emphasis again on defending the Fulda Gap. Once again I was told that the Fulda River was a barrier to an invading Soviet combined-arms army. Since I had seen Germans driving tractors across the eighteen-inch-deep creek, I didn't really consider it a barrier; but I still knew enough not to oppose the school solution. Don Quixote might tilt at windmills; George Dooley doesn't.

Every year approximately one thousand U.S. and allied officers attended CGSC. Unlike other military schools I had attended, there were officers there from every branch and service. The world view was expanded, and almost every course taught was fascinating. The best and the brightest were being taught by exceptional teachers, and the course content was exceptional. The navy taught about sea-lane choke points, while the logisticians described the difficulties in fighting a war in a theater without adequate harbors.

Instruction at CGSC is centered around the section. Each section is broken down into four twelve-person work groups. Each work group is broken down into six two-man tables, with tablemates being of different branches or allied officers. My first tablemate was Bjarne Hesselberg from Denmark. Obviously, Bjarne's view of Europe and the world was different from mine, but the divergent viewpoints brought a better insight into current military affairs.

In addition to the core curriculum centered around defending Europe and the Middle East, there were electives. I took additional courses to supplement my secondary specialty of operations and force development, and learned more about the military budget-planning process than I ever cared to know. As with any organization, the higher level decisions center around money and other assets.

One day, the Infantry School commander visited with the infantry majors attending CGSC. He briefed about the need to coordinate infantry indirect fires with the firepower of the artillery and air force and navy. The problem was being addressed with the formation of FIST (fire integrated support teams) units to be assigned to infantry companies and battalions. He went on to talk about the composition of the teams and how many of the personnel spaces would be artillery and how many were infantry. When one of the students asked why the ratios of infantry to artillery spaces were important, the major general grew angry. From his viewpoint, a FIST team wasn't an army issue, but an infantry vs. artillery manpower issue. I wasn't the person to raise the issue, but I still had doubts as to why the branches and services had to be so parochial. So much for force development; I doubted that I wanted to fight staff battles on branch representation in units.

ORSA (operations research systems analysis) was a force development elective that I enjoyed. Using statistical methods such as linear programming and queuing theory, we learned to optimize various solutions. But since those methods require extensive mathematical calculation, we were also taught how to program for a mainframe computer. It was interesting to watch my engineer branch classmates solve a problem in half the time that my fellow infantrymen took. But we each had different goals and backgrounds.

Like the Advanced Course, CGSC devoted very little time to special operations or Special Forces. More time was devoted to nuclear submarines than to SF. SF was still a stepchild to the army.

Students at CGSC reacted to the course in various ways. On the first day of class, the commandant of the school said that we could sit back and enjoy the course or we could be fiercely competitive and make the course a steppingstone to general officer stars. He went on to explain that even the person who graduated first had no guarantee of becoming a general officer.

I was one of those who saw no future for me in the army, so I decided to enjoy the course. I probably studied less than two hours per day. Instead, I ran, four or five miles per day, and enjoyed a lot of Coors beer. On the other hand, I had classmates who wished to follow in the footsteps of Dwight Eisenhower (who graduated first in his CGSC class). Those classmates worked hard at the course. One of them was Bill Nash, a USMA graduate and armor officer and aviator. Bill was in my work group, and he took the course very seriously. The last I saw of Bill was when I saw him on television as a major general leading a division into Bosnia. I guess that everything boils down to what a person really wants to do. At the time, I wanted to go back to Fort Sheridan and, eventually, retire.

Halfway through the course, we were visited by our branch representatives. For once in the army, Infantry branch did something positive for me. I was given an assignment back to Fort Sheridan, that time to the garrison.

During the 1977–78 time frame, the Soviet Union was still formidable, and the Cold War was still going on. There were proxy wars going on in Somalia, with various powers arming various tribes, along with the other regional conflicts in Africa. There were also hopeful signs that the Cold War might be easing, but we didn't know it at the time.

The Soviet Union sent a military delegation to visit Leavenworth and speak to the CGSC class. A pair of Soviet general officers along with interpreters briefed on the Vistula River campaign, which was the final campaign of the Soviet Union in World War II and ended with the fall of Berlin in 1945. What they didn't brief on was the Warsaw, Poland, uprising and how the Soviets waited along the Vistula while the Nazis defeated the uprising; nor did they brief on the rape of Berlin. The student body was warned ahead of time about what topics were taboo during the question-and-answer period after the presentation. So we all watched and learned how Marxist-Leninist principles triumphed with the Soviet army defeating the Germans. The political rhetoric was enough to gag a maggot.

More important, the visit by the Soviets to Leavenworth was a first tentative step that eventually resulted in the collapse of the Soviet Union. But one more scenario had to develop first. There had to be a Soviet-backed coup in Afghanistan.

Two of the allied officers at CGSC were from Afghanistan. Both were friendly sorts, and they joined the festivities at the officers' club. We exchanged views on each other's countries and talked about military things, the Warsaw Pact and NATO. One of the Afghans pointed out that his country wanted to stay neutral in the United States–Soviet Cold War. In fact, as part of that strategy, the Afghan had attended the Advanced Course in the Soviet Union.

We were all amazed when the Soviet-sponsored coup occurred in April 1978. I was further befuddled when Soviet tanks rolled into the country in December 1979. The two allied officers from Afghanistan were both concerned about their families back home. They obviously were part of the prior establishment and had cause to worry. One had an uncle who was in charge of the defense of the capital city Kabul and who was executed very early in the revolution.

Nobody guessed at the time that Afghanistan would prove to be the Soviet Union's Vietnam. But of course, the United States helped the counterrevolutionary Afghans to defeat the Soviet Union, just as the Soviet Union had assisted the North Vietnamese. As one of the ironies of the Cold War, the 5th Special Forces Group helped train the Afghan guerrillas who opposed the Soviets. The CIA introduced the Afghans first to the Soviet SA-7 and later the Stinger antiaircraft missiles, which ultimately led to the demise of the Soviets. But all that happened much later.

As with the Advanced Course, CGSC brought guest speakers in weekly. We normally had the various service chiefs and the theater commanders from around the world. But we also had generals Westmoreland and Haig come to speak. It was fascinating to get the perspectives of people involved in national affairs. General Westmoreland was a special case, however. He had been my first division commander when I entered the army and joined the 101st in 1959. There was no doubt that he was intelligent and a dynamic leader. He later commanded the XVIII Airborne Corps at Fort Bragg and also commanded USMA (U.S. Military Academy) at West Point. After West Point, General Westmoreland went on to become the MACV (Military Assistance Command, Vietnam) commander. His last assignment was as the U.S. Army chief of staff.

To the Airborne forces of the army, Westmoreland was becoming a legend. Although he didn't command an Airborne unit in World War II, he did command the 187th ARCT (Airborne regimental combat team), the only Airborne unit in the Korean War. Almost every Airborne soldier in the army loved him. I'm probably the one exception.

As smart as he was, I believe that General Westmoreland reached his Peter Principle level of incompetence during Vietnam. If that wasn't the case, then the war just wasn't winnable with the constraints placed upon him. Regardless, he was the man in charge and must take the blame. During the active U.S. participation in the war (1965–73), we spent nine years fighting a war without a strategic goal other than winning. Considering that World War II lasted less than 3½ years for the United States, and the Civil War lasted less than 4½ years, it ought to be understandable why the American people became disenchanted with the war. It wasn't the peace demonstrations that caused the disaffection, it was the lack of definite progress.

In 1977–78 at CGSC, extremely little mention was made of the war that had shaped the lives and careers of the students and faculty. It was as if we knew that we had fought it wrong, and we were mentally rejecting the experience.

Hundreds of books and articles have since been written about our efforts to cut the Ho Chi Minh trail through Laos and Cambodia. But totally neglected is the fact that the Ho

Chi Minh trail would have been useless if there were no supplies or manpower to move south down that trail. If the strategic bombing had been aimed at Hanoi, Haiphong, and the supply lines leading into North Vietnam, Ho Chi Minh would have been confronted with the decision to return to the jungle and fight a guerrilla war or sue for peace to keep what he had.

By allowing the Marines to fight their own version of the war in I Corps, 25 percent of the country was lost early. Later, the joint command superimposed the XXIV Corps onto the I Corps structure, but by that time it was too late. The NVA were romping throughout I Corps, the SF border camps were all gone, and access to the Ho Chi Minh trail was limited. Westmoreland allowed General Walt to set the stage for losing Vietnam to the Communists.

In June 1978, I graduated CGSC and returned home to northern Illinois for my last army assignment.

CHAPTER 12

Fort Shakey by the Lakey

After having been in Recruiting Command at Fort Sheridan, returning to the garrison side of the post was a culture shock. The majority of the senior leadership and staff positions were occupied by civilian employees, none of whom had a college degree or any sort of training to prepare them for their positions, folks who bragged that the military types came and went, while they always stayed and advanced. At least three of them claimed to be the unofficial post commander because they were the real powers on the post. Of the seven hundred plus civilian employees working for the garrison, considerably less than 5 percent had college degrees.

Most of the high-ranking civilians on Fort Sheridan had started out as clerks at the post after World War II and had risen through the ranks. Unlike the military system, however, among the civilians there was no incentive to broaden their knowledge or experience. So they rose to positions in which they were ill-prepared to deal with changing times and situations. The military staff and commanders weren't much better. One primary staff officer was a lieutenant colonel who, on ROTC duty one time in Wisconsin, got drunk and had a shoot-out with the local police. With a shotgun, the lieutenant colonel shot up three squad cars and threatened to kill a bunch of police officers. When he was eventually captured, the secretary of the army intervened, and the officer was sent to Fort Sheridan. However, every weekend he had to go back to Wisconsin to serve the weekend in jail; he had his own private work-prison program.

Since the felonious lieutenant colonel was a USMA

graduate, he was allowed to stay on active duty contrary to all existing policies and regulations. Of course, everyone knew about his exploits and wondered why there were separate rules for enlisted, officers, and USMA officers. Many of the other senior officers and commanders viewed Fort Sheridan as a retirement home for officers who were ROAD (retired on active duty). I once listened to a conversation between three passed-over lieutenant colonels, one of whom was the deputy post commander, as they bragged that they were professionals rather than acknowledging that they were has-beens. Of course, they were rationalizing their continued existence in the army. But then the army must have felt that it needed them for some reason. I only knew that I didn't want to become one of them.

Combining ROAD officers and incompetent civilians produced an organization whose watchword was don't rock the boat. It was no surprise that they referred to Fort Sheridan as Fort Shakey by the Lakey. It was a real life counterpart to Camp Swampy in the Beetle Bailey comic strip. After watching good officers being RIFd in the early seventies, I couldn't understand how the army had sunk to such depths to retain mediocre officers while letting good ones go. This was the situation in the unit to which I was now assigned.

Because of my secondary specialty, operations and force development, I was assigned as the director of plans, training, and security (DPTSEC) which was equivalent to a unit S-2/3. I was in a lieutenant colonel position, but I didn't much care. I was the newest kid on the block, and I didn't like what I saw. Perhaps because I had been in too many good units in the army I didn't like being in a bad unit.

I began to wonder if there was a human counterpart to Gresham's law. Thomas Gresham was a nineteenth-century economist who observed that bad coinage will drive out good coinage. An example was when the U.S. mint began coining clad-copper coins, the new coins rapidly drove the older silver coins out of existence. My concern was that with such a preponderance of mediocre senior officers, that good junior officers would flee. If I ever doubted whether I should retire, the Fort Sheridan garrison convinced me that the army had changed to the point where I didn't belong anymore. I knew that I'd put in the two years required by my attendance at CGSC and get out.

To be fair, it should be recognized that 1978 was the midpoint of the Carter administration and that President Jimmy Carter had done his fair share to screw up the military. It was a period when aviators couldn't fly and vehicles couldn't move because of fuel restrictions, and the "hollow army" was in full bloom. President Carter did more to hurt the military than the Soviet Union ever did. As I recall at the time, to send a lieutenant colonel (O-5) for assignment to Europe, five lieutenant colonels had to be called. The rate of inflation and hardship was such that four O-5s would opt to retire rather than take what was previously a good assignment, particularly for a field-grade officer.

As the DPTSEC, I was responsible for the training of the military units assigned to the garrison, training support for the reserve components within a five-state area, contingency planning, and a few other odds and ends.

Unit and individual training at Fort Sheridan took a backseat to doing the post garrison job. I couldn't argue with that. Doing the job had to come first, but without continual training, soldiers became less competitive and therefore less promotable. An assignment to the Fort Sheridan garrison could and actually did hurt a soldier's career. I had a continual running argument with the post finance officer: He viewed training as a waste of his time that cut into paying bills and providing temporary payments to visiting soldiers and other financial duties. Obviously, someone with my point of view was a detriment to his mission. On the other hand, my view was that in peacetime, soldiers prepare for war. I was still hard charging and should have known better.

I knew immediately that the strong point of the DPTSEC operation was the installation's training and audiovisual support office (TASO). I had previous dealings with the TASO before and was glad to inherit a good operational function.

Francis Axford was the head of TASO. He was a combat veteran of World War II, Korea, and Vietnam. He knew about training and how to enhance it. Better yet, he really cared about his job. Unlike many other employees at Fort Sheridan, Axford actually wanted to help and assist.

When I was the headquarters commandant at Midwest Region in Recruiting Command, I had gone to see Francis Axford about a recent policy decision made by the Department of the Army, concerning audiovisual devices. Without consulting anyone, DA had made it a policy that all audiovisual equipment had to be serviced by the local TASO. What that meant to the local recruiter in West Union, Iowa, was that broken equipment might have to be transported hundreds of miles away for repair, when it could be just as easily repaired locally.

When I explained the position the Recruiting Command was in to Francis Axford, he gave us a blanket waiver to have our equipment repaired elsewhere, instead of at his TASO. Another TASO would have looked on the policy change as a way to draw increased manpower spaces and money to support the Recruiting Command equipment pool. To his credit, Axford cared more about making the overall mission work instead of feathering his own nest. Francis Axford still remains a friend of mine.

Another good area was the planning function. We could and did prepare good plans when it came to real world problems, such as moving units overseas, receiving dependents back from a potential war zone, or augmenting the postal system if it ever went on strike. Unfortunately, the commander at Forces Command in Atlanta, Georgia, lived more in the past than most senior commanders. Instead of wanting to plan for and fight the last war, that four-star general wanted to revert to World War II and fight that war, particularly the mobilization aspect.

So in keeping with the wishes of the Forces Command commander, we all prepared mobilization plans to fight the next war, which would probably be in Europe. Thousands of man-hours were spent in planning to receive reserve component units, equipping them, training them, certifying them as ready, and preparing to ship them off to war. All of that was done in the days of the intercontinental ballistic missile (ICBM) that could reach us from the USSR in about thirty minutes.

When people pointed out that mobilization planning in the nuclear age was rather unrealistic and that the USSR would be stupid to allow the United States to take two years to mobilize and fight a war, the comments were brushed off. The general said that mobilization was the hottest thing that Forces Command could do, and that's what we were going to do. Since other commands outside Forces Command didn't share our commander's same concerns, the planning became downright silly.

Materiel Command was responsible for the logistical supply of the army, and they laughed at Forces Command and mobilization planning. Yet so intent was Forces Command on mobilization planning, that the Forces Command inspector general (IG) demanded that we know where our earmarked tentage was in Material Command, including depot, building number, and shelf or bin number. As usual in the army, when confronted with an impossible situation, we went through the motions and sent messages, letters, and requests, not really expecting an answer. And we never did get any replies.

But the foolish exercise of mobilization planning for Fort Sheridan didn't end there. Forces Command also made Fort Sheridan responsible for mobilization planning for Camp Grayling, Michigan. Normally, that would have been the responsibility of Army Readiness and Mobilization Region V (ARMR V), a two-star general-officer headquarters assigned to Fort Sheridan as a tenant unit. After all, mobilization was part of their name. But ARMR V either didn't know how to write a mobilization plan for an installation or didn't care to. Instead, they tasked Fort Sheridan with the responsibility, while they retained the option to review and criticize. After all, what are higher headquarters for?

Complicating the mobilization planning function for Camp

Grayling was that Camp Grayling was a Michigan National Guard installation that technically didn't belong to the active army. A National Guardsman has no difficulty telling the active army that he works for his state governor and doesn't take orders from the army until the national guard is federalized and called to active duty. Another ingredient in the soup was that Camp Grayling came under the auspices of ARMR VI at Fort Knox, Kentucky.

If the situation sounds complicated, it was. It was a foregone conclusion that nobody would be pleased with any scenario that we developed. I was fortunate, however, that Capt. Andrew Brantley worked for me as the installation plans officer. Drew Brantley was a VMI graduate, Airborne, and a Ranger. Difficult and near impossible tasks were not alien to him.

After many visits and calls to Grayling, we were left with one basic fact: The National Guard at Camp Grayling did not care to participate in mobilization planning for their installation. It was politely explained to them that then we would have no other choice but to designate some other army reserve unit as the command and control element to assume control of Grayling after mobilization. The guardsmen were adamant: They wouldn't play in the mobilization planning game.

Many months went by, and the mobilization plan for Grayling was completed, staffed, and published. Of course, nobody was happy. The interests of ARMR VI were not those of ARMR V; and the Grayling guardsmen refused to cooperate with the reserve unit designated to run the post. The only unifying theme that everyone could agree on was that they all hated the Fort Sheridan DPTSEC people involved in the plan.

There were lighter moments in the planning process, however. Once, I received a call from a rather pompous colonel from ARMR VI at Fort Knox. "What's the status of the Camp Grayling mobilization plan," he asked. On the spur of the moment, I replied: "Sir, it's in dynamic limbo." Dynamic limbo became a catchphrase, used throughout DPTSEC for months thereafter. Of course, the colonel at Fort Knox wasn't going to admit that he didn't know what dynamic limbo meant. After all, he was an all-knowing colonel, and I was a dumb major, so he had to know what it meant. He didn't ask, and I didn't explain.

Planning aside, there were other aspects to the job that made me wonder about the future of the army and my role in it. I was sure that after Vietnam, the army was drifting and wasn't entirely sure of itself anymore. I saw that with Mary Ellen Sonntag, the museum curator at Fort Sheridan when I arrived. Ostensibly, a sweet, smiling dowager, Mrs. Sonntag had run the post museum for a number of years. She had some eccentricities, to be sure, and she was personable although strong willed. For the most part, Mrs. Sonntag was left alone to run the museum. Things changed beginning with my DPTSEC predecessor, Maj. Roy Carlton.

Roy Carlton began to doubt Mary Ellen Sonntag's competence in running the museum. The more he looked and dug, the more he found wrong. By the time that I arrived as his replacement, there was a large suspicion that the post museum was a major problem. Numerous entities evaluated the museum and the curator. What was found was that the collection had never been recorded, so we didn't know what we had. Additionally, we found that we were operating outside the governing regulations for a military museum. There was a real problem with the museum and curator.

In typical fashion in dealing with an army civilian employee, help was offered. Mrs. Sonntag declined any assistance. So pressure was stepped up, and Mrs. Sonntag was warned that if she didn't shape up, we'd have to take action to fire her. That didn't daunt Mary Ellen. She convinced a lawyer to take her case for free and ride interference for her.

The civilian personnel officer (CPO) wavered on a daily basis as to whether we had a case against Mary Ellen. In reality, he didn't want the Sonntag affair to interfere with his pending retirement. The army lawyer advising CPO stated flatly that there was no cause to fire Mary Ellen. I stated, "Well, if that's the case, then we should just back off and forget it. There isn't any reason to fight a battle that we can't win." That attitude drove everyone bonkers. After all, everyone knew that we had a problem with the museum and the curator. But if we couldn't fix the museum problem because of the curator, what were we to do? In the do-nothing era of Fort Sheridan, the CPO and his legal adviser couldn't be challenged. We had a real quandary going. I offered to ask other installations for advice on the situation, but the deputy commander told me that we didn't wash our dirty linen in public. I tried to explain that we were beyond dirty linen and that if Mrs. Sonntag couldn't be fired, then the CPO and his legal adviser were correct, and we should back off and say the problem didn't exist.

But the lawyer advising CPO had an agenda of his own. He wanted to get rid of his army uniform and practice law in New York City. The Sonntag issue was backing him into a corner, and he didn't like it. So a consensus opinion was arrived at: Close the museum, and Mary Ellen Sonntag would be forced to retire at her GS-11 grade. I argued against this.

My position was that I was taking heat from the Forces Command IG because Mary Ellen was still employed and not out on the street. Besides, she had lied to me and others repeatedly about B.A. and M.A. degrees that she didn't have and what she was doing to improve the situation. I was overruled, and the decision was made to close the museum. That's when Mary Ellen filed a suit against me in federal court in Chicago. Case 79C 2876 and subsequent rulings are now a matter of public record, so there's no reason not to discuss them.

When Mary Ellen filed a federal lawsuit, the world changed. I became a pariah, particularly to the post commander and his deputy who had both been advising me on a daily basis. Now, the best advice from the post commander was: "They can't take your house." Later, his replacement as post commander told me that I must have screwed up the Mary Ellen Sonntag thing from start to finish. That from a certified drunk with megalomaniac tendencies who described the world in transactional analysis terms, as I'm okay, and you're not okay. Ah, I loved being in the supportive environment of my fellow officers. I knew then that I didn't want to go to war with any of those guys; they were bureaucratic wimps, and I was still a soldier. I figured, screw it; I was used to fighting in enemy territory, and those guys were all legs who couldn't hack it in the real army.

After the Sonntag lawsuit was received and a federal marshal formally served it to me, the CPO legal adviser came to me and begged me to accept him as my representative in the case. He explained that he knew more about all the particulars of the Sonntag matter than any other legal officer on post, and that it was to my benefit to use him in my defense. I knew that I had the right to other army representation, but I figured that the lawyer with the most knowledge of the matter would help. I reasoned that even if he was going to try to clean up his own responsibility to do the right thing originally, he couldn't hurt me or change the facts. Obviously, I wasn't very good at legal matters.

About a month after I received the lawsuit, I received a letter from TJAG (the judge advocate general of the army) office in DA. Enclosed was a waiver that I had to sign before the army would agree to represent me before handing the matter over to the U.S. attorney. The waiver said in part that I agreed to accept responsibility for penalties, awards, and damages if the government lost the case. I crossed out what I didn't like in the waiver (to include personal responsibility) and sent it back. TJAG called and told me that I was on my own if I didn't sign the waiver as written; I backed down and signed. With hindsight, I wish that I would have gone with my instincts. I'm sure the army would have been ordered to represent me without me signing the waiver.

Eventually, the Sonntag issue went from the hands of the army into the control of the U.S. attorney's office in Chicago. Along the way, Sonntag retired, and the army washed its hands of me and my fellow defendants. The Forces Command IG refused to release its documentation about the sorry state of the Fort Sheridan museum because these findings were only "opinions." The army lawyer who represented me in the Sonntag matter told me that his job wasn't to represent me, but to represent the army. I had fallen into a snake pit.

The Sonntag case was thrown out after a year or so, because other remedies were available. Sonntag's free lawyer appealed, and the case was reinstated. Later, in Bush v. Lucas, 462 U.S. 367 (1983), the Supreme Court ruled in a similar case to the one that Mary Ellen had filed. Justice Thurgood Marshall in a concurring opinion cited Sonntag v. Dooley, 650 F. 2d 904, 907 (CA7 1981). What this means to nonlegal scholars is that Thurgood Marshall cited a case that had never been tried! I couldn't believe that a Supreme Court justice could be so stupid, but I now know that stupidity is an everyday occurrence.

For years after I retired from the army, the assistant U.S. attorney would call me every six months and tell me that Sonntag's attorney would be willing to settle for a token payment. I'd reply that the army hadn't made me buy my ammunition in Vietnam, so why should I pay now for something the army told me to do?

When the Sonntag matter finally came to be tried, Judge Milton Shadur was stuck with making the case go forward. After all, a Supreme Court justice had cited an untried case and one couldn't correct someone like that by dismissing the matter. After three weeks and hundreds of thousands of dollars, Mary Ellen Sonntag's allegations were dismissed. I was held liable for five thousand dollars, but Sonntag's free lawyer agreed to waive the money if I agreed not to appeal. I jumped at the opportunity. I wasn't about to expose myself any longer as the army's point man. I knew that I had had to do some harsh things to Mary Ellen, at the direction of the post commander and some of his advisers. During the trial, the army had offered to settle the matter with Mrs. Sonntag for some sum less than one hundred thousand dollars. Mary Ellen refused; she said she was going "for the big bucks." Poor Mary Ellen; I always questioned her judgment.

The best part of the trial for me was when the CPO representative who had handled the Sonntag matter admitted that there was ample evidence to have terminated Mary Ellen Sonntag's employment previously. There was no explanation why this never occurred.

Because of the Sonntag matter, my remaining time in the army was under a cloud. I applied to retire as soon as my CGSC two-year commitment was met.

By 1980, I had prepared myself for civilian life. I had gone to school (more studying at nights and on weekends) while at Fort Sheridan and had gotten an M.A. in management. I was ready to leave my green suit behind! I didn't much like the army anymore, and I reasoned that with my attitude, the army and I were both better off if I left.

I began to do job interviews. I had a promising job lined up at the University of Chicago when the army told me that I couldn't retire. Interestingly, the deputy post commander, who had been a perpetual thorn in my side, asked me if I would recommend him to replace me in this civilian job. Yeah, sure, when hell freezes over.

Department of the Army contrived to connect my CGSC two-year service obligation with my three-year service obligation for going to Columbus College. In effect, DA said $3 + 2 = 4$, even though our own regulations say that we can't make you serve beyond a four-year total obligation. I pointed out that my personnel records at Fort Sheridan said that my service obligation ended in 1980, but DA didn't care. Instead, DA told the Fort Sheridan personnel officer to change my records to reflect a different retirement eligibility date. My retirement refusals would be signed by a lieutenant colonel or colonel.

I figured, okay, I'll give the army an honorable and easy way out. I created a "most important" job opportunity and again applied for retirement. Again, the army refused. I wondered why the army would want to retain an obviously dissatisfied officer? Did the army think that I was proarmy at that point in my life? Finally, I said to hell with it.

I applied for correction of my military records to the administrative board in Washington that has to review those things prior to filing a federal court action. I can't imagine that the army didn't see that I wanted out by then in the very worst way. Still, the army ignored me. In effect, I was told, you'll be let go when we want to let you go. In my writings to the army, I explained that slavery wasn't legal anymore, that I wasn't a draftee looking for a way out, but that I had served a full career and wanted out. The army said no.

Ironically, although I didn't know it at the time, Judge Shadur was the person who ruled in my favor and told the army to let me retire. When my retirement orders were FAXd in from DA, they were signed by a major. The unofficial rule is that you don't attach your name to a losing battle. The senior officers who had refused my earlier retirement requests had all vanished.

During this fight for my retirement, I always kept in mind that I was dealing with noncombat officers. These were people who wouldn't go to the woods and shoot people, but preferred an easier life. That was okay, as far as I was concerned, I just wanted out. The army's response to my lawsuit for release was classical staff officer thinking: How dare Major Dooley challenge the position and authority of the secretary of the army? Easy, just let me go.

While my retirement lawsuit was pending, an NCO from the DA staff called and told me that DA couldn't reply to my suit because my records were before the lieutenant colonel selection board. I told the sergeant that his problem was easy to solve: go to the lieutenant colonel selection board and ask for my records back. Even if I was selected for lieutenant colonel the next day, I would not stay in. The NCO accepted my response. The key here is that an officer on the staff didn't call me. I suspect that one of the adjutant general types made the NCO call me instead of calling me himself. Yeah, officers in my army didn't have balls anymore. Keeping from getting tainted and covering your ass was becoming important.

So I left Fort Sheridan and the army that I had entered twenty-three years earlier. I had fun and enjoyed myself along the way. I lost friends also and shed some of my own blood. But I felt like a dinosaur in the army of the eighties. I was an

SF type who didn't fit in anymore. I recognized that; why couldn't the army?

Along the way, my life was changing. After years of low-key disagreement with my wife, I knew my marriage was over. I was concerned about my children, but I watched as my spouse criticized me to them. I recognized that was a no-win situation. To fight meant I had to respond and tear her down and make the children choose sides. That wasn't for me, and I refused to give battle. I moved out of the house, hoping that space and time would help. That didn't happen. A supposed lifelong friend advised my wife to hire a lawyer. My "friend" killed any chances at reconciliation. One doesn't need friends like that, so I dropped the friend along with the wife. Okay, Buddha must have willed it. Perhaps that was my destiny.

When I first went in the army, I had bought into the idea that I was married to the army and that the army had to come before family. I didn't know that the army would prove to be a faithless spouse. I accepted that, however; the army had changed, and I didn't want to change along with the army. There was still a real army out there in the SF groups and the Airborne units. But I wasn't in the real army anymore. Unlike a lot of others, I was very glad to leave the army.

CHAPTER 13

Free At Last!

Retiring from the army meant freedom for me. For too long, I had met people who expected respect because of their rank. After all, in their minds, rank equated with intelligence. But I had grown up in a system in SF where respect was earned. To hell with your rank. If you didn't do as good as I in the bushes, respect lagged.

Shortly before I retired, I was having a beer after work at the post officers' club when a lieutenant colonel joined me on my left side. He had looked at my right shoulder patch, which was the combat patch of SF (combat unit patches are worn on the right shoulder) and announced: "Special Forces, don't show me shit!"

"Okay. I can understand that," I replied.

"Yeah, Special Forces are overrated and can't do anything that other units can do."

"Okay. I can understand that," I replied again.

"Yeah, Special Forces think that they're hot shit, but I'm not impressed," said the lieutenant colonel.

"Sorry you feel that way," I said.

He went on: "You fuckin' people think you're good, but you're not."

"Okay, maybe you're right. So what?" I asked.

"Well, Special Forces doesn't impress me at all!"

I realized that I had a belligerent drunk on my hands and thought that I could reason with him. "Sir, look at the rest of the bar. Could you form an A-team from this group of people?"

"Of course I could, Major!"

"Okay sir, who would be the commo sergeants? Who would be the demo sergeants? Who would be the weapons sergeants? Who could possibly attempt to be the medical NCOs? Then we have to choose two operations and intelligence sergeants, along with a pair of officers that can hopefully control these superachieving guys."

Rationality went out the window. "Well, I can't do that with this group of people," replied the lieutenant colonel. "But in my control group, back home, Special Forces doesn't show me shit!"

The mention of a control group showed that the lieutenant colonel was a reservist. Okay, all restraints went off. "Do you mean that you're not a real lieutenant colonel and that you're screwing with me?" I replied.

The conversation went downhill from there, but it illustrates how many felt at the time about Special Forces. The hard jobs were always given to SF, and SF always wanted those hard jobs. But at the same time, there was quite often a view of disdain. An A-team commander was viewed as the equivalent of an infantry squad leader because he only commanded eleven other men; no thought was given to the battalion of men that he might actually command or influence with that A-team. The army knew that SF was necessary, but the army didn't have to like it. So SF service was made to be not career enhancing for officer or enlisted. Many SF officers were passed over for promotion and were forced out of the army. The same thing happened with SF NCOs, but they usually were able to retire at twenty years.

Well, I had made the decision to leave the army, so I thought it best not even to think about the army anymore. All that was in the past, or so I thought at the time.

Before I left the army, I figured out over a period of weeks what I wanted to do as a civilian. I knew that I didn't want to work for any form of government as, to my mind, government work tended to stifle personal initiative. Besides, I had a decided bias against government employees because of what I had seen at Fort Sheridan. On the other hand, I had twenty-three years in the largest educational institution in the world.

In peacetime, the armed forces train for war. Additionally, there was always an educational motivation to learn more about the rest of the armed services and potential enemies. The education field seemed to be a natural choice for me, but I knew that I didn't want to be a teacher. I accepted that I no longer had the patience to teach repetitiously. So I had written my resume and hoped to become an educational administrator.

I lucked out in 1983 when I was hired to be the business manager and treasurer at St. John's Military Academy (SJMA) in Delafield, Wisconsin.

Col. Charles Watkins was the president of the school when I was hired. Charlie Watkins was a retired West Pointer who had been an air-defense artilleryman on active duty. The last years of his career had been in various assignments at West Point. At the time, he was running a military academy of his own, albeit for sixth through twelfth graders.

SJMA was founded by an Episcopal priest, "Doctor" Smythe, who had nourished the institution into a large organization that called itself a college-preparatory school. The reality was that no record could be found that Smythe had earned his doctorate or been granted an honorary degree. Another reality was that SJMA was no longer doing such a good job preparing young men for college. But that wasn't to be my concern; my objective was to keep the books for the school and improve the physical plant.

Although I had hated the concept of eyewash in the military, I knew that if something looked good not much else mattered. We concentrated on the maintenance and appearance of the campus, and in a few years, SJMA looked like a prosperous enterprise. Along the way, a bunch of leaky roofs were repaired, and nine tennis courts were built. I had a fun job and was given the opportunity to make things better.

When Charlie Watkins announced that he planned to retire in the summer of 1984, a year-long search was instituted. The faculty were brought into the selection process, and that may have been the ultimate downfall of the successor to Colonel Watkins. But I'm getting ahead of the story.

Retired Brig. Gen. David L. Buckner was eventually hired to become the new president of SJMA. Dave Buckner was hard-core to the bone. He was Airborne, Ranger, Pathfinder, and SF qualified, had commanded a battalion in the 173d Airborne Brigade in Vietnam, and had a back-to-back tour commanding a battalion in the Berlin Brigade in Germany. He later commanded a brigade in the 82d Airborne Division and then went to the Infantry School as head of the Airborne Department. Buckner was the deputy assistant commandant of the Infantry School when he was selected for brigadier general. He was a thoroughly hard-charging individual who wanted things done in the fastest time possible.

Dave Buckner had served in command and staff positions at almost every level in Airborne units. He wasn't very tolerant of mediocre performances. Many said that he was difficult to work for. That was probably true. He wanted SJMA to change almost immediately, but there was resistance. Most forgot that Buckner had also once been a teacher. After serving as an enlisted man in the Korean War, Dave Buckner left the army, obtained a college degree and taught English at the elementary and high-school levels. He had served his time in the classroom and knew what was expected of teachers.

Under his leadership, SJMA was no longer the complacent Wisconsin school with pretentious airs. Most of the students loved him as he was the perfect role model for a young teenager. Yet, many of the faculty disliked him because of his decisive manner and perceived arrogance. Another reason for the faculty to dislike him was that Buckner soon found out that SJMA students were not being taught to grade level and were falling behind on standardized tests.

Dave Buckner and his wife, Ellen, brought an aura of class to the school. They involved themselves in community activities and enhanced the reputation of St. John's. Ellen Buckner was a serious opera singer and enjoyed entertaining. They both began to put St. John's on the road to recovery.

My dealings with Dave Buckner were ideal. I had worked with his type forever in the military and knew what he wanted: absolute excellence. He let me increase the summer camp business and expand the auxiliary enterprises so that we were making much more income from nonacademic sources.

Unfortunately, during that period, the board of trustees was mostly composed of earlier graduates of St. John's, most of whom had not bothered to go on to college after their own graduations and had usually inherited family wealth. When faculty members began complaining to them, they didn't have the breadth of knowledge to realize that heeding those complaints could only undercut General Buckner's position. As Buckner began to get rid of deadwood teachers, the complaints increased, and the trustees didn't know how to respond.

The trustees hired numerous consultants and were dismayed to find out that the consultants couldn't find anything wrong with the way the school was being run. Rather than accept what their own consultants told them, the trustees decided to investigate on their own, and each found what he thought was the problem. Ultimately the board of trustees polarized into factions. The pro-Buckner group couldn't agree with the anti-Buckner group and the chairman of the board wavered between the two.

At one point, the anti-Buckner group of trustees were sending their sons and other graduates onto the campus, asking: "What is really going on at St. John's?" I spoke to a few of the trustees and asked them how they would feel if I went to their place of business and asked the janitor how he felt about the place. They didn't like the analogy, but persisted in their research to find out what "bad" things Dave Buckner was doing.

Eventually, on Veterans Day (November 11), 1987, Dave Buckner was fired, and the school began an immediate decline, although the trustees didn't recognize it. Donations and support fell off, as did recruiting. But the faculty and their supporters won. They had gotten rid of their nemesis. It's ironic that the firing had to occur on such a symbolic day, but it does point to the insensitivity of the board of trustees.

A temporary president was hired, and he allied himself with the anti-Buckner group. He probably thought that by pandering to the revolutionaries that they would support his bid to become permanent president. The temporary president lasted less than three months, and he, too, was gone.

Then, one of the trustees decided to assume the presidency of the school. Of course, since this particular individual didn't have a college degree and was therefore professionally unqualified to run a school, nobody thought to question the decision. Since the new president-trustee had to have perks, his grandson was admitted to the academy, even though he was a truly troubled student. When he broke into his grandfather's house—and mine—his pranks were overlooked, and the boy was not expelled. That didn't enhance discipline among the rest of the students.

I resigned in March 1988, before I became too tainted with what was happening at SJMA. The faculty were in joyous rebellion because they had toppled Buckner, and one previously fired individual was brought back. Observing what went on, I knew what the French Revolution was like. Sadly, it took many years for the trustees to understand what they had done to themselves and fire the people who had led the anti-Buckner revolution.

During my SJMA period, I tried to distance myself from the army and SF. After all, the army set me up for the Sonntag affair and then failed to support me. And since I didn't care much anymore about the army, I didn't know too much about what was going on in SF. I was content receiving my monthly retirement check. Then, one day, I met my first wannabe.

In the late spring on a Sunday afternoon, I was sitting on the front porch of the alumni house at SJMA watching the maintenance crew tear down after that year's graduation. Folding chairs were being stacked, sound systems were being boxed up, and I was thinking that another academic year was over and that I'd have about two weeks to prepare for the coming summer camps. The hostess of the alumni house introduced me to Sergeant Somebody, a former ROTC (Reserve Officer Training Corps) instructor at the school who had left the army and now lived in northern Wisconsin. Sergeant Somebody had returned to watch the graduation.

We conversed and, as usual with former military men, traded bona fides. I said that I was a retired major. Sergeant Somebody told me that he used to be a Green Beret. That rang a gong with me as SF people don't usually call themselves "Green Berets."

I asked, "Where were you at in Group?"

Sergeant Somebody replied, "I was a Special Forces Green Beret." I already knew that the guy was an obvious phony or that SF had changed entirely since I had been there.

"Well, I was in Group, too. I was in the 7th and had two tours with the 5th. Where were you?"

I guess by that time Sergeant Somebody realized that I knew he wasn't telling the truth. He left shortly thereafter. I wondered why somebody would say that they were something that they weren't. I've scuba dived, but wouldn't claim that I was a SEAL. I couldn't figure it out. For years, during Vietnam, SF manpower needs were so acute that we would almost take anything breathing. But we had the highest unit casualties of the war, and that tended to keep people from volunteering.

With the Vietnam War safely over and years past, there were thousands of people passing themselves off as former Green Berets. With one of the brotherhood, the wannabe can usually be exposed in less than a minute. The typical wannabe just doesn't know the vernacular when dealing with a real SF person, but the usual wannabe doesn't normally deal with real SF people. The wannabes of the world save their stories for those who don't know any better.

About this time, I found Ed Sprague again, and he told me about his experiences with wannabes. After leaving the army, Ed said, he met hundreds of people who claimed to have been a Special Forces Green Beret in Vietnam. I wonder where all those guys were when we really needed help?

* * *

During the 1960s and 1970s, I had stayed in touch with Ed Sprague and Roger Knight. But as with all things military, our various assignments drove us apart, and we lost each other. Roger Knight was a lieutenant colonel in Iran (before the Shah was deposed) when I lost him.

One day, my wife, Nina, returned home from teaching at Carroll College in Waukesha. Nina has a Ph.D. in history and spends a lot of time in libraries. She had been browsing through the Waukesha Public Library that day, and she had run across a reference book that purported to be a guide to fraternal and veteran organizations in the United States. She had stumbled across a reference to the Special Forces Association and told me about it. I asked her to get me an address, and I would write to see if I qualified for membership. That was in 1988, and I had never heard of the SF Association. I knew that there was a Decade Club for members of SF, but since I never accrued ten years of SF service, I had never bothered finding out more.

I wrote the Special Forces Association inquiring about membership and also asked if Ed Sprague, my old team sergeant at A-226, was a member. About a week later, I received a membership application for the SFA along with their membership requirements. I found that I was qualified for membership, and written across the top of my original letter was an address for Ed Sprague in New Hampshire. That evening, I wrote the SFA requesting membership and wrote Ed Sprague. Three or four days later, Nina received a phone call that she swears sounded like it was from a foreign person. She said that the caller asked: "Is Ghawege there?" It wasn't until a few more sentences that Nina realized that the caller was asking for George and that it was Ed Sprague. Ed's deep Boston accent had thrown her! Nina has since been able to understand Ed.

When I returned home that evening, Nina gave me a message to call Ed Sprague in New Hampshire. I was finally reunited with my old team sergeant and the person that I now consider my best friend. Eventually, between us, we found most of the original members of A-226 and many of the re-placement members. We had our first reunion in Fayetteville, North Carolina, in 1992, in conjunction with the SFA convention. Many of us have been going to the annual convention ever since.

Aside from reuniting with my old SF buddies, I still wanted to pursue a career in educational administration. I thought that I was taking a big leap when I accepted a job at Northwestern University in early 1989. Ironically, I turned down a facilities administration job in Milwaukee to take the Evanston, Illinois, job. With hindsight, I wasn't too bright.

I was hired to be the director of finance at Norris Center on the Northwestern campus. Norris Center was the student union on campus, along with being the hub for student organizations and some alumni functions. Finally working at the university level perhaps blinded me to the realities that working in an educational setting can be just as treacherous as working anywhere else.

Norris Center was part of the student services division of the university. I used to think that the military was hidebound in its thinking, but I quickly found out that universities can surpass the military in staid thinking.

Homosexuality was not uncommon in the student services division, but I didn't worry about that. After all, I had dealt with homosexuals in the seventies, protecting them from the army rules that would draft a gay man, then give him a bad administrative discharge when the person's orientation was figured out. Although I considered myself a political conservative, I thought that I was enough of a social liberal to tolerate and accept everyone. But in the politically correct (PC) era of the late eighties and early nineties, I found that I still didn't fit in. Some examples are necessary.

Each freshman class had a week-long orientation period. The people presenting the orientation had great difficulty explaining to the new students that if you get on an elevated train in Evanston and ride south into Chicago, there are some stops that are not safe. They even had to explain that it wasn't safe to take the elevated train to the University of Chicago on Chicago's South Side. That the elevated train stops were in predominantly black neighborhoods caused consternation in their PC minds. But I had grown up and lived in a working-class, "bad" neighborhood on Chicago's South Side and knew that attitude was everything. If you acted afraid and like a victim, you'd become a victim; but then, I had the experience of wandering around "bad neighborhoods" in Southeast Asia.

One day, my boss was required to receive training by the women's center because he was perceived as antifemale. So to deflect personal criticism, he went to the training, taking along his primary staff. We all sat around a large table with the two "cadre" from the women's center. As usual with these things, each participant had to introduce himself. I listened around the table as each of my colleagues said how happy he or she was to be at the session and how they looked forward to becoming further enlightened. When the introductions got to me, I said who I was and that I was scared and apprehensive.

"Why do you feel that way, George?" asked one of the discussion coordinators.

"Because you're from the women's center and espouse the dogma of the feminists. And, since one of the authors and leaders of the feminist movement (Susan Brownmiller) says that all men are rapists, I'm scared. I'm a man, but not a rapist, and I think that you may already have a preconceived agenda."

In explaining myself, I won the battle but lost the war. The two women spent the remainder of the hour session apologizing to me. My boss later told me that he was embarrassed by my comments. I didn't understand how he would be embarrassed by my words, since his comments on various women's eye shadow and lipstick colors being wrong caused the self-criticism session in the first place. It was my destiny at Northwestern not to be one of the guys.

It was only a matter of time before I knew I had to quit Northwestern. I had always heard that a university was a center for ideas and thought; but I came to realize that that wasn't the case if the thought was conservative.

One day, I was sitting in as a student financial adviser to the board that funded student activities. The group being considered for funding was called For Members Only (FMO), which was the campus black organization. Now, some people might think that FMO might sound a bit exclusionary and racist, but not people at Northwestern. FMO proposed funding for a series of mailings to accepted black students and presented the literature that they wanted to send. I read the literature and thought it profoundly racist. I asked: "Would you agree to send this literature, if everywhere it said 'black' I substituted 'white' and vice versa? Frankly, I think that this stuff is extremely racist." It hadn't been explained to me that minority blacks couldn't be racist. By the same token, it hadn't been explained to me that mainstream blacks also couldn't be racist. Aw hell, what does a white man know, particularly one who has lived among black, brown, and yellow people for a whole bunch of years?

In October 1992, I quit Northwestern University. Eleven years after I retired from the army, I knew that educational administration wasn't for me. It was time to find out what else I could do.

While at Northwestern, I used to joke (as much as one could joke at Northwestern) that there were only five straight men in Student Services and that I was one of them. Aside from that, however, I also adopted the slogan that: "I ain't racist, sexist, or homophobic; I'm an equal opportunity misanthrope." At Northwestern, being a misanthrope was okay.

Another incident had soured me on academia, years before when my wife Nina was working at Carroll College in Waukesha. At the start of the school year, Carroll College hosted a convocation dinner for the faculty and their spouses. Nina asked me to attend with her. The dinner was held in the school dining facility, and we sat at twelve-person tables. Since we were all strangers to each other, the conversation was tentative. I introduced myself as the business manager at

St. John's and as the husband of Nina. I added that I was a retired army officer.

Two people across the table introduced themselves as geographers, faculty at Carroll. One of them replied that he was a retired military officer also. We traded the usual bona fides and the geographer explained that he was a retired lieutenant colonel from the USAR (army reserve). I responded that I was a retired regular army major and that my branch was infantry, but that my primary qualification was SF. Nina responded to the table, "Yes, my husband is a retired Green Beret."

Immediately, to my side, an individual looked up from his salad and said: "Of course, you must know that I detest everything that you stand for."

I looked at this wormy, scrawny fellow, who I later learned was a French teacher, and said, "I can understand why you might feel that way, but I don't understand."

I was then treated to a short dialogue about people-oppressing militarists and the usual leftist word-trash. Later, I learned that the leftist French teacher was in his fifties, had never married, and lived with his mother. For the rest of the dinner, he regaled us with such un-PC remarks as Africa begins in the south suburbs of Rome!

Academia now seemed strange to me. Most academics appeared to be intelligent (average IQ 119, if we can believe Richard J. Herrnstein and Charles Murray, authors of *The Bell Curve: Intelligence and Class Structure in American Life*), yet so many of them appear to be far outside the mainstream of modern American thinking. I've since concluded that truly intelligent people are not academics. Many academics think that military officers are bloodthirsty warmongers, without realizing that most field-grade officers today have advanced degrees and prefer negotiation to combat. I learned long ago, however, that the world doesn't have to make sense.

Since leaving Northwestern, I've learned the best ploy for me to remain employed in a civilian job is not to worry or care too awfully much. Unlike the army, civilian life doesn't seem to value dedication very much. Also, unlike the army, performance doesn't mean as much as what you say you can do. Back in the bad old days of the military, I used to tell junior people not to tell me what they could do, but show me what they could do. Few ever did.

I've mellowed over the years. But that's good. I don't care to do great things anymore. The people that I most like and respect aren't really civilians either. My attachment to the army is minimal. I don't advertise the fact that I'm a retired officer. When people ask me what I think about their son or daughter joining the military, I tell them to really think about it. The post-Vietnam military is more mercenary and really doesn't care very much about the troops. I advise that, based on my own experiences, flipping hamburgers still probably has more potential for advancement than the army, and it's considerably safer.

Fitting in and being part of the community is a normal thing to want. Never having been a joiner in the past, I've tried to join other organizations, but nothing satisfies very much. I joined the VFW (Veterans of Foreign Wars) and then quit when I realized that they cared more about how much I cared to contribute than my desire for an affinity group. While I would never consider joining the American Legion, it bothered me that the VFW hounded me for money. Writing their development office didn't work, so I finally returned my membership card. Then the local VFW post decided to keep me on as a charity case and pay my dues for me. I guess that they haven't figured out that I really don't care to be a member.

The local Masonic lodge proved to be a correct choice for me. But they, too, want more than I care to give. Brotherhood aside, many in my local lodge often seem more to want to argue among the brethren than to cooperate. Damn, doesn't anyone realize the power of cooperation and teamwork?

I've found my group in the Special Forces Association. These are the folks that I can most identify with. They are what I am. Chapter 73 of the SFA is based mainly in Wisconsin. From its membership, I can identify with people who were in SF from the start, through Vietnam SF vets, to newer Special Forces people who served in the Gulf and Haiti. Jerry Poe served twenty years in Airborne assignments; he understands. Steve Schofield was in Vietnam and Laos; now retired from the army reserves, he works with the local Hmong who have been resettled in Wisconsin. Craig Halpert served with SF in Iraq and Haiti; today he suffers from Gulf War syndrome, and the VA tells him that nothing is wrong. But this is the same VA that said that there was nothing wrong with Agent Orange victims from the Vietnam War.

Life is better now. I've seen and done things that most men haven't. I've enjoyed myself along the way. Looking back, I probably would change very little if I had the chance.

CHAPTER 14

Reflections

As Charles Dickens wrote, "It was the best of times, it was the worst of times." The same could be said for Special Forces in Vietnam. Vietnam was the high point for SF: There were seven active duty Special Forces groups, with many other reserve and National Guard units. Unfortunately, as the power structure in the army came to dislike Special Forces, all of SF fell on hard times throughout the world. Just as OSS was inactivated after World War II, and the same thing happened to the divisional Ranger companies after the Korean War, it was time to make SF go away or at least pare it down to a bare minimum, even though the Vietnam War wasn't yet over. Too bad that success doesn't always win supporters; more often than not in the army, success breeds enemies.

It's doubtful that anyone can point to any specific thing that Special Forces did wrong, even the Rheault affair, to use as a basis for reducing the size of Special Forces. After all, the entire SF program was dramatically successful worldwide. Cuban subversion in Latin America was stemmed, Soviet expansionism was contained, and 5th Group was performing so splendidly in Southeast Asia that the unit set army records for the numbers of Medals of Honor and lesser combat decorations earned. But Special Forces was unfortunately associated with the army that didn't "win" in Vietnam.* And so, by

---

*During the sixties, a lot of SF soldiers and teams referred to Special Forces as USSF (United States Special Forces) rather than USASF (United States Army Special Forces). Undoubtedly, the army was never happy with their grammatical secession.

association, Special Forces had to take part of the blame. Okay, we did some things wrong, and other things could have been done better.

Clemenceau said that war is too important to be left to the generals, and he's probably right. But it's also much too important to be left to politicians and bureaucrats. Throughout the Vietnam War, President Lyndon Johnson tried to use limited war as a form of negotiation. By not bombing Hanoi and Haiphong and the Red River dikes, he thought that he could maneuver Ho Chi Minh into negotiation and a settlement. After all, President Johnson thought that he was behaving rationally and that his adversaries would act the same. It wasn't until President Nixon initiated the Christmas bombing of 1972 (Operation Linebacker II) that the United States got Hanoi's attention, and serious negotiations began for withdrawing the remaining few U.S. forces from the war. But the United States failed much earlier in the war.

Let's consider what happened earlier in the war. At the national level, there was always concern about bringing the USSR and China into the war. The United States wanted to avoid that at all costs. Okay, then let's do a bit of game playing here: What would the Soviets and Chinese have done if we had bombed the Red River dikes and all the bridges into North Vietnam, along with mining Haiphong Harbor? Feeding North Vietnam would have become the paramount problem, not supplying the war. Does anyone think that the Soviet Union and China would escalate to World War III and let the North Vietnamese starve? Besides, the ages old antagonism between the Chinese and North Vietnamese still existed. The two nations have never liked each other, and it's doubtful that Communist China would seriously fight for North Vietnam. There were substantial numbers of Chinese in North Vietnam, and I suspect that the average Vietnamese could not have been happy about it.

Bombing at the source of the problem would have negated the problem with the Ho Chi Minh trail. Sadly, Washington thinks that conflict is a surgical thing that can be administered nicely, neatly, and softly. The folks in Washington have been constantly surprised since Vietnam that war is brutal and that brutal measures at the onset keep total casualties down.

Perhaps based on the model of Korea, we decided to quit fighting wars and to fight small conflicts, or police actions, instead. The phrase that grew out of this, limited war, is an oxymoron. There is no such thing as limited war. You either fight or don't fight. Anything else is a betrayal of the American people who send their sons (and now their daughters) off to war. Going to war without an intent to win is not furthering U.S. policy, and it is never in the best interests of those troops who have to fight that war.

The administration failed to mobilize the reserves and National Guard and use them as we did in Korea. In conjunction, we could have relied less on the draft and thereby avoided much of the protests against the war. But perhaps, the biggest mistake that the government made was not recognizing that a protracted war would not be supported by the American people. The alternative then was to bring the war to North Vietnam and to make that country hurt, and hurt badly. Also, we could have done away with the one-year tour of duty for career soldiers and stayed and fought. That alone would have given an impetus to ending the war. But so far, those factors all relate to actions at the national level. The army in Vietnam also must share some blame.

After Tet 1968, it should have been apparent that the days of the guerrilla war were over; the guerrillas were nearly all dead. USARV failed to concentrate on the destruction of the main force NVA units and allowed conventional U.S. units to continue to be tied down in area pacification roles. Maybe the ARVN units should have had the pacification mission and the U.S. Army the ass-kicking role, assuming of course that the air war was properly taken to the north (and Laos) and that infiltration of supplies and troops could be curtailed.

But we in Special Forces were also not blameless. Our mistakes were legion. One of the major errors, along with the one-year tour of duty and the posh living for B- and C-teams, was the building and manning of Special Forces camps.

The Vietnam Studies book, U.S. Army Special Forces,

1961–1971,* published by the Department of the Army, lists many A-camps with old and new sites. Like Mai Linh replacing Buon Beng in Phu Bon Province (a difference of five miles), the replacement of camps shows a fortress mentality rather than a recognition that an SF camp was an operational patrol base. In unconventional warfare (like the OSS in World War II), the location of the often-changed headquarters site is immaterial; the important location is the operational area.

In reality, what it meant when an SF camp was relocated was that the old camp was abandoned and a new camp had to be built. And that affected combat operations for at least six months. It could be argued, however, that there just weren't enough SF personnel assets to meet all the Vietnam requirements. That argument would be valid, but the solution is plain: extend the tour of duty. Anybody who truly wanted to be in SF would have accepted a longer tour. Besides, when SF was in country, we controlled the terrain, and when SF left, it fell apart rapidly. But the mood of the United States back in the 1960s and 1970s wouldn't have accepted this solution either; not after we had garnered large casualty figures without any end in sight. The NVA dictated the game, made the rules, and the United States played the game by the NVA rules. Coincidentally, at the same time that the United States was building up in Vietnam, the British were fighting and winning a war in Malaysia, along with other lesser wars throughout their old empire. The British fought with professional soldiers and mercenary troops such as the Gurkhas with little public outcry back home. Maybe they figured out something that the United States hadn't.

Partly as a consequence of Vietnam, Special Forces had wrongly gotten an image as a bunch of armed thugs. And, of course, the Rambo movies didn't help either. From seven ac-

---

*A notably inferior reference book, there are mistakes throughout. As only one example, in Map 6 the locations of Mang Buk, Plateau Gi, and Polei Kleng are wrongly depicted or named. That's three errors out of seven camps in Kontum Province. The reference gives new meaning to the term, "close enough for government work."

tive duty groups, SF was reduced to only the 5th, 7th, and 10th Groups in the seventies. Third SF Group closed in December 1969, followed by 6th Group in 1971. Eighth SF Group closed in June 1972, and 1st Group closed in 1974. Fortunately, the army eventually realized that the SF missions still existed, and the 1st and 3d Groups were later reactivated. But the reserve groups didn't fare as well. They were cut constantly and never recouped. The army, however, knew what to do with the SF soldiers that were released from SF duty.

Due to the turmoil of Vietnam, the army had been falling apart in the late sixties and early seventies. Fraggings were common; there were thousands of soldiers who had gone AWOL or deserted, and the U.S. Army was taking on the aspect of a mob rather than a disciplined force. It was logical to take the experienced and professional noncommissioned officers out of Special Forces and put them to work in troop units as platoon sergeants and first sergeants. So the army did what had to be done, and overall, the army got better.

During the sixties and seventies, an SF NCO would quite often call Mrs. Billye Alexander of the SF enlisted assignments branch in Washington to get an SF assignment of his choice. Mrs. Alexander was famous within the enlisted ranks because she really cared about getting SF soldiers proper assignments. As a result, she received a lot of birthday cards, flowers, and gifts. But with the drawdown of SF groups, there were few SF assignments available anymore.

Eventually, the benign neglect of Special Forces showed up. The debacle of Desert One in Iran was a textbook example of how not to employ Special Forces.

When the Iranians took over the American embassy in 1979 in Tehran, the army responded with a hostage rescue effort in 1980 built around SF Operational Detachment DELTA, which was a trained counterterrorist organization. Unfortunately, the field commander, Col. Charlie Beckwith, had to yield to the demands of joint operability, which resulted in untrained navy, air force, and Marine participation in a raid for which they had no training or skills to perform. The raid was aborted when participating aircraft dropped out and other aircraft crashed into each other in a remote Iranian airstrip named Desert One. I watched the operation in Iran in 1980 and truly grieved for my army. We couldn't fight anymore. If the best that the army had couldn't defeat a bunch of Muslim students, or even achieve a base in the desert, we were in trouble. At that point in history, I was ashamed of SF.

Throughout the dark period of the seventies and eighties, Special Forces still had clandestine missions in Lebanon, Central America, and Africa. But even after the resurgence of SF in the eighties, the cloud of suspicion was still strong. During the buildup to Desert Storm in Iraq, General Schwartzkopf, the theater commander, was still reluctant to accept and employ SF. When he did get them, they proved that they had reconnaissance and force multiplier skills that made them invaluable. They chased scud missile launchers throughout Iraq, performed bomb damage assessments (BDAs), did point reconnaissance missions, assisted in finding evading aviators who had been shot down, and all of the numerous things that Special Forces can do within their mission statements.

Yet General Schwartzkopf was reluctant to accept SF into his theater. Schwartzkopf was an old Airborne soldier, but did he really think that the jobs that SF did could be accomplished by squads or platoons out of the 82d? Yeah, and I also believe in the tooth fairy, Santa Claus, and the Easter Bunny.

Sadly, Special Forces were still tainted from the Vietnam experience. Even as Vietnam faded from memory, SF still received ripples of comment as social "progressives" sought to use the armed forces as an instrument of social change. After all, if women can be in the army, then why can't homosexuals? And why can't everyone be eligible for service in elite organizations such as SF? I'm sure that future-looking spokespeople for the disabled will wonder at some point why their clientele can't serve. That isn't meant to criticize anyone. By experience, mentality, and training, SF can do things that other people can't. Why not use those people who volunteer for a hard job, for hard jobs? If that means excluding lesser qualified people, so be it.

* * *

There has recently been a renaissance for Special Forces. With the debacle of Desert One, Congress forced the armed services to form a Joint Special Operations Command. Finally, all the special operations forces of the Department of Defense were unified under one authority. The army followed suit and formed a specified command, the Special Operations Command, which also controls the Ranger units of the army. Subordinate to that command is the Army Special Forces Command. The ultimate improvement was when the army designated SF as a separate branch for noncommissioned officers and officers in 1987. Not even that is a universal solution, and it has resulted in a situation where professional commissioned officers can challenge the team sergeant, the mainstay of the A-team. Additionally, with the advent of warrant-officer executive officers, there is a further challenge to the team sergeant's authority. Not overlooked at Department of the Army level is the fact that SF now has quitters and terminators, just like the old 101st and 82d. To *this* old soldier, that is intolerable. How do you induce the best soldiers in the army to quit? You really have to work at it.

Jim Zachary and I have been in touch over the years. We don't always agree, but we've been friends since 1966 when we were roommates together at A-226, Mai Linh. Those of us at Mai Linh used to think that if any team commander had a chance at general officer, it would be Jim. That was not to be, but it hasn't lessened our respect for him. Zachary either just wasn't enough of a politician or the army plain screwed up.

It was from Jim Zachary, however, that I first heard about the SF branch difficulties with warrant officers. Let's paint a scenario: Captain X is an infantry officer, and he graduates from the infantry officer advanced course and applies for a branch transfer to SF. After evaluation and selection, he becomes an A-team commander. Later, he serves time on the B- or C-team staff. A few years later, he commands another A-team.

Sergeant First Class Y has been the intelligence or weapons sergeant for an A-team for a lot of years. He looks at his future career and sees that the best that he can hope for is to become a sergeant major (E-9) and retire thereafter. But if he applies to become an SF warrant officer, he can stick around for a long time and probably retire as a warrant officer with pay comparable to a major or lieutenant colonel.

Master Sergeant Z has come up through the ranks in SF. He might have been a commo man, medic, weapons, or demo sergeant. But now, he's an SF team sergeant. He knows SF because he's been doing it for the last ten years or so.

Master Sergeant Z and now Warrant Officer Y are almost guaranteed to collide. It's normal to expect Y to challenge Z, because both have been around for a while. Now enters Captain X with his four or five years' experience, and he also thinks that he knows a bit about SF. Now SF has new problems. The team sergeant has always run the team, but he has a warrant officer and captain looking over his shoulder.

None of this is meant to say that creation of SF as a branch is bad. Just as every new solution may create new problems, the SF branch solution still requires work.

Special Forces is finally coming back and being accepted by the army. Supposedly, some in the new branch believe that SF has to be "sold" to the rest of the army. That's like saying that military intelligence or army aviation has to be sold. SF branch is still new and insecure.

Another aspect, however, is the fact that some army commanders realized that they had *in extremis* forces at their disposal. Literally, "in extreme circumstances," the SF units have capabilities that make them field-army assets.

But all is still not rosy. Anna Simons's book *The Company They Keep* details some of the dissatisfaction felt by SF noncommissioned officers as SF officers seek to impose more conventional control. Rock painting exercises are still taking place, and some SF battalion (equivalent to the Vietnam era C-team) commander actually massed his A-teams into a company for a conventional rifle company assault on an objective; but what is being lost sight of is that SF has always had some foolish commanders with what they think are good ideas. I still recall an SF major in 1965 who was going to teach four A-teams' worth of people how to kill by throwing knives. Contrary to Hollywood movies, it is most difficult to gain enough acceleration and velocity with a thrown knife to cause serious injury or death. Weighing the bad against the good, SF is still better off as a separate branch than it was when it survived purely at the whim of general officers who used to be tankers.

Perhaps the ultimate improvement for SF is the low-key profile that they now enjoy throughout the services. The navy SEALs now get a lot more public affairs attention than the army SF, and that's to the benefit of SF. When SF was too prominent, it was too big a target for the rest of the army. Perhaps SF has learned something from how the British Army doesn't showcase the Special Air Service, Special Forces' counterpart organization in Britain. The 22d SAS Regiment, based in Hereford, England, has the same kinds of missions as SF, but the media are not allowed to concentrate on them, and they benefit from the lack of exposure.

For a number of years, SF has been at a crossroads. There are those who want to perform guerrilla missions deep behind enemy lines and others who want to perform daring Ranger-type raids. There's room for both missions. The quiet guerrilla (or counterinsurgency) missions still exist in the real world. On the other hand, the antiterrorist door breakers can still thrive.

The army of the nineties has returned to the "zero defects" mentality that it once had briefly in the fifties and sixties. With no tolerance for mistakes, officers and NCOs will not experiment or improvise. Why waste a promising career for creativity or innovative activity? To leap ahead of the pack is to be devoured by the pack. To return to my earlier analogy, army management now punishes success (or at least stifles it), while rewarding mediocrity. Maybe this is the army that we deserve.

As I read biographies of the great generals of World War II, I wonder if they would make it in today's army. Eisenhower and Patton would certainly not thrive now. Both had written in the thirties that the horse cavalry was dead and that the time of the armored tank was at hand, a remarkable idea at the time that earned them both a reprimand. Omar Bradley and many others were plodders and might make it today. MacArthur surely wouldn't have. Times and standards change, and that has to be accepted. But would the outcome of history have changed?

Special Forces has survived as an organization when there were those in the seventies who predicted that SF would fade away into nothingness. Likewise, the older veterans of Vietnam SF service look at the selection process, funding, assignment, and training of the current SF groups and feel proud that the traditions are being carried on. We're proud of the people who have come along after us. They proved themselves in Central America and Somalia. They will do so again for as far into the future as situations requiring their unique skills will arise. And that's probably forever. But SF is still somewhat tainted because of Vietnam.

It has become fashionable nowadays for liberal commentators to talk about how "we" lost the war in Vietnam. Sometimes the we is defined as the U.S. government, or the army, or even SF. But to this unreconstructed soldier, SF never lost anything. Sure there were some battles where we had our ass kicked, such as losing the camp at A Shau, but we were always able to go back and retake any camp or objective that we wanted.

I recognize that the typical liberal needs to feel guilt, and losing in Vietnam helps to assuage some of that guilt. But it's a disservice to the two-score friends and acquaintances that I knew and who died in Vietnam to claim that we lost. The facts speak otherwise: We never signed a surrender document, and the United States was never occupied. We did significantly reduce the male population of North Vietnam, but who cares about facts!

Fifth Special Forces Group (Airborne) gathered the greatest number of decorations of any U.S. unit in Vietnam. Even though the commander of 5th SFGA couldn't approve anything above a Bronze Star, SF people garnered a disproportionate share of Silver Stars, Distinguished Service Crosses (DSC), and Medals of Honor. The facts of the truth cannot be denied: SF soldiers performed better than most units and can be proud of their exemplary service.

As an aside, the matter of individual decorations has always been a minor irritant to SF soldiers. Soldiers in divisional organizations would typically earn decorations one or two steps higher than SF soldiers for comparable valor just because a division commander could award Silver Stars, but the 5th Group commander couldn't. When a recommendation for award of a DSC or Medal of Honor was forwarded by a divisional commander, it carried much more weight than one submitted by a colonel commanding 5th Group. In at least one division in Vietnam, there was what was called a commander's packet, which meant that almost every captain leaving a company command received a Silver Star, a Bronze Star for achievement, and a Purple Heart.

SF soldiers knew that they had to adhere to a higher standard than most, and they did. What was bothersome was when the war was winding down, the reductions in force (RIF) targeted the "nonachieving" SF personnel who couldn't favorably compare. Oh well, we all knew that life and the U.S. Army weren't fair.

Ed Sprague spent more time with the montagnards than any other Westerner. He sincerely tried to help and assist them. He has summed up his experience as follows:

First year with the montagnards: "Boy, I really got to know these people."

Second year with the montagnards: "Shit! I don't know a damn thing about these people."

Third year with the montagnards: "Ah! I'm getting to know these people."

Fourth year with the montagnards: "Hell! I don't know a frigging thing about these people."

Fifth year with the montagnards: "Hmm! I'm starting to understand a bit about these people."

Sixth year with the montagnards: "I think I understand these people. I wonder if I do?"

Seventh year with the montagnards: "Okay! I got it. I understand."

Minister Nay Luett once told Ed Sprague that Sprague was the only outsider who understood the montagnards. At the time, Sprague thought that was the greatest compliment that he had ever received. Luett went on: "I am Phu Bon, you are Phu Bon." Phu Bon and Cheo Reo are the ancestral homes of the Jarai.

Perhaps as compensation or guilt, over the years I've been trying to assist montagnards to leave Vietnam under the Orderly Departure Program (ODP). There have been some successes and many more failures. My most prominent failure has been with Ksor Sung, also known as Mike.

Mike was the chief interpreter at Mai Linh on my first tour in Vietnam. He was eligible in every respect to leave Vietnam under the ODP. Unfortunately, the Clinton administration decided that with the reopening of relations with Vietnam that the ODP didn't need to stay active and ought to be closed down. In doing so, Clinton ignored the reports of Amnesty International, which still list the montagnards of Vietnam as an oppressed people. But then, Clinton was also making Vietnam go away for himself, and that helped rid him of guilt feelings. After all, there're not too many montagnards in the United States to answer to.

Despite my four years of work on Mike's behalf, the ODP brushed off Mike's request for an interview. To the Immigration and Naturalization Service and State Department, Mike's right to an interview and subsequent entry to the United States was meaningless. It didn't matter that Special Forces held the Central Highlands with the essential help of the montagnards in the sixties and seventies, the policy now is to ignore what the montagnards did for us. Besides, the administration can garner more Asian money if we ignore the montagnards.

In the fall of 1999, I asked my congressman (Phil Crane, Republican, Illinois) to sponsor a bill authorizing Mike and his family to come to the United States. The response of my congressman has been to do nothing. His staff people have ignored my letters, and when I call, there is still no response. I guess that I'm one of the few people in the United States without representation. Not talking to your constituents seems to be one of the latest gambits with congressional representatives. Why would I expect otherwise? After all, everyone wishes Vietnam would just go away.

I still hurt for my government's failure to do the right thing. We declared an amnesty for draft dodgers to come home, but we can't admit former allies to the United States who have been persecuted by their own government because they helped us. Go figure.

I feel that I've earned my right to be a cynic. As I once heard a Department of Army civilian employee say: "I love this fucking army, and this army loves fucking me!"

CHAPTER 15

FULRO

It was a sunny afternoon on April 13, 1975, when they came for Nay Rong. The Americans had begun to make a hurried departure, and Saigon would fall on April 30, 1975. But in the Central Highlands of Vietnam, the North Vietnamese had already been victorious, had spread out, and were an occupying force. The monsoon rains were coming every afternoon, and the Central Highlands villagers were beginning to plant their rice.

The highlands villagers were apprehensive about the change in government. Under the South Vietnamese, an accommodation had been worked out, and the Central Highlands montagnards didn't know if they would keep the autonomy that they had fought so hard to gain. Since the montagnards had mainly supported the American effort, and by default the government of South Vietnam, few knew what to expect under the North Vietnamese.

After World War II, Nay Rong grew up under the tensions caused by the domination of the ethnic Vietnamese over the montagnard tribes. Although the French had ceded a Montagnard Autonomous Region consisting of the Central Highlands to the montagnards in 1947–49, the ethnic Vietnamese never agreed with the French action. Nay Rong belonged to the Jarai, one of the more populous of the thirty-two tribal groups. After the French left in 1954, the Vietnamese government moved ethnic Vietnamese onto montagnard land and slowly began to repress the montagnards. Taxes were imposed on the montagnards, but no government services followed. No education or health care was provided. In spite of that, Nay Rong was able to receive an education at the National Institute and to dream of a promising future. While he prepared for that future, the montagnards sought their accommodation with the South Vietnamese government.

A leadership coalition of all the montagnards was organized and named BaJaRaKa after the four major tribes: Bahnar, Jarai, Rhade, and Koho. In 1958, tribal leaders went to Saigon to present their grievances and were promptly jailed. Unrest and agitation continued over the next few years. Finally, the montagnards formed an alliance with the Chams (an Islamic Malayo-Polynesian people) and Khmers (ethnic Cambodians) called FULRO (*Front Unifié des Luttes des Race-Oprimées*/United Front for the Liberation of the Racially Oppressed). Under the leadership of a Rhade government official (assistant to the chief agricultural services) named Y B'ham, FULRO became more demanding and militant. A revolt took place in the highlands in 1964, which forced Saigon to establish a Ministry of Ethnic Minority Development to deed land to the montagnards, to recognize tribal courts, and to begin education and health programs. That wasn't enough for some younger members of FULRO, who prompted two smaller but bloodier revolts in 1965. The Vietnamese response was to kill more than eight hundred men, women, and children in reprisal and to stage public executions of captured revolutionaries at a soccer field in Pleiku. In one case, a montagnard appropriately named Jarai was tortured to death by slowly shooting him in the legs and arms before finishing him off; all to the cheers of the Vietnamese crowd and the ignored pleas of a French Jesuit priest.

Special Forces began operating in Vietnam in 1962 in the Central Highlands, and as increasing numbers of U.S. Army Special Forces arrived in Vietnam, more attention began to be paid to FULRO. First working with the Rhade tribesmen to train them to find and destroy the Viet Cong, they later expanded throughout the highlands and through all of Vietnam. Although the Vietnamese considered the Bronze Age montagnards to be savages, the Americans came to like the montagnards and developed a lasting friendship for their tribal allies. As the FULRO movement grew and revolt became more imminent, it was not possible for the Special Forces to stay uninvolved with FULRO and yet still work closely with the various tribal groups. Eventually, the Special Forces found that one of its roles was to foster reconciliation between the montagnards and Vietnamese if the war against the Viet Cong was to be successfully prosecuted.

By the late 1960s, at American urging, the Vietnamese had come to terms with FULRO and the montagnards, although Y B'ham wisely remained with the FULRO movement in Mondolkiri Province, Cambodia. Montagnards were accepted into officer training programs in the Vietnamese army, and Y B'ham virtually disbanded the FULRO army by ordering entire battalions to volunteer for service under the leadership of the U.S. Special Forces. In the Central Highlands, most of the CIDG (Civilian Irregular Defense Group) Strike and Mike (Mobile Strike) Force units were affiliated with FULRO. In effect, the United States trained, supplied, and paid the FULRO army.

Unlike the majority of montagnard men who joined the Special Forces strike forces for counterguerrilla warfare, by virtue of his education Nay Rong was destined for a political role. In 1968, he began working for the Ministry of Ethnic Minority Development in Pleiku. Pleiku and Ban Me Thuot were the centers of montagnard culture and influence and both were bastions of Jarai and Rhade power in the Central Highlands. The ministry was a mechanism for cooperation between the Vietnamese and montagnards, but the montagnards' ultimate goal was always to regain as much autonomy as possible from the Vietnamese.

Nay Rong fitted himself into this difficult job in Pleiku, representing the Vietnamese government to the montagnards and the montagnards to the Vietnamese government. While most of his age group fought in the Vietnamese army or in the Special Forces strike forces, Nay Rong contented himself with issues of agriculture, education, and civic action on behalf of the montagnards. He also led a double life, as he knew about FULRO and frequently sat in on Sunday strategy sessions with FULRO leaders and representatives from Y B'ham's headquarters in Cambodia. Nay Rong knew that FULRO didn't feel strong enough to take on the South Vietnamese government and that the military option was not yet feasible for the montagnards, so they were content to fight the North Vietnamese and keep the South Vietnamese out of the highlands.

As the tide of war changed and the Vietnamese began to evacuate the highlands in 1975, Nay Rong returned to his wife and children and village south of Pleiku near the province capital of Cheo Reo. He was sure that the North Vietnamese occupation would only be a replacement of one Vietnamese group by another and that regard for the montagnards would not really improve. Yet he still dreamed of the autonomy that his race prayed for. As the North Vietnamese began taking montagnard men for interrogation, imprisonment, and "reeducation," he was sure that his minor political activities would exempt him as he had not actually fought against the North Vietnamese. He was wrong. He found that he was considered a worse threat to the North Vietnamese than the soldiers who had actually fought.

Earlier in the war, the North Vietnamese tried to subvert the montagnards by promising them autonomy and equality if they would ally themselves with the North. The North Vietnamese even took a few montagnard leaders to North Vietnam to show off their model minorities programs. The Potemkin Villages were not believable to most montagnards, and the North Vietnamese never really gained the support of the montagnards, although some montagnards did stay in the north and were used for propaganda purposes. However, the North always believed and practiced that political action was just as important as military action. To them, then, Nay Rong's very existence was threatening.

Nay Rong was taken to Pleiku, beaten, interrogated, and beaten again. He was held for four months, including twenty-three days in a hole with only a small trapdoor for light and air. Without trial, he was sentenced to a reeducation camp for political prisoners. As one of a group of two thousand prisoners, he was force marched to Plei Bong, northwest of Pleiku. Rations and water along the way were minimal, and medical care was nonexistent. Nay Rong's group was the first to arrive, and its job was to create the Plei Bong camp. Wake-up was at 4:00 A.M., then exercises, two to three hours of indoctrination each day, and then work until 9:00 P.M. Roll call was at 10:30 P.M., and then Nay Rong could sleep until 4:00 A.M. and begin again.

When he arrived at Camp Plei Bong, Nay Rong found that his reeducation was to be a combination of indoctrination, interrogation, slave labor, self-criticism, and extermination. When not working on dike and road repair or in the rice fields, the prisoners were required to constantly write and update their life histories back to four generations with an emphasis on the "crimes" that they had committed against the Vietnamese people. Later, the histories would be read by an interrogator and compared with earlier histories for discrepancies. Omissions and discrepancies were the basis for further interrogation and punishment. If errors were found, the errors were judged as lies. Lies were a crime against the people, for which the only punishment was death.

After two months, Nay Rong realized that he was marked for death. Along with four others one night, Nay Rong escaped. Moving slowly toward Pleiku, Nay Rong went hungry for six days. He eventually met a montagnard villager who fed him. Thirty days after his escape, Nay Rong made it to his village, where his wife gave him food and clothing, and he learned of the execution of friends and family members. Nay Rong, the former bureaucrat, had returned to his tribal roots and vowed to join FULRO and fight the North Vietnamese. He began a walking trip southwest into Darlac Province, heading home.

As he moved through the jungle, Nay Rong met numerous groups of armed FULRO squads composed of former Strike and Mike Force troopers (at that point, approximately twenty thousand montagnards had joined FULRO and "gone to the woods"). The squads were organized into ten-man cells to limit knowledge of others in FULRO, and Nay Rong was surprised to learn that the former troopers who had fought the Vietnamese were not high on the North Vietnamese's list for reeducation. The real threat to the North Vietnamese were the montagnard politicians, bureaucrats, teachers, and educated people, not soldiers. FULRO cells were freely roaming the jungle and attacking North Vietnamese checkpoints and soldiers. Weapons and ammunition for the FULRO forces were plentiful as the fleeing South Vietnamese had abandoned their equipment in their zeal to escape.

By the fall of 1975, FULRO was growing in size and becoming more active, but there were organizational problems. Y B'ham and the other top members of FULRO had been killed, but it's necessary to digress to tell the story accurately.

When Ban Me Thuot fell to the North Vietnamese in early 1975, the South Vietnamese leadership made a decision to abandon the Central Highlands, which soon led to the destruction of the South Vietnamese regime. Shortly after Kontum and Pleiku fell, the Vietnamese army began to desert and run for safety to the coastal areas. As the U.S. embassy watched the mounting panic, liaisons to FULRO were told at the U.S. embassy that FULRO should attempt to hold the highlands and that they would be supported with arms, ammunition, and supplies. The offer was put in writing (the letter would later be disavowed and be destroyed by a U.S. embassy staffer in Bangkok, Thailand) and carried by Cowboy, a Jarai with a colorful history of working with Special Forces. Cowboy met with Y B'ham and the leadership council in Cambodia, and FULRO was only too happy to begin combat operations against the North Vietnamese in Cambodia and Vietnam. However, complications began to ensue.

As Vietnam was experiencing the beginning of the North Vietnamese victory, Cambodia was having a similar experience. The Khmer Rouge (Cambodian Communists) had been in revolt for a number of years, with many of their troops having been trained in U.S. Special Forces camps in Vietnam (as one of the oddities of Southeast Asia, Cambodian Communists didn't mind fighting North Vietnamese Communists while earning U.S. pay). Under the leadership of Pol Pot (whose horrible regime was later and most vividly exposed in the book and movie *The Killing Fields*), the Khmer Rouge began to expand their area of influence in Cambodia as Cambodian government troops retreated. Moving into the FULRO-dominated area in northeast Cambodia, the Khmer Rouge forced Y B'ham and the FULRO leadership council to flee to Phnom Penh. When the Khmer Rouge took Phnom Penh, the FULRO leadership took refuge in the French embassy. When the Khmer Rouge demanded that the French turn Y B'ham over to them, the French complied, and Y B'ham and his group were all immediately executed. Doesn't say too much about the French, does it?

FULRO rebuilt its leadership and continued to fight the Vietnamese. It was to that new organization that Nay Rong traveled. He joined, becoming one of eight thousand montagnards still fighting. Because of his earlier contacts with FULRO and his work in Pleiku, Nay Rong rapidly moved through the ranks and ultimately became a regimental commander and part of the new FULRO leadership council.

By 1980, the Vietnamese had invaded and occupied Cambodia. Pol Pot fled to the jungle and began his own guerrilla war against the Vietnamese. As they were both now fighting a common enemy, the Vietnamese, an uneasy alliance developed between the Khmer Rouge and FULRO. At that point a new nation/player enters the scene: Communist China (People's Republic of China).

Although China had supported North Vietnam against the Americans during the war, by 1980 the centuries-old national rivalries had resurfaced, and China and Vietnam had begun to clash militarily along their common border. China also sided with Pol Pot against the Vietnamese in Cambodia. As a result, the Khmer Rouge took their instructions from Beijing. The result to FULRO was that their mobility in Cambodia was decreased, and FULRO units could not move without Khmer Rouge and Chinese permission. There was one benefit though: The Chinese rearmed FULRO.

Seeking U.S. support, Nay Rong and other representatives

from FULRO went to the U.S. embassy in Bangkok, Thailand. The embassy turned the montagnards away and confiscated the letter that the U.S. embassy in Saigon had provided in 1975. Now short of weapons, ammunition, and supplies, FULRO realized that they could not continue to fight the Vietnamese without outside help from somewhere. A Thai army general (Gen. Savit-Yun K-Yut) told the Chinese embassy in Bangkok of the montagnards' predicament, and the Chinese responded. After negotiation and insuring that the montagnards would continue to fight the Vietnamese, the Chinese provided five thousand rifles and other weapons and ammunition.

FULRO continued to fight, and has been fighting for over twenty years. The Vietnamese have responded in kind and oversee the Central Highlands as a military tactical zone. Roadblocks still exist, villages are concentrated along access routes, and travel is difficult into or out of the highlands. Westerners are not allowed to enter the highlands because of the continuing FULRO war, although the Vietnamese have allowed Japanese and Taiwanese lumber companies access. The logging operations have assisted the Vietnamese government because vast tracts of land have been denuded, thus making guerrilla operations by FULRO more difficult. Since 1975, more than 200,000 montagnards have been killed by the Vietnamese in a genocidal campaign unequaled since World War II.

Tired of war and angered by the refusal of the United States to help, Nay Rong crossed into Thailand in 1980 with a band of two hundred other montagnards. He and the others have since settled in the United States and have been attempting to get their relatives out of Vietnam. This has proved to be difficult because the Vietnamese consider the FULRO montagnards to be pawns of the CIA. Additionally, the montagnards have begun to bicker among themselves. Factions have developed, one group preaching accommodation with the Vietnamese (both in the United States and overseas), others remaining more militant, and yet others straddling the fence. Needless to say, most have lost the devotion to FULRO that led them to the jungle in 1975.

But the story of FULRO and the montagnards in the United States isn't finished. With the "normalization" of relations established by the Clinton administration, the Communist Vietnamese remain paranoid about the intentions of the U.S. montagnards. They have even gone so far as to send at least two agents to the United States to find out what the montagnard community is up to. The two agents were quickly caught and turned over to the FBI, and the agents confessed.

Perhaps it's the policy of the Clinton administration not to make waves with the Vietnamese (after all, Asian funds helped to reelect Clinton), or maybe there are other reasons. Nevertheless, the agents have not been prosecuted and have been allowed to remain in the United States. Another more troubling aspect is the administration's dismantling of the Orderly Departure Program (ODP).

After 1975, hordes of refugees (mostly Vietnamese) began to flee Vietnam to escape the Communists. Many fled by foot across Cambodia to Thailand, others went by boat to Thailand and to Hong Kong. Most of the people were refugees who had affiliations with the United States during the war and were being discriminated against by or had good reason to fear the Communist conquerors. Those who fled overland were met by Pol Pot's people in Cambodia and many were killed or starved during the trek. The ones who went by boat were often attacked by Thai pirates that preyed on the exodus from Vietnam. Embarrassed by the slaughter still going on, Congress passed the ODP.

The ODP was designed to identify Vietnamese (and ethnic minorities) who had assisted the United States during the Vietnam War and faced discrimination by the Communists. To keep their departure "orderly" and safe, an ODP office was established at the American embassy in Bangkok, Thailand. Since there was no U.S. recognition of the Communist regime in Vietnam, international voluntary agencies (also known as nongovernmental agencies, NGOs) screened the applications and made recommendations to the State Department and the Immigration and Naturalization Service.

Individuals who should be granted political asylum in the United States were to be identified and given visas to enter. It all sounds wonderful, doesn't it? But the reality has not been.

First, the Vietnamese were not about to let montagnards leave Vietnam. Their goal since 1975 has been to kill off the montagnards or to force their assimilation.

Second, the venal Vietnamese Communists recognized an opportunity to make money with the ODP: They began selling exit permits and even false certificates of incarceration (required sometimes by ODP as proof of having undergone reeducation) to people having the money and wanting to leave. Unfortunately, that didn't apply to montagnards as they are mostly poor and have no money.

Many montagnards who had been approved by the U.S. government for entry into the United States have not been able to buy exit permits. The ODP has ended, and they are still in Vietnam. Less than a thousand montagnards have made it to the United States.

For montagnards without money, the Communist officials offered them a deal: leave your spouse and family in Vietnam and take a Vietnamese spouse and children on your passport to the United States. Then when the "family" arrives, the "spouse" says I don't know this person and want to be resettled on my own. So the United States had to accept the situation and then allow the spouse to move her/his real family to this country.

But the problem is not just one with the Communist Vietnamese. Fundamental U.S. government official policy is to deny the montagnards exist as former allies.

For those montagnards with FULRO connections, the State Department now says that FULRO is an insurrectionary organization, and no legitimate government has the right to deal with revolutionaries. By the same reasoning, the American colonists' revolt against the British was illegitimate, and their alliance with France was therefore illegal.

Even though Amnesty International still lists the montagnards as an oppressed people, the State Department has taken the side of the Communists. Why then was it official policy to help the montagnards in the 1960s and 1970s?

To many former SF people, the United States has simply abandoned its friends, and that is shameful.

I was one of the first who reported the false "family" and "spouse" trick, but still have been unable to get some montagnard friends out. Even after extensive letter-writing campaigns to Illinois and Wisconsin senators, the State Department refused to act. One Jarai friend of mind was designated an applicant of "special concern." He has been refused even an interview.

I can understand the antiwar movement crowd now in the White House does not like me or my kind. After all, we went and did what they didn't have the guts to do. But is Vietnam still so personally embarrassing that we have to compromise our integrity and leave our friends behind? I guess it is. No wonder some allies of the United States consider us not very dependable.

Like many others, I'm ashamed of how our government now treats the montagnards left in Vietnam. Future insurgent movements that the United States may sponsor may look at how the U.S. government treated past insurgent movements. Is there any wonder that the Kurds of Iraq haven't sided with the United States? The United States has abandoned the montagnards; the Kurds know that they'll be abandoned, too. There's no reason for me to be proud of being an American.

CHAPTER 16

Update

Throughout this manuscript, a lot of names have been mentioned. Maybe the reader and I might have something in common, such as acquaintance with one or more of the people mentioned. In this last chapter, I'll try to point out what the various characters have done or what they're doing now.

I can't swear to the accuracy of what follows as the list represents my understanding of things through much word of mouth and rumor:

Francis Axford has finally retired from working for the army. His military retirement grade was as a major; his civilian grade is GS-12. He and his wife Beverly live in northern Illinois.

William Balfanz remained behind as the S-3, 3d Brigade, 3d Armored Division when I left Germany in 1973. I haven't seen or heard from him since.

Ray Barry retired from the army in 1976 as a colonel. Before he retired, he pursued a law degree and later accepted a job at Kent School of Law in Chicago.

Bob "Sam" Bass retired from the army as a sergeant major. He has since been active in the Special Forces Association and attends every annual convention. He now lives in Florida.

Oscar Biehl eventually took over the team at Cung Son. He was the team leader there when he was killed on May 30, 1967.

Premond "Bob" Bowen had a very successful career after Mai Linh, and he eventually retired as a sergeant major. He later went to language school for Chinese and served with 1st Group on Okinawa. After he retired, he moved back to North Carolina to work for Rose's Department Stores.

Dave Boyd was a Special Forces commander when he was killed in IV Corps on November 14, 1966. His wife, Barbara, eventually remarried and divorced.

Andrew Brantley rose in rank to lieutenant colonel and retired in the early nineties. He now works for a defense consulting firm in Virginia. As of this writing (July 1999), he's working in Bosnia.

Siu Broai was a major when captured by the North Vietnamese in 1975. He served seven years in a reeducation camp and eventually emigrated to the United States. He settled in Utah, but returned to Vietnam to die when he was diagnosed with inoperable cancer. Broai was one of the few Jarai to advance in the Vietnamese army.

David L. Buckner returned to Tennessee after leaving St. John's Military Academy. He now works for the City of Chattanooga. As a retired brigadier general, he is active in Chattanooga's annual Armed Forces Day activities.

Henry Caesar has been a difficult search for me. I assume that he's retired from the army, but have not been able to locate him. An address in Texas showed that he had moved, and the retired army locator wouldn't assist. There are rumors that he's been seen in Korea.

Richard Campbell retired as a sergeant major and is now living in Guam.

Roy Carlton, my predecessor as the director of plans, training, and security for Fort Sheridan, retired as a major and was living and working in central Illinois, last I heard.

Wilbur Childress was a sergeant major when he was killed in Southeast Asia on April 29, 1972. He's officially listed as a nonhostile death, but rumors persist that he was "fragged." At the time of his death, he was working with *Forces Armee Nationale Khmer*, the U.S. sponsored advisory element to the Cambodian army.

Michael B. Dooley kept extending in Vietnam until he was killed at Duc Lap on August 25, 1968. By then, Mike had been in Vietnam for two and a half years.

George Dunaway later went on to become the sergeant major of the army and eventually retired. He lives in Nevada and is active in the SFA.

Daniel French eventually retired as a major general. He was a colonel in Germany when I left in 1973, but it was obvious that the army had marked him as a fast burner. I don't know more about his subsequent career.

Sidney Haszard retired as a colonel. After he left 3d Brigade, he became the 3d Armored Division chief of staff. I heard that he later was chief of staff at Fort Knox, Kentucky. Despite an exceedingly gruff personality, Colonel Haszard was one of the very few officers who truly cared about the welfare of his troops.

John Hennigan later moved to an ROTC assignment somewhere in the south. I believe that he has since passed away.

Bjarne Hesselberg is still on active duty as a colonel in the Danish army. My old tablemate from CGSC sends annual Christmas cards telling all his old classmates how he and his family are doing. After CGSC, among other assignments, Bjarne commanded a battalion in the breakup of Yugoslavia. I suspect that his wife Inge is as vivacious as ever.

Houston Houser eventually retired as a general officer. He was a brigade executive officer in the 3d Armored Division when I next (and last) saw him in 1972. Later, he had assignments in the newly formed Ranger units.

Roger Knight is a retired colonel living in New Mexico. Following a career path that meant certain death for an armored officer, it was expected that Roger wouldn't do well. He had just too many Airborne and SF assignments. But after commanding a psychological operations battalion at Fort Bragg, Roger was selected for promotion to colonel. After retirement, he managed a physical fitness complex in Albuquerque and has since retired from that job, too.

Bob Kvederas retired as a colonel and now lives in Connecticut. An extremely quiet man, he is often mistaken for shy. The reality is that Bob is extremely intelligent, and his attributes have contributed to help the army through the years.

Steve Leopold remained active in the army reserves after his release from the Hanoi Hilton in 1973. He is a USAR colonel and an administrative law judge in Milwaukee, Wisconsin. After a career as a successful practicing attorney, Steve is still active in supporting Chapter 73, SFA.

Mike Lewis and I both attended the same advanced course class in 1973–74 at Fort Benning. I don't know what he did subsequently, but I've read that he was a lieutenant colonel in the USAR.

Carl Mayse retired as a sergeant major, but I'll always remember him as Field Marshal Mayse. He has not joined the SFA, and I've been unable to locate him.

John McFadden was a master sergeant when he retired from the 10th Special Forces in Germany. He and his wife opened a vacation lodge in Fall, Germany, in the Alps near the Austrian border. For a small-town boy from Sterling, Illinois, John did well. His second tour in Vietnam was in MAC-SOG (CCN), and he had mostly SF assignments until he retired. John has since died of Agent Orange–related cancer and is buried in Bavaria.

Clarence Mobley was the sergeant major of the 407th S&T Battalion. Although he tried to keep me from going to SF, he told me enough SF stories to make me want to become a snake eater. I last saw him in 1969 in Qui Nhon as a sergeant major in the 1st Cavalry Division.

John Mullins retired from the army as a major. Among other things, he has been writing books based mostly on his SF and Project Phoenix experience. I had contact with him in Oklahoma, but have since lost contact.

Nay Rong, after coming to the United States, has since been reunited with his wife and family. It took a directive from Hanoi to the Communist warlord in Ban Me Thuot to release Rong's family, even though they had already paid thousands of dollars in bribes. The family has since bought a house in North Carolina.

Zane Osnoe retired from the army and became a police officer in Fayetteville, North Carolina. Later, Zane transferred to the Washington, North Carolina, police department and rose through the ranks. He eventually retired as the deputy chief.

Lorenzo Perea was the first sergeant of HHC, 3d Brigade, 3d Armored Division when I left in 1973. I've lost contact since that time.

Wayne Price retired and is living near Fort Campbell, according to George Dunaway. Sergeant Major Price not only convinced me to make the army a career, he shaped me and pointed me in the right direction. If the army were full of men like Price, it would be invincible. I admire him to this day.

Joe Simino retired from the army as a colonel and is living in Louisiana. He works for a defense contractor, teaching artillery tactics at Fort Polk.

Arnold Sims is one of the people that I was unable to get in contact with when I organized the A-226 reunion. On my second tour, he was a staff sergeant with the II Corps Mike Force. I suspect that he has long since been retired from the army, but I don't know what he's doing or where he lives.

Bucky Smith is retired from the army and now living in Utah. I last saw him at the Colorado Springs convention in 1997. After I left B-24, he was transferred to be the team sergeant at Ban Het.

Mark Smith is a retired major and now lives in Thailand.

Mary Ellen Sonntag moved to a retirement community in Colorado.

John Southworth went to artillery OCS and eventually retired a major. He taught school for a second career and retired from that in June 1999. He and his wife now live in central Wisconsin. John contributed a detailed and extensive description of Ed Sprague's team A-10 when they went to Norway in early 1963 for the Winter School for Infantry. John was considered A-10's strongman, to the point that he was called Clark Kent. John was in his sixties when he scaled Pike's Peak during the SFA convention in 1997.

Bill Spencer was a sergeant first class when he was killed December 29, 1969, while serving with MAC-SOG (CCC). Leigh Wade described Bill's death in *Assault on Dak Pek* (New York: Ivy Books, 1968).

Ed Sprague: After Camp Chaffee, Ed Sprague had State Department assignments in the Sinai Desert along the Israel-Egypt cease-fire line and in Tanzania. While in Israel, he began anew his hobby of carving and painting gourds, an art form that he began experimenting with as a child. His gourd creations are now in art museums throughout the world.

In 1983, Ed Sprague retired from the State Department at its highest grade, Foreign Service Officer-1. Ed Sprague achieved more than most men dream of. Along the way, he became venerated by the montagnards of Vietnam and his Special Forces friends who served with him.

But Ed Sprague never completely forgot his Special Forces roots. Proud to have one son who served in Special Forces, he also has a retired Special Forces son-in-law. Every year, he attends the Special Forces Association convention, meets with his old friends (particularly Sam Bass), and remembers the service that he gave to his country. Ed and his friends know that they won the Cold War.

Today, Ed Sprague and Eve live on a ten-acre plot in rural New Hampshire, surrounded by an apple and peach orchard. The montagnards, media people, and researchers still contact him. He's more withdrawn now than before. He's still troubled by the montagnards and our abandonment of them. But he knows that he did the best that he possibly could and that nobody else could have done it better.

I am one of those proud to have known and to have served with him.

Mark Sprague married Kathleen after watching the fall of Vietnam. Mark has a degree in anthropology and is now an officer in Northern Light, a computer search-engine firm he founded.

Jim Stewart served 19½ years in Special Forces. Jim retired from the army as a sergeant major and now lives in Alabama. He taught junior ROTC until he again retired. Jim's Special Forces service in Southeast Asia has generally gone unrecognized because his SF assignments were outside the organized SF structure. Jim has served in MAC-SOG and Project 404 in Laos (a CIA sponsored activity), along with an earlier tour in the Dominican Republic.

Gordon Strickler won a Silver Star while serving at Dak Pek. Previously, he had been the S-1/adjutant at B-24. There was a rumor once that he died while on active duty.

Wayne Summers was the junior medic at Mai Linh. It's believed that he left the army and returned to his home in California. He is not a member of the SFA, and I've been unable to contact him for our various A-226 reunions.

Andrew Szeliga I never saw again (after Pole: Kleng). I believe that he retired from the army and is living in Florida.

Jean Uszakow died at Mai Linh on September 24, 1966.

Jim Welsh was assigned to B-22 in Qui Nhon, and we lost touch. He's not listed as a member of the SFA.

Jim Zachary probably had the most illustrious career, aside from Ed Sprague. Everyone expected Jim to eventually make general officer, but that was not to be. After various SF assignments, Jim commanded the 10th Group at Fort Devens, which had a Soviet-bloc orientation. Ironically, when he retired as a colonel, Jim worked for a while with Tatarstan (a former member of the Soviet Union), helping that country export oil.

Jim is fond of telling a story that when he was commanding the 10th Group, he attended a Special Forces commanders conference at Fort Bragg. In irritation at something Jim said, a general officer commented to Zachary that Jim "had never been able to think beyond the A-team level." I personally can't think of a nicer backhanded comment, one which also shows the stupidity of some general officers.

A-teams are the foundation of Special Forces; everything else is just support. If a general officer wasn't able to recognize that, it's no wonder that SF has had trouble in dealing with the rest of the army for over forty years.

Index